The Political Economy of Japanese Monetary Policy

The Political Economy of Japanese Monetary Policy

Thomas F. Cargill
Michael M. Hutchison
Takatoshi Ito

The MIT Press
Cambridge, Massachusetts
London, England

Set in Palatino on the Miles 33 system by Graphic Composition, Inc.
Printed and bound in the United States of America.

Library of Congress Cataloging-in-Publication Data
Cargill, Thomas F.
The political economy of Japanese monetary policy / Thomas F. Cargill, Michael M. Hutchison, Takatoshi Ito.
p. cm.
Includes bibliographical references.
ISBN 0-262-03247-3
1. Monetary policy—Japan. 2. Banks and banking, Central—Japan. 3. Nihon Ginkō. 4. Japan—Economic policy—1945– I. Hutchinson, Michael M. II. Itō, Takatoshi, 1950– III. Title.
HG1275.C37 1997
332.4'952—dc21 97-3717
CIP

Contents

Acknowledgments

Our collaboration on this book began in 1993; however, the book would not have been possible without the assistance and encouragement of a number of individuals and institutions. All three authors have benefitted from discussions with many Bank of Japan officials, in particular Mitsuhiro Fukao, Kunio Okina, and Hiroo Taguchi. All three authors have had past and present affiliations with various international agencies and central banks in the capacity of being a staff member, a visiting scholar, or a research associate. All data used in this book, however, come from publicly available sources, and the opinions expressed in this book are solely the authors'.

Cargill especially thanks the Bank of Japan and the Federal Reserve Bank of San Francisco for providing a research environment in several forums over the past decade that importantly contributed to his research on Japanese financial and monetary issues. Cargill also acknowledges research support from the Japan–United States Friendship Commission and the Hoover Institution at Stanford University. Hutchison especially thanks the Center for Pacific Basin Monetary and Economic Studies at the Federal Reserve Bank of San Francisco for a stimulating and hospitable environment in which to conduct research on Japanese monetary policy during the past decade and acknowledges research support from the Japan-United States Friendship Commission, the Japan Foundation, and the Social Sciences Division and the Committee on Research at the University of California at Santa Cruz. Ito especially thanks Charles Goodhart for his sharing deep insights on the literature of central banking during a shared-teaching assignment on central banking at Harvard University in 1993–94.

The Political Economy of Japanese Monetary Policy

1 Introduction

This book is about the formulation and execution of Japanese monetary policy within a broad political and institutional context. We explore the creation and the evolution of central banking in Japan, the institutional structure, how policy is formulated and how it has evolved in the face of Japan's changing domestic and international environment, and how policy is influenced by Japan's political institutions and by the Bank of Japan's formal and informal relationship with the Ministry of Finance. Our primary focus is on recent experience, especially since the collapse of the Bretton Woods system. Though we also discuss the historical record and the "high growth" with a fixed exchange rate in the period 1959–1971, the fundamental changes on the real and financial sides of the Japanese economy that have occurred in the past 20 years have done much to diminish the relevance of the previous periods to the present workings and policies of the Bank of Japan.

1.1 Macroeconomic Background

Moving from the chaotic conditions and the economic and political instability that followed World War II, Japan was well on its way to reindustrialization by 1950. Forty years of unmatched economic growth and rising prosperity ensued. Japan's rapid GNP growth and low unemployment were impressive by any standard—especially between 1950 and 1973, when annual growth of 10 percent doubled the size of the economy every seven years.

Economic growth began to slow in the 1960s but suffered its first real setback after the 1973 oil-price shock, when Japan experienced a deep recession and a burst of "wild inflation." The inflation was soon brought under control, and Japan returned to a path of impressive growth (especially by the standards of mature industrial economies), with real GNP rising 2.5–5.0 percent each year between 1975 and 1991. While this strong growth was being achieved, inflation was gradually reduced to the lowest level among the industrial economies. Japan became the most dynamic economy in the world during this period, characterized not only by rapid growth and low inflation but also by growing technological and manufacturing prowess, unprecedentedly large trade surpluses (despite a series of deep tariff reductions), and the establishment of Tokyo as a major financial center. By the mid 1980s, Japan was the number-two economy (after the United States) and the number-one creditor nation in the world.

The Japanese economy went into a new phase in the second half of the 1980s as growth accelerated and asset prices skyrocketed. Land, commercial buildings, golf club memberships, art objects, and other assets often increased in value by factors of 3 or more in just a few years. Real GNP grew at an average rate of more than 4 percent, though consumer-price inflation was kept below 1.5 percent. This "bubble economy" (i.e., an economy characterized by rapid growth and asset-price inflation) was widely viewed as reflecting confidence in Japan's continued bright economic prospects. Underlying the bubble, however, was a growing and largely unrecognized problem having to do with banking: because of inflated asset prices and increased exposure to the volatile real-estate and construction sectors (where loans were often extended on little or no collateral other than the expectation of future price increases), the quality of banks' balance sheets had deteriorated sharply.

The bubble began to burst in May 1989, when the Bank of Japan raised the discount rate. By the summer of 1991, stock prices had fallen 60 percent from their peak values. Land prices started to decline in 1991 and fell continuously through 1996. A downturn in the economy soon followed the collapse in asset prices, and in the four years during which real GDP grew at a rate below 1 percent (1992–1995) Japan experienced its worst postwar recession. Japan is still struggling with the burst of the bubble, particularly with its consequences in banking and finance. In the mid 1990s, Japan's financial system faces its most serious challenge since the financial crisis of 1927. Nonperforming loans exceeding 10 percent of GDP (6 percent of total loans) put the magnitude of the problem at least on a par with the collapse of the US savings-and-loan industry in the 1980s. Moreover, a slow and piecemeal regulatory response by the Japanese authorities long hid the magnitude of the problem and prolonged its adverse effects on the real economy.

With the focus on current economic problems, the remarkable performance of the Japanese economy for the greater part of the postwar period is often forgotten. Not since the 1974 recession and the wild inflation, during which Japan struggled to restructure its economy to cope with the high prices and uncertain supplies of imported energy, have such fundamental questions and doubts about economic and financial structure been raised and the policies critically evaluated.

1.2 The Political Economy of Monetary Policy

Recently Japan's monetary and financial policies have come under close scrutiny and have been criticized for their role in the rise and collapse of the bubble economy. Policy shortcomings are more evident with the benefit of hindsight. For the greater part of the postwar period Japan's monetary and financial policies were praised for supporting strong and stable economic growth, and since 1975 they have been praised for achieving the lowest average rate of increase in consumer prices among the industrial countries.

The Bank of Japan is usually given credit for its role in creating a stable economic environment; in several instances it has also been credited for responding quickly to changing economic circumstances. For example, in response to the 1979 oil-price shock it raised interest rates very quickly, kept inflationary expectations in check, and allowed Japan to avoid the worst of the economic slump that hit the other major industrial countries. The Bank of Japan's performance is all the more impressive in light of financing pressures arising from the central government's large budget deficits though most of this period, the extensive measures to liberalize financial markets, and the steps taken to internationalize the yen. This performance has led some academics to view the Bank of Japan as a model central bank.

The particular factors that determine policy successes and failures in central banking are often difficult to identify, and they depend in part on the general economic environment and on the institutional and political structure. To fully appreciate the formulation and execution of Japanese monetary policy, it is helpful to view the Bank of Japan within this broader context. Monetary policy is, of course, the responsibility of the Bank of Japan. But the Bank of Japan, similar to other central banks, always faces constraints on its choices of policy actions, and these constraints have varied greatly in nature.

During the Bretton Woods period, Japanese monetary policy was institutionally constrained by a myriad of controls and regulations (largely dictated by the Ministry of Finance) on interest rates and international capital flows, and by the commitment to maintain a fixed exchange rate. (From 1950 to 1971 the exchange rate was 360 yen per dollar.) International constraints on the operation of monetary policy have also been evident since the move to flexible exchange rates. Moves to coordinate monetary policies at various Group of Seven meetings and attempts at influencing the value of the yen exchange rate serve as two clear examples.

More direct political influence on policy is also occasionally exercised. The mistake of monetary policy in creating the wild inflation of 1974 is, in part, attributable to the delay in raising interest rates despite clear signs of inflationary pressure. And this delay is related to political interference in policy. In 1972, Prime Minister Kakuei Tanaka insisted on lowering the discount rate when Bank of Japan officials had recommended precisely the opposite. After the wild inflation, direct political interference lessened and public support for greater price stability rose. Under these circumstances, the Bank of Japan introduced a new "money-focused" policy.

More recently, the financial crisis has been a policy concern of the Bank of Japan, and that institution may be confronted with conflicts in its roles as regulator of banks, lender of last resort, and provider of liquidity to the economy. Japan's monetary policy turned expansionary in 1993 after the burst of the bubble and the slowdown in the economy. Beyond considerations of stabilization policy, concern over the banking system is a motive for monetary ease. Lower interest rates and a larger "spread" between lending rates and deposit rates helped to restore banks to profitability and to limit the spread of the financial crisis. Japanese banks enjoyed record operating profits in 1995, partly as a result of discount-rate cuts that brought the rate down to a historic low of 0.5 percent. In the period 1993–1996, monetary ease was consistent with the objectives of countering the economic downturn, maintaining price stability, and supporting financial stability. By 1997, however, clear evidence of an economic upturn had again raised the potential for conflict between these objectives.

1.3 The Focus of the Book

In this book we explore Japan's economic and political institutions to the extent necessary to explain the workings of monetary policy. Financial institutions and markets play particularly important roles here, as does the evolving "real" structure of the Japanese economy—the flow of fund changes, the phases of growth, the growing trade surpluses, the increasing internationalization of the economy, and so on. Other changes in the Bank of Japan's operating environment, including political developments, are also discussed.

The contribution of monetary policy to the successful performance of the Japanese economy since World War II is one of the central issues we investigate. This contribution took on a new dimension with the move to managed exchange rates and the introduction of a "money-focused" policy orientation in the early 1970s. The Bank of Japan's success in gradually reducing inflation and then maintaining price stability in the face of large government budget deficits, oil-price disruptions, structural changes in the economy, and financial liberalization is discussed in detail.

Of course, Japan's policy has not been without shortcomings. We discuss policy mistakes such as the wild inflation and the banking crisis in detail. Indeed, we give these cases particular attention, because they have had such important effects on the economy and because policy implications may be drawn from them. The recent experience with asset inflation and deflation raises important questions about Japanese monetary policy: Was expansionary policy the reason for the asset inflation? Did policy "accommodate" and prolong the asset inflation, and thereby exacerbate the adverse effects when asset prices fell precipitously, by passively providing liquidity to asset markets? How is the deterioration of the financial system likely to influence Japan's monetary policy in the future?

Against the backdrop of these developments, questions about political influence on the Bank of Japan's policy actions naturally arise. How independent is the Bank of Japan to pursue policies of its own choosing? Are there pressures to pursue expansionary policy at specific times, such as before elections, in times of international policy "coordination," and when monetary expansion is deemed desirable to foster stability in the financial system? We take up these issues at several points, offering an extended discussion of the influence of international policy coordination on monetary policy and devoting separate chapters to political business cycles (i.e., the links among elections, politically motivated policy moves, and the business cycle) and to the links between central-bank independence and other institutional and structural factors that have contributed to Japan's good inflation record.

The independence of central banks has become particularly interesting as financial liberalization has offered opportunities for countries to restructure their central-banking institutions and as political developments in parts of the world have made this restructuring necessary. The collapse of the Soviet Union necessitated the development of new central-banking institutions in transitional economies, the impending European Monetary Union generated the need to develop a new central-banking institution for countries comprising multiple sovereign states, and the recognition that price stability is a necessary condition for sustained economic growth created movement toward enforcing explicit accountability of the central banks for low inflation in several countries.

The conventional view is that central-bank independence helps to insulate the monetary authority from political interference and, if not a necessary condition, certainly helps to create an environment conducive to price stability. A large body of empirical evidence, including cross-country data, indicates that greater central-bank independence is associated with lower inflation rates. The case of the Bank of Japan and Japan's inflation performance during the past two decades does not fit the conventional picture, however. The Bank of Japan is legally and institutionally dependent on the Ministry of Finance, and it has no price-stability mandate in its charter. Japan achieved a price-stability record on a par with Germany and Switzerland—two of the countries with the most independent central banks—with a completely different institutional structure and a completely different political environment.

In November 1996, despite the impressive inflation record of the Bank of Japan, an official working group (the Central Bank Study Group) presented Prime Minister Ryutaro Hashimoto with a report proposing major changes in the formal structure of the Bank of Japan and in the Bank's relationship with the Ministry of Finance. It is widely anticipated that these changes will provide the Bank of Japan with much greater formal independence. The motives for these changes, however, are related to dissatisfaction with the Ministry of Finance and its handling of the banking crisis rather than to poor performance by the central bank.

The links among monetary policy, regulatory policy, and the banking crisis in Japan are also explored in depth. We devote a chapter to the rise of the bubble economy in the second half of the 1980s. The confluence of events leading to asset inflation—financial deregulation, relaxation of lending restrictions on banks, competitive pressures on banking institutions, a strong real economy, and monetary accommodation—is not unique to Japan. Special factors in Japan, however, contributed to the most dramatic speculative bubble in the industrial world in recent memory. But the "burst" of the bubble and its real and financial consequences may be even more important in the present context. This is explored in some detail, and the depth, extent, regulatory implications, and likely resolution of the banking crises are analyzed carefully.

As a result of these issues, Japan is embarking on another major reform effort. In November 1996 Prime Minister Ryutaro Hashimoto announced that his government would undertake an extensive deregulation of Japan's financial system by 2001. Senior officials referred to this as the "Big Bang" approach to financial deregulation in reference to proposed deregulation in the United Kingdom more than a decade ago. This may very well lead to major strucural changes in Japan; however, it is far too early to assess the impact of this call for reform.

1.4 The Organization of the Book

In chapter 2 we review the historical evolution of central-banking institutions in Japan through the early 1950s. In chapter 3 we continue the historical and institutional discussion, focusing on the period from the early 1950s to the present; we also discuss the role of the Bank of Japan in the "high-growth" period and in the "wild inflation," and how financial liberalization has influenced the Bank of Japan's policy since the mid 1970s. In chapter 4 we discuss the international context of monetary policy, how the Bank of Japan's policy evolved after the end of the Bretton Woods system of fixed exchange rates in 1973, the efforts to coordinate foreign-exchange intervention in the second half of the 1980s, and the conflicts between foreign-exchange-rate objectives and domestic price stability; we also consider the international efforts to coordinate policies and the potential for a yen currency bloc in East Asia. In chapter 5 we focus on the bubble economy and its collapse, and on the role of monetary policy in that process. The resulting banking crisis and its implications for future Bank of Japan policy are discussed in chapter 6. In chapters 7 and 8 we discuss the influence of political business cycles on Bank of Japan policy, on the nature of the electoral system, and on how institutional structure and the political system have influenced the Bank; we also consider why Japan has avoided an "inflation bias" over the past two decades. We conclude with a short chapter summarizing our major themes.

2 The Evolution of Central Banking in Japan, up to the 1950s

The history of the Japanese financial system can be roughly divided into three phases: the pre-modern system (before 1872), the prewar system with a central bank (from 1882 to the start of World War II), and the present system. This brief historical review is not intended to be comprehensive; however, we will discuss the financial system before the Meiji Restoration of 1868, the establishment of the Bank of Japan in 1882, and relevant banking and monetary events before World War II. We will also consider the revised Bank of Japan Law of 1942 and the controversy surrounding the current status of that law.

Even before the modern system with a central bank was introduced, in 1882, a foundation of money exchanges (quasi-merchant banks) and financial markets had existed for several centuries. The national government had also minted gold coins, which were treated as legal tender nationwide. The current banking system is largely based on the Banking Law of 1928, which was a product of the financial panic of 1927. It is noteworthy that the basic framework of the Bank of Japan Law and the (commercial) banking law dates from before World War II.

The evolution of central-banking institutions in many countries share a common thread. Goodhart (1991) convincingly summarizes the case for establishing a central bank, as opposed to "free banking" (i.e., bank notes issued by private banks). History has shown that notes issued by private banks often result in quality problems and trigger runs on individual banks, which then affect the rest of banking system.[1] Information asymmetry (noteholders or depositors have less than perfect information on the soundness of a specific bank's asset and management) opens the door to moral hazard (bankers are tempted to issue more notes than is warranted, or there is free riding on the reputations of good banks).

A central bank is established to ensure quality control over bank notes and to supervise the operation of banks.[2] The potential for systemic risk (the insolvency of one bank can lead to a chain reaction) distinguishes banking from other industries. Hence, there is a strong theoretical argument for establishing a central bank that, on the one hand, issues notes and maintains price stability and, on the other hand, serves as a lender of last resort and provides liquidity to limit contagion. A central bank's monopoly over the issuing of notes, however, also provides a tempting means of financing government expenditures. The existence of a central bank has often tempted a government to use money creation for financing a war or a populist domestic agenda, the end result being severe inflation.

Yet the exact reason for establishing a central bank differs from country to country, as does a central bank's legal status (especially its relationship with the treasury or the ministry of finance). Sweden's Riksbank, established in 1668, is usually considered to be the oldest central bank.[3] The Bank of England began operations as a private bank and developed into the central bank of a regional clearing system. Some of the European central banks, such as the Banque de France, were created by central governments and were subject to political influence from the beginning. Before the Federal Reserve was established, in 1913, the United States twice established and then abolished an institution (the First Bank of the United States (1791–1811) and the Second Bank of the United States (1816–1836)) that had some of the characteristics of a central bank.

Eventually, governments learned that a stable financial and monetary environment required the establishment of specialized institutions to regulate the overall money supply, keep prices stable, and provide prudential regulation of the banking system to ensure public confidence in the money supply. The monetary authorities also grew to assume other responsibilities, such as regulating the inflow or the outflow of foreign exchange.

In 1872, Japan's newly created central government, aspiring to rapid industrialization, "imported" the national banking system of the United States, which did not incorporate a central bank. The Bank of Japan was established in 1882 as the country's central bank and in 1884 was declared the sole note-issuing bank; however, it required another 20 years to retire all notes previously issued by national banks. The Bank of Japan was designed to provide central control over the nation's money supply, ensure price stability, and regulate foreign exchange; however, it was not assigned a major regulatory or supervisory role and was declared to be formally part of the government, specifically the Ministry of Finance.

Our prewar review is no substitute for the more detailed discussions of the subject by Patrick and Rosovsky (1976), Schiffer (1962), Tamaki (1995), and Teranishi (1990). It is intended to provide historical background for our extended discussion of Japanese monetary policy during the past two decades, which begins in the next chapter. Our specific objectives are to show that the evolution of central banking in Japan follows a pattern witnessed in many other industrialized countries, to show how special institutional features of the Bank of Japan were established early, and to show that price stability and (often) exchange-rate objectives were important aspects of the Bank of Japan's responsibilities.

2.1 Money in Japan before the Seventeenth Century

Until the end of the sixteenth century Japan was ruled by a combination of an Imperial Court in Kyoto, an aristocracy, and numerous local warlords. Unified governance over Japan (excluding Hokkaido and Ryukyu) was first achieved by Hideyoshi Toyotomi in 1590. The first strong central political control over Japan was established in 1603 by a military government under the Tokugawa family. A series of Tokugawa *shoguns* (generals) ruled the country through strong military and political control for the next 260 years.

The first Japanese currency, *wado-kaihou,* coined by the government,[4] was introduced in 708 AD. The coin, modeled after the Chinese *kaigen-tsuhou,* had a round shape with a square hole in the middle, a shape that became the standard for subsequent copper coins in Japan until 1868. Twelve copper coins, two silver coins, and one gold coin were minted and in circulation from 708 to about the tenth century. The coins, however, circulated only in the western part of Japan, where Kyoto, Nara, and Osaka are now located.

Money coined by the Imperial Court tended to follow Gresham's Law, that is, newer coins contained less precious metal as the rulers frequently debased the money supply to finance their expenditures. As a result, the value of a coin, measured by the purchasing power of rice, fell to 1/150 of its initial level over the 150 years from the beginning of the eighth century to the middle of the ninth century (Bank of Japan 1972). Consequently, by the end of the tenth century, money circulation ceased and the economy regressed back to a barter economy.

Japan entered an age of feudalism around the thirteenth century, and for the next 300 years local warlords fought one another almost continually. Despite the lack of political and military stability, the expansion of the economy increased the demand for money. The lack of central authority prevented the establishment of a money supply responsive to the increased needs of trade. In the absence of a Japanese money supply, Chinese currency acquired through increased trade with China circulated within Japan. The circulation of Chinese money continued until the Tokugawa era started, in 1603; however, it was not sufficient to satisfy the demand for money. In order to fill the gap, coins were minted privately. These homemade coins, usually of low quality, were traded at varying discounts and were sometimes rejected.

2.2 The Tokugawa Period (1603–1868)

The Tokugawa shogunate, located in Edo (later to become Tokyo), ruled Japan from 1603 to 1868. However, the nation was divided into regions and certain power was delegated to *daimyos* (local lords). The Tokugawa period was characterized by *sakoku* (isolation from foreign countries) and *shino-kosho* (a rigid caste system that divided the citizenry into *samurai* warriors, peasants, artisans, tradesman, and an underclass of untouchables such as landless peasants). While the center of government was in Edo, the commercial center was in Osaka. The economic system revolved around rice. The "tax" on farmers, collected by samurai and daimyos, was in rice, and a daimyo's ranking was measured by the amount of rice sent to the Tokugawa shogun. Rice was both the basic food source and a means of wealth. Surplus rice from the samurai class was sent to Osaka for sale to city dwellers and merchants. As a result, spot and futures markets in rice developed in Osaka.[5]

The Tokugawa government introduced gold, silver, and copper coins nationwide. Whereas the silver coins varied in weight and thus in value, the minted gold and copper coins were standardized. Exchange rates among the three metals were determined daily in the market. The minted gold coins were prevalent in the eastern part of Japan, including Edo; the silver coins were prevalent in the western part, including Osaka.

Around 1600, a merchant in the Ise region began to issue paper notes in lieu of change for silver coins. This was the first paper money in Japan. A number of daimyos then began to print money. The first daimyo to do so on a regular basis was Matsudaira in the Fukui region. Subsequently, many daimyos printed local paper money backed by silver or gold. It is notable, and unusual from the evolution of monetary systems in other countries, that national coins and local paper money coexisted for a long time in Japan.

Economic policy during the Tokugawa era resembles present-day Japanese economic policy to a surprising extent. In the late seventeenth century, foreign trade was allowed on Dejima, an island near Nagasaki. In 1715, the government reduced the number of Dutch and Chinese ships allowed to come to Nagasaki in order to curb the outflow of coins. This parallels an import quota triggered by a reduction in foreign reserves. Partly because of a lack of silver and gold due to this outflow, and partly because of the government deficit, which was financed by borrowing from the tradesman (merchant) class, the Tokugawa government reduced the content of gold and silver in coins on two occasions: once in 1695 and once during the period 1706–1711. This was a classic case of seigniorage (profit from recoinage). Inflation resulted from the increases in the monetary stock.

In 1713, the Confucian scholar Hakuseki Arai advised the government that inflation was caused by too much money and recommended that the gold and silver content in coins be raised. The government adopted Arai's recommendation to reduce the money supply by increasing the gold and silver content in 1714 and 1715. Severe deflation resulted from this action. In particular, the price of rice decreased so much that daimyos and warriors, who taxed peasants in rice, were adversely affected. Because it had become a way of life for daimyos and warriors to sell their surplus rice, declines in the real price of rice reduced their wealth. In 1736 the government reversed its course and increased the money supply, and the price was more or less stable for the next 80 years.

In the early nineteenth century the Tokugawa government tightened its budget in reaction to inflationary pressure caused by natural disasters, the Tokugawa family's extravagance, and military expenditures. Large amounts of seigniorage were collected in the periods 1818–1829 and 1832–1837. The money stock increased by 60 percent on the first occasion and 20 percent on the second. As a result, the price level, most reliably recorded in rice prices, more than doubled from 1820 to 1837.

During the Tokugawa period, the merchant class steadily increased its wealth through trading as the economy expanded. Several merchants established exchanges that might be regarded as crude merchant banks. These exchanges, which first functioned as carriers transferring money from Tokyo to Osaka, eventually expanded their operations to include lending to farmers and local daimyos. The Mitsui Exchange, for example, was established in Edo in 1683 as a side business of a fabric store named Echigoya to transfer money from Tokyo to Osaka, and the current Sakura Bank is a direct descendant of the Mitsui Exchange.

In 1686 the Mitsui Exchange opened a Kyoto branch, and in 1691 the Mitsui Exchange in Osaka was appointed to be a government trading bank. The latter involved an operation to accept payments in Osaka from government offices and transfer the funds to Edo. This helped the Mitsui Exchange, because it could now offset the flow of gold from Tokyo to Osaka. By this time there were a dozen major exchanges in Osaka. These exchanges gradually increased their operations to lend money to farmers and daimyos.

Although the social and political system ranked the commercial class below samurai, farmers, and craftsmen, the commercial class contributed importantly to the accumulation of economic wealth during the Tokugawa period. As a result, establishment of a stable money supply and concern for price stability won broader support as economic activity increased relative to the pre-Tokugawa period.

It is important to note that some of these wealthy merchants later became bankers in the early Meiji period. When modern banking started, there was a group of people who had accumulated capital and expertise in some aspects of banking during the Tokugawa period.

2.3 The Meiji Restoration and Rapid Industrialization

One hallmark of the Tokugawa period was the policy of *sakoku,* under which Japanese citizens were prohibited from making contact with foreigners and from traveling to foreign countries. This policy evolved in steps and was aggressively enforced.[6]

Foreign pressure against the sakoku policy intensified in the nineteenth century, and the critical turning point was reached with the decision of the United States to send Commodore Matthew Perry in 1853 to force Japan to open ports for international trade. In 1854 the Tokugawa government signed a treaty to establish diplomatic and trading relationships with the United States. Similar treaties with other governments followed shortly afterward and effectively ended the sakoku policy.

Debate between those who wanted to return to the sakoku policy and throw out the foreigners and those who wanted to further open Japan to the outside world and take advantage of the superior technology of the West intensified in the late 1850s and the early 1860s. The opening of Japan became inevitable, partly because of the superiority of foreign fleets with modern weapons. In 1867 political power was transferred from the last Tokugawa shogun to a 16-year-old emperor.

In January 1868 the *Meiji Ishin* (Meiji Restoration) handed ultimate political power back to the imperial family. Major efforts to "modernize" the country's political, economic, and social institutions were mounted. Missions were sent to Europe and the United States, and advisers were invited to Japan from abroad. During the Meiji period, which lasted until 1912, Japan achieved a major transition from an agricultural to an industrialized economy. The Japanese economy sustained a steady increase in real output until World War II.[7] The emperor was the head of state and had power to oversee a central government formed under a prime minister and a cabinet as a constitutional monarchy.

The first task of the Meiji government was to push for a wealthy nation and a strong military. The Meiji government inherited a number of favorable conditions from the Tokugawa era that were important for the task at hand. Specifically, the Tokugawa era contributed an educated work force, accumulated capital, comparatively high technological level of agriculture, and an infrastructure of roads and irrigation. The Meiji government's push for military power and economic wealth, however, was based on the realization that past isolation had rendered Japan backward relative to the West because it had limited economic growth by denying Japan access to Western technology. Thus, the Meiji government sent numerous missions to the West to learn about modern technology and about the modern social and political infrastructure. The objective was thus to transform Japan from a feudal and agricultural economy to an industrial and military power in order to achieve parity with, and ultimately surpass, the economic power of the West.

Rapid industrialization was to be accomplished by establishing a strong central government, by removing the Tokugawa period's barriers to labor mobility across regions and economic class, by making education compulsory, by instituting fiscal reforms to base government revenue on currency payments rather than agricultural produce, by enhancing the country's infrastructure, and by establishing a modern banking system and a central bank.

2.4 A National Banking System

The Meiji government's budget had two major goals. First, to ease the transition of the new government, about half of the spending was directed to paying off members of the samurai class before their stipends were eliminated, repaying debts of former daimyos and the Tokugawa shogunate, and dealing with scattered rebellions against the new government. Second, to accomplish the objective of economic and military parity with the West, the remainder of the spending was directed to building an industrial infrastructure and a military. The new government did not have liquidity in the form of tax revenues, and thus it ran large deficits.

One of the first actions of the Meiji government, in 1868, was to order a specie-minting machine from the United Kingdom. At the same time, the government started to issue paper money (*dajokansatsu*). In 1869, the government started to mint coins which were intended to replace the paper money. It became immediately clear that the objectives of the government could not be achieved unless a stable financial and monetary environment could be established. At a minimum, the country needed a mechanism to provide a domestic money supply and a financial system that could mobilize the country's savings and support the accumulation of capital.

In 1870, Hirofumi Ito (a politician who later became prime minister) visited the United States to study the American national banking system, which had been established in 1863 by the federal (Union) government to establish a unified currency issued by private but government-chartered banks and backed by government bonds. Although the inefficiencies of free banking in the United States were often mentioned as having made the national banking system necessary, it is also clear that a primary objective of the national banking system was to finance the Union side in the Civil War. Ito recommended upon his return that the Meiji government duplicate the American system as a means of unifying Japan's currency by substituting national bank notes for the mixture of inconvertible government money, specie, and various forms of private money; that a banking system be established to mobilize Japan's financial resources to support industrialization; and that a market for government debt be created through this national banking system. The Japanese version did not incorporate a central bank, but it accepted the US premise that in the absence of a central bank a national banking system would be sufficient to provide a stable financial and monetary environment.

The burden of the stipend to samurai on the government budget became an important fiscal issue during the first years of the Meiji Restoration. Daimyos and shoguns lost power, as did many samurai. The government decided to terminate samurai stipends in exchange for a one-time lump-sum payment in government bonds, some of which were used to provide capital for national banks.

In 1872 Japan established a national banking system. A national bank could be established with capital of more than 50,000 yen, 60 percent of which was to be deposited with the Ministry of Finance in the form of previously issued government paper money, which was then exchanged for government bonds paying 6 percent. The government bonds could then be used as backing for new national bank notes. Only national banks were permitted to issue national bank notes. In this manner three objectives were achieved: the previously issued government notes were retired, a market for government bonds was established, and the new national bank notes issued by specially chartered banks were placed in circulation. The remaining 40 percent of capital was to be held as a specie reserve. The high reserve requirement, the relatively low yield on government bonds, and the lack of public acceptability of the bank notes limited the number of new national banks. Only four national banks (in Tokyo, Yokohama, Niigata, and Osaka) were established before the system was restructured in 1876.[8]

In 1876, the national banking system was revised so that national bank notes were now inconvertible into specie but exchangeable with government notes, and 80 percent of capital in the form of government bonds could be deposited with the Ministry of Finance in exchange for bank notes.[9] The remaining 20 percent of capital was to be held as a reserve against bank notes in the form of government bonds. These changes were sufficient to make operating a national bank profitable; as a result, the national banking system expanded rapidly after 1876.[10]

By 1879, 153 national banks had been established. In fact, the 1876 revisions rendered the issuing of bank notes so profitable that the government eventually stopped the formation of new national banks. National banks were also taxed on their issuing of notes, at the rate of 0.7 percent (after 1878).

In 1877, a rebellion against the Meiji government occurred in Kyushu. To finance the "Seinan War" to put down the rebellion, the government and the national banks issued money without restraint. A period of severe inflation followed. The experience convinced the government that the national banking system was only a partial solution to the problem of achieving a stable financial and monetary environment and offered no means to limit the overall amount of money in circulation. Since the United States did not have a central bank at the time, Japan looked to Europe for central-bank models.

2.5 The Bank of Japan

The Bank of Japan, established in October of 1882, became the sole bank to issue convertible notes two years later. National banks were converted

Table 2.1
The transition from national banking to central banking.

	Number of national banks in business	Capital (yen)	Bank notes in circulation (yen)
1872	National Banking Act		
December 1873	2	3,000,000	852,520
December 1874	4	3,450,000	802,703
December 1875	4	3,450,000	233,861
June 1876	4	2,450,000	62,456
August 1876	National Banking Act modified		
December 1876	5	2,550,000	1,654,976
December 1877	26	22,986,000	13,021,976
December 1878	95	33,351,101	24,455,159
December 1879	153	40,616,100	33,965,282
December 1880	143	44,206,100	34,385,349
1880	No more national banks allowed		
October 1881	"Fiscal consolidation" by Masayoshi Matsukata		
1882	Bank of Japan established		
1884	Bank of Japan issues notes		
December 1885	136	45,838,851	28,565,829
1897	Gold standard adopted		
1899	National Bank notes suspended as legal tender		

to "ordinary" banks accepting and issuing deposits and specializing in short-term business lending but were no longer permitted to issue notes against reserves (table 2.1). Private commercial banking was officially legalized by the 1890 Bank Law. In addition, the government established several other types of financial institutions. In 1874 the Postal Savings System was created to provide savings assets to the citizenry, and in 1902 the Industrial Bank of Japan was established to provide long-term business financing.

On the management of foreign exchange, the Bank of Japan worked closely with the Yokohama Specie Bank, which was established in 1880 (two years earlier than the Bank of Japan). The Yokohama Specie Bank was operated under the direction of the Bank of Japan to regulate the flow of foreign exchange and to encourage exports.

The Bank of Japan was initially modeled after Belgium's central bank; however, as is pointed out by Goodhart (1991, pp. 154–155), the Bank of Japan developed into a much different institution than the National Bank of Belgium. For example, although the governor was appointed by the king, the National Bank of Belgium was independent from political force, and operated by profit motives of shareholders. The Bank of Japan from the outset was under the direction of the Ministry of Finance, although it was a corporation (half of the capital was provided by the government and the other half by the private sector). The Bank of Japan was originally licensed under the Bank of Japan Ordinance for a 30-year period. Convertible currency (convertible to silver and two years later into gold) was not issued until 1885. The Bank of Japan's license was extended for another 30 years starting in 1912. The original Bank of Japan Law was revised in 1942 to reflect wartime conditions. The 1942 version of the law has remained essentially unchanged. It now appears likely, however, that in 1997 legislation will be proposed to grant the Bank of Japan greater institutional and legal independence from the Ministry of Finance.

The structure of the Bank of Japan as established in 1882 was characterized by several features which, in varying degrees, continue to the present. First, the Bank of Japan was established as a formally dependent central bank under the direct supervision of the Ministry of Finance. Little change occurred in the formal relationship between the Bank of Japan and the government. Indeed, the wartime revision of the Bank of Japan Law remained in force more than 50 years after the end of World War II. In 1996 serious efforts were underway to provide the Bank of Japan with more formal independence, and legislation is expected in 1997. Nonetheless, the Bank of Japan has achieved considerable de facto political independence since 1975. Second, the Bank of Japan was designated to play a minor role in the regulation and supervision of the financial system. Even today, the Bank of Japan plays a small role in the overall regulation of the financial system relative to the Ministry of Finance, and examinations of banks are done alternately by the Bank of Japan and the Ministry of Finance.[11] Third, the Bank of Japan was designated to support the developing banking system by encouraging a money-supply mechanism in which large banks depended on the discount window for funds, which were often provided at rates well below market levels. The large banks would then become suppliers of funds for smaller banks. Fourth, the Bank of Japan supervised foreign-exchange flows and the financing of foreign trade. The Bank of Japan did not actually undertake these activities; however, it provided funding and supervision over the Yokohama Specie Bank, which did.

The Japanese financial system expanded significantly after the revisions in the national banking system and the establishment of the Bank of Japan. In 1913, there were 1,457 ordinary banks, 52 specialized banks, and 684 small savings-type institutions (Schiffer 1962, p. 20), in addition to a large number of postal savings offices. During the period from the establishment of the national banking system through the 1920s, Japanese banking developed in an environment of limited government regulation compared to postwar Japan. Self-regulation and cartelization of the market did exist, however, with tacit approval from the government. Teranishi (1990) has argued that the prewar Japanese financial system was more competitive than is commonly believed, although it would be difficult to compare pre-World War I Japanese banking with the free banking in the United States in the period 1837–1863.

The prewar Japanese banking system consisted of essentially two sets of banks: a large number of small, poorly capitalized institutions that financed small businesses which were subject to credit and liquidity risks and a small number of very large, better-capitalized banks which became part of the industrial structure referred to as *zaibatsu* (in which families controlled industrial conglomerates by means of holding companies). In addition, the large banks had direct access to the Bank of Japan's discount window, while smaller banks had only indirect access through the larger banks. The small banks, being poorly capitalized and not monitored, were subject to credit and liquidity risks. In fact, many small banks were organized to provide funds for a single borrower or a small group of borrowers and thus provided no effective means of evaluating and monitoring borrower risk. The system was inherently unstable and susceptible to abuse.

2.6 The Financial Crisis of the 1920s and the Mobilization for War

Japan's most severe banking collapse occurred in 1927, primarily as an aftereffect of the major Tokyo earthquake of September 1, 1923. The 1923 earthquake was devastating in terms of lives lost (133,000) and property damage. The Bank of Japan aggressively discounted commercial bills drawn on banks in the affected areas to assist the reconstruction, with the understanding that losses would be covered by the government. By 1927 the "earthquake bills" totaled ¥2.1 billion, of which the Bank of Japan had rediscounted almost one-fourth of the outstanding amount.[12] The rediscount period had been extended twice, and in 1927 the legislature began debating a bill to extend measures for compensating earthquake-bill losses. The government was forced to reveal details about the earthquake bills, and as a result inside arrangements between companies and banks were made public. In March 1927, the debate and the mistaken claim by the Minister of Finance that the Tokyo Watanabe Bank had gone bankrupt triggered a run on that bank. The Watanabe Bank had been experiencing problems with nonperforming loans and deposit outflows but was still in operation.[13] The subsequent failure of the bank triggered runs on other banks and ultimately caused many banks to fail in 1927. In the absence of deposit insurance, depositors moved their saving from smaller and weaker banks to stronger ones. Large banks that failed were known to hold bad assets in the form of earthquake bills, but it was mainly small banks that failed (because of their high credit risk and lack of access to the Bank of Japan's discount window).

In the aftermath, the Bank Law of 1928 significantly expanded government regulation and supervision of the banking system and encouraged consolidation of banking (which continued for the next 15 years). The Ministry of Finance introduced bank examiners after the wave of bank failures in late 1927 and encouraged bank mergers as a means of disposing of bad assets. The number of commercial banks declined from 1,420 in 1925 to 466 by 1935, and by the end of the war only 61 banks remained in operation (along with a number of specialized financial institutions).

In the 1930s the government increased control over the financial system as part of its general war mobilization. The Provisional Fund Control Act of 1937, the National Mobilization Act of 1938, and the 1942 Bank of Japan Law were all designed to bring the financial resources of the country under the government's control and to support its war efforts. The government also required a company to designate one bank to handle all its finances. This is considered to be an origin of the "main bank" system.

2.7 The Bank of Japan Law

The Bank of Japan Law as revised in 1942 was consistent with putting all the nation's resources into the war effort. In this context, the Bank of Japan was required to support whatever objective was determined by the government. The central bank was placed entirely under the control of the Ministry of Finance.

Article 1 of the Bank of Japan Law states: "The Bank of Japan has, for its object, the regulation of the currency, the control and facilitation of credit and finance, and the maintenance and fostering of the credit system, pursuant to the national policy, in order that the general economic activities of the nation might adequately be enhanced." Article 2 states: "The Bank of Japan shall be managed solely for achievement of national aims." The stated objective is to achieve the potential of "economic activities" (alluding to potential output?) and other "national aims." There is no explicit mention of price stability. These articles clearly reflect the wartime concerns and objectives of the Japanese government.

Article 25 says: "The Bank of Japan may, with the permission of the competent Minister, undertake such businesses as are necessary for the maintenance and fostering of the credit system." This article, which has been invoked when the Bank of Japan has extended uncollateralized loans to financial institutions, is interpreted to justify any action if the lack of that action threatens the stability of the orderly credit system. Special loans to Yamaichi Securities in 1965, for example, were based on this article. Article 25 was also used to justify special loans to support various schemes to deal with nonperforming loans and bank failures in 1995.

Article 42 states: "The Bank of Japan shall be under the supervision of the competent Minister." Article 43 specifies: "The competent Minister may, whenever deemed necessary for the attainment of the object of the Bank of Japan, order the Bank to undertake any necessary business, or order alterations in the By-Laws as well as other necessary action." These articles are interpreted to mean that the Bank of Japan is under the control of the Finance Minister, and that if the minister objects to certain proposed actions (say, the change in the official discount rate) the Bank of Japan may not implement the plan. As a result of Articles 42 and 43, many researchers regard the legal "independence" of the Bank of Japan as very weak.

After the war, the Bank of Japan Law was revised under the supervision of the Supreme Commander for the Allied Powers (SCAP). Joseph Dodge, an American banker who had already helped end Germany's immediate postwar inflation, came to Japan in 1949 to help establish financial stability and became an economic advisor to SCAP. Dodge later became known in Japanese economic history as the individual who introduced the austerity budget and stopped inflation. He was also personally involved in an attempt to revise the Bank of Japan Law, although his main concern was that the Ministry of Finance might continue to force the Bank of Japan to finance fiscal deficits.

In 1949 the Policy Board was introduced as a decision-making forum and as a means of bringing down inflation and stabilizing the economy. The Policy Board is composed of five voting members representing banking, manufacturing, and agriculture; the Governor of the Bank of Japan serves as chairman, and there are two observers representing the Ministry of Finance and the Economic Planning Agency. Separate legislation was enacted prohibiting government-deficit bond issues. In this process, however, the Bank of Japan Law itself was not fully revised, and the infamous Articles 1 and 2 survived. Moreover, the Policy Board was a disappointment to Joseph Dodge:

> There has been no evidence the Policy Board has proved to be effective as a control device. . . . Apparently it is not a satisfactory substitute for statutory controls or for the personal administration and authority heretofore exercised by the Governor of the Bank of Japan and the Finance Minister.
>
> As far as we know, the Policy Board has taken no constructive action to strengthen the position of the Japanese banks.
>
> There does not appear to be close coordination of the financial policies of the Bank of Japan and Government fiscal policies.[14]

The disappointment to Dodge was that the Bank of Japan continued its easy-money policy while he was attempting to craft a fiscal-austerity plan that required tighter monetary policy. However, the Policy Board and the revision of the Bank of Japan Law envisioned by Dodge were never seen as a means to independence from the fiscal authority. It may not have been a coincidence that Articles 1 and 2 were not revised.

There was another attempt to revise the Bank of Japan Law in late 1950s to the early 1960s. The forum for this attempt was the Committee on Financial System Research (*Kinyu Seido Chosa kai*). The report was submitted in 1960 to the Minister of Finance. Discussion over the official relationship between the Bank of Japan and the government occurred in the 1950s in an effort to revise the Bank of Japan Law to suit peacetime conditions. The Committee for Financial System Research, an advisory committee of the Ministry of Finance, framed the debate in terms of two plans (Suzuki 1987, pp. 314–315) for resolving conflicts between the Bank of Japan and the Ministry of Finance. Plan A required the Bank of Japan to simply follow the instructions of the ministry as long as they did not violate the bank's guiding principles; plan B limited the ministry to a request for postponement of a policy for a certain period of time. Despite considerable discussion, the issue was never resolved and the Bank of Japan remained formally under the influence of the 1942 Bank of Japan Law. In fact, even if the Bank of Japan Law had been revised according to plan B, the bank would still remain formally dependent on the ministry. The recommendation for revision was not unanimous in the report, and the revision was not made. According to Shionoya (1962, p. 10),

> it became clear that the committee of experts was divided into two groups opposed to each other regarding the character of the central bank. It appeared that these two groups were represented by two committee members—the first group by Osamu Shimomura of the Ministry of Finance and the second group by Shigeo Matsumoto of the Bank of Japan. . . . Mr. Shimomura stressed the inevitable subordination of the central bank to the Government from the two standpoints—that the policy of the central bank should be managed and operated in full coordination with the general economic policy of the Government and that the Government on its part is called upon to hold itself responsible to the nation for the outcome of its financial policy. Mr. Matsumoto emphasized the necessity of maintaining the independence or neutrality of the central bank from the Government on the ground that the central bank is first of all assigned with the task of contributing to the stabilization of currency value. . . . It may be said that the greatest obstacle in the way of the revision of the Bank of Japan Law after all existed in the great difficulty in harmonizing these two different views.

This eloquently summarizes the state of understanding about central banking in 1960.

Serious debate about reforming the 1942 Bank of Japan Law was not initiated again until early 1996. Widespread dissatisfaction with the Ministry of Finance, and with its handling of the banking crisis in particular, generated political pressure to reform the ministry. Although the Ministry of Finance appears likely to escape many of the reforms initially proposed, one likely outcome is a reformation of the Bank of Japan Law to provide the Bank of Japan with more institutional independence (along the lines of the Federal Reserve System in the United States). In November 1996 an official working group issued a report dealing with this issue; the group's proposals are slated to be acted upon in 1997.

Concluding Comment

The evolution of Japan's financial and monetary institutions reflects a pattern common to other countries with only a few notable differences. The Bank of Japan's original functions were to provide a stable source of currency issue, to influence exchange rates, and to support the large banks. Little has changed since the Bank of Japan was organized in terms of these objectives. The Bank of Japan pursued these objectives as a formally dependent central bank with a limited role in the prudential regulation of the financial system. Although the formal relationship between the Bank of Japan and the government has changed little over the years, we will argue below that since the middle of the 1970s the Bank of Japan has often operated with considerable independence from political pressure.

3 Phases of Japan's Monetary-Policy Experience

The institutional, political, and macroeconomic environment in Japan has changed dramatically since World War II, in turn affecting the operating conditions and constraints faced by the central bank. The Bank of Japan has adapted and responded in various ways, ranging from adjustments in the technical details of operating procedures to significant shifts in the broad approach to policy design and implementation. In considering these changes, it is useful to divide the postwar period into five monetary-policy phases of varying length: 1945–1950, 1950–1971, 1971–1975, 1975–1985, and 1985–1996.

Each phase identifies a distinct period in the Japanese economy. The first phase was a period of great trauma, economic devastation, and high inflation after a war that virtually destroyed Japan's industrial capacity. The second phase was the "high-growth period," so named because of rapid real GNP growth and moderate inflation. This was also the Bretton Woods period of fixed exchange rates. The third phase was a brief, turbulent transitional period of inflation, oil-price increases, and end of the Bretton Woods system. In the fourth phase, with real GNP growth fluctuating between 3 and 5 percent per year and low rates of inflation, Japan emerged as the second-largest economy in the world. The fifth and current phase is another turbulent one. Whereas the first five years of the period saw asset-price inflation, asset-price deflation dominated the next five years. The asset deflation generated Japan's most severe recession since 1950 and weakened the financial system.

Monetary policy played an important role in each of these phases of economic performance.

3.1 1945–1950: Postwar Adjustment and a Foundation for Rapid Growth

Japan at the end of World War II was a devastated nation. The majority of its industrial capacity was destroyed, and the first postwar years witnessed major economic and financial disruptions manifested by high rates of inflation generated by government deficits and monetary growth. Japan's prospects improved in 1949 when the government embarked on Joseph Dodge's austerity program of reduced government spending and monetary growth.

At the same time, Japan embarked on a major transformation of its political and economic institutions—a transition comparable in some ways to the one that occurred during the Meiji Restoration. Reindustrialization was a major component of the postwar transition. Again, the prime objective was to achieve economic parity (at least) with other countries. Financial and monetary policies and institutions were structured to assist in the reindustrialization effort.

The stabilization effort initiated in 1949, the start of the Korean War in June 1950, and the end of the occupation in 1952 set the stage for rapid economic growth and for the emergence of the Bank of Japan as a major component of Japan's reindustrialization effort.

The Dodge Plan

Japan's transition from devastation to rapid economic growth involved inflation, austerity, potential recession, and the economic stimulus of the Korean War. The three-digit inflation (365 percent in 1946, 196 percent in 1947, and 166 percent in 1948) caused by rapid increases in the money supply and in government spending was brought under control in 1949 by the series of emergency measures referred to as the Dodge Plan. The policy Joseph Dodge initiated restrained the government budget, lowered the growth of the money supply, and committed Japan to the fixed exchange rate of ¥360 = $1.00. The inflation rate declined from 166 percent in 1948 to 63 percent in 1949 and to 18.2 percent in 1950. The Dodge Plan can be regarded as a successful experiment in stabilizing a high-inflation economy.

Disinflation is often accompanied by a sharp decline in output. However, Japan was able to avoid a severe recession by becoming an important supplier of goods for the United Nations forces in the Korean War, which began in June 1950.

The Financial System

The occupation, which lasted from 1945 to 1952, played a meaningful role in Japan's postwar financial and monetary policies; however, the role is often exaggerated. The financial system that remained after the occupation was not a new system; it strongly reflected prewar trends. It is more proper to view the postwar Japanese financial system as an evolution of the prewar structure with only minor changes introduced by the Allies during the occupation (Hamada and Horiuchi 1987).

The occupation dissolved *zaibatsu*, redefined the relationship between the Bank of Japan and the government, and established a Glass-Steagall type of regulatory wall between commercial and investment banking. However, these efforts did not achieve their intended goals entirely.

The rigid structure of the prewar *zaibatsu* was indeed dissolved; however, it was replaced by a looser structure of company groups with leadership provided by a large bank (sometimes referred to as enterprise groups) and the main bank system. The fiscal law written under the occupation force prohibited direct acceptance of government debt by the Bank of Japan and established a policy board to give the Bank some independence, but it left the Bank subordinate to national goals as defined in the Bank of Japan Law of 1942. Hence, the Bank could be pressured to keep interest rates low in order to minimize the costs of government debt finance. The Allies imposed a regulatory wall between banks and securities companies; however, this did not prohibit Japanese banks from holding equities of nonfinancial corporations.

The dissolution of *zaibatsu* holding companies and the breakup of monopolistic manufacturing companies did have a significant impact on the financial system, but in a manner not intended by the Allies. The new policies established bank dominance in enterprise groups and bank dominance in the flow of funds, both of which were special characteristics of Japanese finance during the period 1950–1971 (Cargill and Royama 1988). The advent of financial liberalization in the mid 1970s began to weaken the role of banks in Japan's industrial and financial structure, but only gradually.

3.2 1950–1971: The Bank of Japan's Policy Objectives and Instruments

Under the Bretton Woods system, Japan maintained a fixed exchange rate of 360 yen per dollar. Monetary policy during this period "passively responded" to international developments: the primary task of monetary policy, supported by extensive capital controls, was to maintain the fixed exchange rate. Discretionary actions by the Bank of Japan were limited, and monetary policy was often driven by adjustments in foreign-exchange reserves to offset exchange-rate pressures. Since movements of private capital were heavily regulated, trade-balance deficits (surpluses) placed pressure on the exchange rate to depreciate (appreciate) and were set by contractionary (expansionary) monetary-policy responses.[1]

The primary instruments of monetary policy in the 1950s and 1960s were "window guidance" (i.e., quantitative limits on commercial bank lending), quantitative limits on discount loans, and changes in the discount rate. Japanese monetary policy was able to rely on quantitative controls because Japan maintained a heavily regulated and protected financial system until the early 1970s, as did many other industrial countries,[2] though Japan's financial structure was probably one of the most rigidly and administratively controlled in the world. The government virtually prohibited flows of capital into or out of Japan. The monetary authorities explicitly or implicitly fixed most interest rates at low levels. The only significant exceptions to the policy of fixed interest rates were the interbank rate and the unofficial *gensaki* (repurchase) market in government bonds that emerged in the 1960s.

Quantitative credit controls and interbank lending were used in tandem to influence economic activity.[3] The Bank of Japan influenced the interbank rate in three ways: through the purchase and sale of bills in the interbank market (effectively setting the interbank rate), through administrative guidance of interbank transactions, and through credit rationing at the discount window. Changes in the interbank rate influenced the portfolio decisions of the city banks, particularly since they were large net borrowers in the interbank market. Increases (decreases) in the interbank rate contracted (expanded) the amount of funds banks could lend to the business sector and increased (decreased) the effective cost of funds. Banks increased the effective cost of funds by varying the required loan-to-deposit ratio. Borrowers were required to maintain compensating balances with the bank as a condition for obtaining loans. Banks could also change the effective cost of funds by altering the amount of loans that qualified for the fixed prime rate of interest.

The interbank rate also played a role in transmitting the effect of policy changes to other financial institutions. While city banks were net borrowers in the interbank market, other financial institutions were net

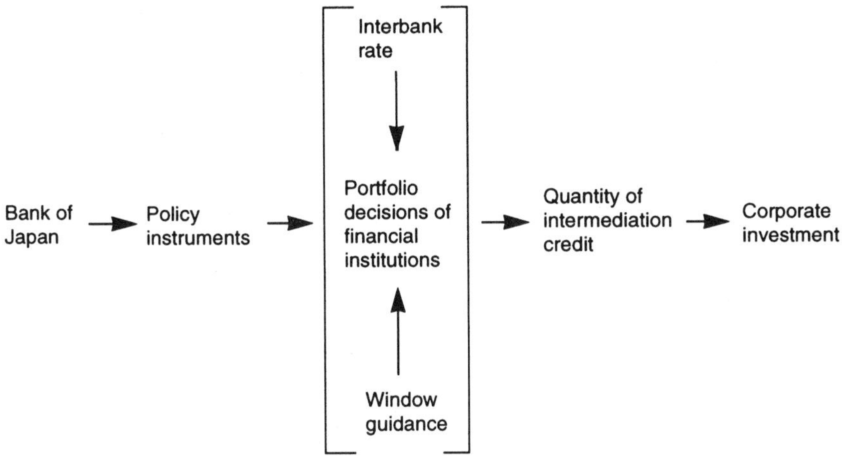

Figure 3.1
Pre-liberalization transmission of monetary policy. Source: Cargill and Hutchison 1988, p. 233.

lenders. Changes in the interbank rate influenced the portfolio decisions of the other financial institutions in that increases (decreases) in the interbank rate shifted funds away from (toward) business lending.

In addition to controlling interest rates, the Bank of Japan's window guidance limited the amount by which banks could increase loans in a month. To restrict monetary growth, the Bank of Japan would direct city banks to restrict business loans by lowering the lending limit. To encourage monetary growth, the Bank of Japan would raise the lending limit.

Figure 3.1, a schematic outline of pre-liberalization monetary policy in Japan, identifies two channels: Bank of Japan actions to change the interbank rate (which in turn influenced portfolio decisions of financial institutions to change lending to the corporate sector) and Bank of Japan actions through window guidance to change the quantity of funds available to financial institutions and the corporate sector.

The low-interest-rate policy and the emphasis on credit rationing meant that the loan market was often in disequilibrium. During the high-growth period it was usually in a state of excess demand for loans. Credit limits had a constraining effect on the behavior of banks and firms. Ito and Ueda (1981) conducted an econometric test of the rationing of business credit in Japan for the period 1968–1977 compared to the United States for the period 1965–1979. They found that the market in business loans was in disequilibrium more frequently in Japan, and that the adjustment of interest rates to excess supply or demand was much slower in Japan. Changing quantitative limits on bank loans was apparently effective as a monetary instrument influencing business investment and aggregate demand.

The High-Growth Period

The most remarkable aspect of the Japanese economy during this period was its rapid growth. Between 1950 and 1973 the economy grew at an average rate of 10 percent a year, doubling its size every seven years. Rapid productivity growth, technological development, and dynamic industrial transformation characterized the period. Unemployment was below 2 percent for most of the period, and Japan's manufacturing sector became increasingly competitive in the world's export markets. Only the recession of 1954 saw a decline in output; otherwise the only economic downturns were growth recessions. These growth recessions—short episodes in which output growth slowed to average rates of 3.7–5.0 percent—were generally induced by restrictive monetary policy designed to restore equilibrium to the balance of payments.

Although Japan's average growth during this period was the highest among the industrial countries, volatility was also fairly high. The standard deviation of real GNP growth was 3.9 percent for Japan during the period 1955–1973, compared to 2.0 percent for the United States. However, standardizing for the high average rate of growth (coefficient of variation: standard deviation divided by average growth rate) gives more comparable measures of volatility: 0.43 for Japan and 0.58 for the United States. In any case, Japan's volatility was associated with rapid industrial transformation, with rebuilding an economy devastated by war, and with playing technological "catch up" with Europe and the United States[4] (Denison and Chung 1976).

Average inflation during this period was also moderately high by the standards of the industrial countries, with the consumer-price-index inflation rate averaging about 4.5 percent (1950–1972). Inflation was not a top policy concern; however, the focus was on growth, and in any case the overall stance of monetary policy was constrained in large measure by the balance of payments. In addition, no industrial economy matched the growth of GDP experienced by Japan during this period (table 3.1).

Table 3.1
Macroeconomic performance of Japan and various other industrial countries (average percentage changes). "Germany" is the Federal Republic until unification. G7 includes Japan, the United States, Germany, France, Italy, the United Kingdom, and Canada. OECD includes G7, Australia, Austria, Belgium, Denmark, Finland, Greece, Iceland, Ireland, Luxembourg, Mexico, the Netherlands, New Zealand, Norway, Portugal, Spain, Sweden, Switzerland, and Turkey. Growth rate and CPI inflation rate are annual percentage rates of change between the years indicated. Unemployment rate is unemployment as a percentage of the total labor force and the average of the years indicated. Source: *Historical Statistics, 1960–1993* (Organization for Economic Cooperation and Development, 1995).

	Real-GDP growth rate	Inflation (CPI)	Unemployment rate
1960–1973			
Japan	9.6	6.2	1.3
US	3.9	3.2	4.8
Germany	4.3	3.4	0.8
G7 average	4.8	3.9	3.1
OECD average	4.9	4.1	3.2
1973–1979			
Japan	3.6	9.9	1.9
US	2.5	8.5	6.7
Germany	2.4	4.7	3.4
G7 average	2.7	9.8	4.9
OECD average	2.8	10.8	5.0
1979–1989			
Japan	4.0	2.5	2.5
US	2.5	5.5	7.2
Germany	1.8	2.9	6.8
G7 average	2.7	5.6	6.9
OECD average	2.6	8.9	7.2
1989–1993			
Japan	1.7	2.3	2.2
US	2.5	3.9	6.5
Germany	2.9	3.6	7.3
G7 average	1.6	3.8	6.7
OECD average	1.7	5.5	7.2

3.3 1971–1975: "Wild Inflation"

Japan's transition from the high growth of the 1950s and the 1960s to the more moderate pace of the 1970s was not smooth. Policy errors and external stocks had profound influences on the Bank of Japan's policy. In 1968 and 1969 the Japanese economy was in a boom, with the GDP growing at a rate in excess of 12 percent. But a current-account surplus, substantial for the time, of more than ¥720 billion ($2 billion at the fixed exchange rate of ¥360 per dollar) failed to generate a monetary "brake" on the economy. At the fixed nominal exchange rate of ¥360 per dollar, Japan's improved competitiveness had led to a structural trade surplus, which had brought automatic pressure for monetary expansion (Organization for Economic Cooperation and Development 1969).[5] Consumer-price inflation was hovering at 5.5 percent in 1968–69. By 1970, real growth was still growing at a rate over 10 percent, and the current-account surplus was still over $2 billion, but the inflation rate had climbed to 7.7 percent.

The obvious macroeconomic policy course at this point would have been to revalue the yen. The Japanese government resisted revaluation for several reasons: defending the exchange rate of ¥360 to $1 was part of the foundation underlying its commitment to the Bretton Woods system, the ¥360 rate was viewed as fundamental in the success of the preceding two decades, and the government wanted to protect export-based industries. However, continued imbalances in the international economy (primarily balance-of-payments deficits of the United States juxtaposed against surpluses in Japan and Germany) made the Bretton Woods system untenable.

The United States unilaterally abandoned the Bretton Woods system when it took the dollar off the gold standard in August 1971 after being frustrated with Germany and Japan (especially the latter) for refusing to revalue their currencies. A short period of floating rates was followed by another attempt to fix parities in the context of the Smithsonian Agreement in December. The yen was set at ¥308 per dollar. Even this attempt failed to adequately redress international imbalances, however. After massive foreign-exchange interventions to support the dollar, governments eventually gave in to market forces. The present period of floating rates began in February 1973.

Against this background, Japan's economy slowed considerably in 1971, partly in response to the tightening of monetary policy in 1969 and the revaluation of the yen from 360 to 308 per dollar. In 1971, the growth rate of Japan's real GNP was only 4.4 percent, with private investment falling by 0.4 percent. The Bank of Japan responded quickly to the slowing economy, apparently overestimating the adverse effect on output growth associated with yen appreciation, and cut the discount rate six times between October 1970 to June 1972.

Despite the yen appreciation, Japan's current-account surplus grew between 1971 and 1972. At the same time, the "inflation adjustment" argument that inflation should be tolerated so as to induce real appreciation of the exchange rate without changing nominal parities gained support in Japan. The government planned for deliberate inflation in 1972, and money growth rose very rapidly in 1971 and 1972. Moreover, political pressure to maintain a rapidly expanding economy, leading to excessive cuts in the discount rate, was exerted by Prime Minister Tanaka to support his Reconstruct the Japanese Archipelago plan (Ito 1992; Henning 1994).

Despite these moves, measured inflation was stable in 1972 (table 3.2) because the revaluation of the yen masked the underlying domestic inflationary pressure. Built-up demand pressures associated with monetary expansion emerged in 1973, however, and price inflation accelerated substantially. The CPI registered annual rates of increase of 7.4, 10.7, and 12.6 percent during the first three quarters of 1973. This was followed by OPEC's announcement of the oil embargo and the sharp oil-price increases starting in the middle of October.

This sequence of events led to the "wild inflation" of late 1973 and 1974. CPI inflation was 12 percent in 1973 and jumped to over 23 percent in 1974. The concern over the high inflation rate and the associated disruption in the real economy (including the worst labor disputes since the late 1940s) quickly made price stability a policy priority. In addition, the high rates of inflation rekindled memories of the inflationary conditions immediately after World War II. The Bank of Japan's new approach to tackling the inflation problem coincided with two significant changes in the bank's operating environment: the end of the fixed-exchange-rate system in 1973 and the start of financial liberalization.

3.4 1975–1985: The "Money-Focused" Monetary Policy

The Bank of Japan's *Monthly Review* of July 1975 contained an article entitled "On the Importance of the Money Supply in Japan." This article announced a new monetary-policy procedure emphasizing the importance of the money supply as a fundamental determinant of inflation

Table 3.2
CPI inflation rates during the "wild inflation" period.

1971	
first quarter	5.9
second quarter	6.4
third quarter	7.6
fourth quarter	5.4
1972	
first quarter	4.7
second quarter	4.9
third quarter	4.9
fourth quarter	5.1
1973	
first quarter	7.4
second quarter	10.7
third quarter	12.6
fourth quarter	16.0
1974	
first quarter	23.3
second quarter	22.4
third quarter	23.3
fourth quarter	23.2
1975	
first quarter	15.3
second quarter	13.3
third quarter	10.4
fourth quarter	8.7
1986	
first quarter	8.9
second quarter	9.5
third quarter	9.7
fourth quarter	9.5

and the usefulness of monetary growth as an intermediate policy indicator. Consistent with the policy pronouncement, the growth rate of the broad money aggregate (M2 + CDs) gradually declined between 1975 and 1985 (figure 3.2). Money growth was permitted to fluctuate between 15 and 30 percent per annum between 1956 and 1973, but since that time monetary growth was brought down gradually, dropping to just over 7 percent in 1983. Although some fluctuation around the declining trend

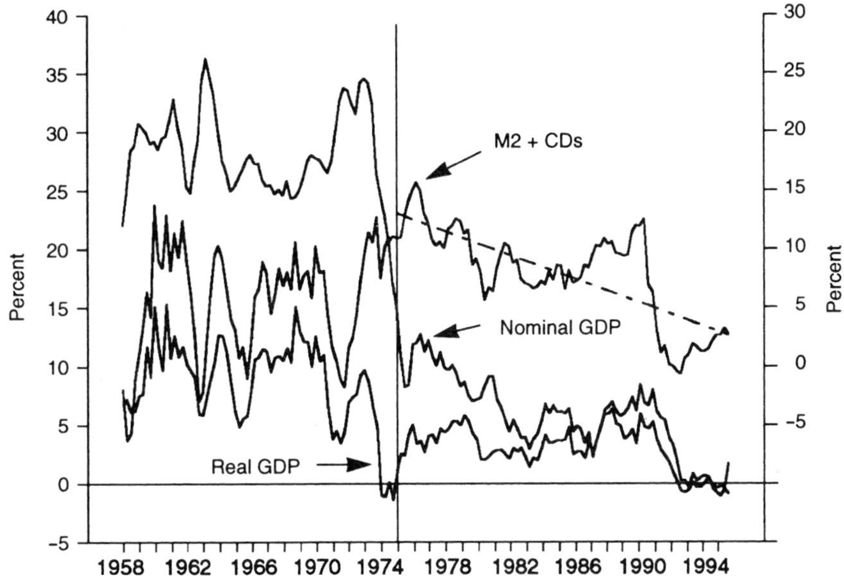

Figure 3.2
Growth rate of money supply (M2 + CDs) relative to right scale, growth rate of nominal GDP relative to left scale, and growth rate of real GDP relative to left scale. Difference between middle line and bottom line is GDP inflation rate. All growth rates measured against same quarter of preceding year. The trend of the top line after 1975 was calculated by regressing the monetary growth rates on the time trend from 1975 to 1995. The "M2 + CDs" data (before 1979:1 "M2" because CDs did not exist) are the three-month averages of end-of-month observations in the quarter.

was evident, figure 3.2 shows that much greater stability in money growth was achieved during this period.[6]

Another feature of the new policy approach, beginning in July 1978, was public announcement of the quarterly "forecasts" of the broad money growth rate. (See table 3.3.[7,8,9]) These announcements emphasized the Bank of Japan's new focus on monetary growth in the formulation of policy. They may also have provided information useful to the public in forming expectations about the future course of policy.

The announcements are for the projected annual rate of growth for one quarter ahead with the previous three quarters of monetary growth already realized. For example, the forecast for monetary growth in the first quarter of 1995 over the first quarter of 1994 is announced at the beginning of the first quarter of 1995. The forecast represents an average of three quarters' realized money growth and one quarter's projected or forecast money growth. Each quarter, the base for the new projection is

Table 3.3
"Forecast" and actual M2 + CDs growth rate compared to same quarter of preceding year. ("Shocks": actual minus mean. "Large shocks": outside range.)

	Forecast					
	Floor	Mean	Ceiling	Actual	Shocks	Large shocks
78:3	11.0	11.75	12.5	12.1	0.35	
78:4	12.0	12.5	13.0	12.2	−0.3	
79:1	12.0	12.5	13.0	12.3	−0.2	
79:2	12.0	12.5	13.0	12.1	−0.4	
79:3	11.5	12.0	12.5	11.7	−0.3	
79:4	10.5	11.0	11.5	11.2	0.2	
80:1	9.75	10.0	10.25	10.6	0.6	+0.35
80:2	10.0	10.5	11.0	10.1	−0.4	
80:3	9.5	9.75	10.0	8.4	−1.35	−1.1
80:4	7.75	8.0	8.25	7.8	−0.2	
81:1	6.75	7.0	7.25	7.6	0.6	+0.35
81:2	7.0	7.5	8.0	7.9	0.4	
81:3	9.0	9.5	10.0	9.6	0.1	
81:4	10.0	10.5	11.0	10.6	0.1	
82:1	10.5	11.0	11.5	10.6	−0.4	
82:2	9.5	10.0	10.5	9.2	−0.8	−0.3
82:3	8.5	9.0	9.5	9.0	0.0	
82:4	7.5	8.0	8.5	8.1	0.1	
83:1	7.0	7.5	8.0	7.6	0.1	
83:2	7.0	7.5	8.0	7.6	0.1	
83:3	6.5	7.0	7.5	7.1	0.1	
83:4	6.5	7.0	7.5	7.2	0.2	
84:1	7.0	7.5	8.0	7.9	0.4	
84:2	7.5	8.0	8.5	7.6	−0.4	
84:3	7.5	8.0	8.5	7.8	−0.2	
84:4	7.5	8.0	8.5	7.9	−0.10	
85:1	7.5	8.0	8.5	7.9	−0.10	
85:2	7.5	8.0	8.5	8.3	0.30	
85:3	7.5	8.0	8.5	8.3	0.30	
85:4	8.0	8.5	9.0	9.0	0.50	
86:1	8.5	9.0	9.5	9.0	0.0	
86:2	8.0	8.75	9.5	8.5	−0.25	
86:3	8.0	8.5	9.0	8.8	0.30	
86:4	8.0	8.5	9.0	8.3	−0.20	
87:1	7.5	8.0	8.5	8.8	0.80	+0.3
87:2	8.5	9.0	9.5	10.0	1.0	+0.5
87:3	9.5	10.0	10.5	10.8	0.80	+0.3

Table 3.3
(continued)

	Forecast					
	Floor	Mean	Ceiling	Actual	Shocks	Large shocks
87:4	11.0	11.5	12.0	11.8	0.30	
88:1	11.5	12.0	12.5	12.1	0.10	
88:2	11.5	12.0	12.5	11.3	−0.70	−0.2
88:3	10.0	10.5	11.0	10.9	0.40	
88:4	10.0	10.5	11.0	10.6	0.10	
89:1	10.0	10.5	11.0	10.3	0.20	
89:2	10.0	10.5	11.0	9.7	0.80	−0.3
89:3	9.0	9.5	10.0	9.7	0.20	
89:4	9.0	9.5	10.0	10.0	0.50	
90:1	9.0	9.5	10.0	11.7	2.20	+1.70
90:2	11.0	11.5	12.0	13.0	1.50	+1.0
90:3	12.0	12.5	13.0	12.0	−0.50	
90:4	10.5	11.0	11.5	10.0	1.0	−0.5
91:1	7.5	8.0	8.5	6.0	−2.0	−1.5
91:2	3.5	4.0	4.5	3.7	−0.3	
91:3	3.0	3.5	4.0	2.8	−0.7	−0.2
91:4	2.0	2.5	3.0	2.2	−0.3	
92:1	2.0	2.5	3.0	1.7	−0.8	−0.3
92:2	1.5	2.0	2.5	1.2	−0.8	−0.3
92:3	0.5	1.0	1.5	0.0	−1.0	−0.5
92:4	−0.5	0.0	0.5	−0.5	−0.5	
93:1	−0.5	0.0	0.5	−0.2	−0.2	
93:2	0.0	0.5	1.0	1.1	0.6	+0.1
93:3	1.0	1.5	2.0	1.7	0.2	
93:4	1.5	2.0	2.5	1.6	−0.4	
94:1	1.0	1.5	2.0	1.7	0.2	
94:2	1.0	1.5	2.0	1.8	0.3	
94:3	1.0	1.5	2.0	2.1	0.6	+0.1
94:4	2.0	2.5	3.0	2.7	0.2	
95:1	2.5	3.0	3.5	3.5	0.5	
95:2	3.0	3.5	4.0	3.2	−0.3	
95:3	2.5	3.0	3.5	2.9	−0.1	
95:4	2.0	2.5	3.0	3.1	0.6	+0.1
96:1	2.5	3.0	3.5	3.0	0.0	

the actual level of M2 + CDs three quarters earlier.[10] Bank of Japan officials have noted that the announced figures should be interpreted as projections rather than targets (Shimamoto 1982, p. 81). That is, they represent the Bank of Japan's estimates of the money growth consistent with policy settings and macroeconomic developments in the past, as well as those anticipated over the next quarter. In addition, as part of the process, the Bank of Japan makes an "estimate" of its own policy stance (which is not publicly announced).

The "Forecasts" in More Detail

The Bank of Japan started announcing forecasts of money-supply growth in 1978, and the subsequent low-inflation policy outcome for the next decade has attracted considerable attention in the literature. How valuable were the publicly announced forecasts in helping to achieve a more stable monetary and inflationary environment in Japan? Three main questions arise in this regard:

How accurate were the forecasts of monetary growth ? Only reasonably accurate forecasts could presumably help stabilize public expectations about the future course of monetary policy.

How much information about future monetary growth did the official forecasts provide that was not available from other sources? Additional information provided by the forecasts is the relevant criterion by which to judge whether they helped the public form a more accurate picture of future policy development.

Were the official forecasts really monetary targets, forming an important part of a broader "monetarist" strategy followed by the Bank of Japan? This interpretation has been offered by some analysts.

This section addresses these questions in turn.

Official description

The Bank of Japan explains in several publications why it adopted a "money-focused monetary policy" in the mid 1970s and how that policy was implemented. (See, e.g., Suzuki 1987, pp. 328–331.) This signaled a change in monetary management in Japan. Beginning in July 1978, the Bank of Japan made it a rule to announce, at the beginning of every quarter, an estimated value for the growth rate of the average outstanding balance of the money supply relative to the same period in the previous year. This estimated value, called a *mitshi* (forecast), applies to the current quarter. The following is a summary of an official description of the Bank of Japan's forecast announcement:

> . . . the annual rate of increase is the focus of attention. . . . Monetary policy in Japan focuses on M2 + CDs but does not determine "targets" in the strict sense of the word. Only "forecasts" [*mitshi*] are announced. However, the policy actions of the Bank of Japan itself are included in the determination of these forecasts, and in this sense the forecasts represent increases in the money supply that the Bank of Japan is willing to permit. (Bank of Japan 1986, p. 465; translation, p. 331)

The above description allows some degree of interpretation over whether a *mitshi* is a "forecast" or a "target." One way to resolve this issue is to examine the characteristics of the "forecasts" and determine whether they are equivalent to monetarist "targets."

Track record

Ito (1989a) examines the track record of "forecasts" measured both by the official description (four-quarter growth rate) and the quarter-to-quarter growth rate. The announced "forecasts" and ex post actual growth rates of M2 + CDs are summarized in table 3.3 (updated to 1996). The difference between the mean of the forecast and actual growth rates are shown in the "shocks" column of table 3.3. The "large shocks" column shows that the actual path strayed outside the forecast range only four times during the "money-focused" episode through 1985, but ten times between 1986 and 1991. The most notable deviations occurred in 1987, when there were three straight quarters of underpredicting monetary growth, and in 1990, when there were two successive quarters of large errors underpredicting monetary growth.

The forecasts during the "money-focused" period appear highly accurate; however, a few caveats are in order. First, in the original official announcement, the range of the "forecasts" is not accurately specified. Instead, only descriptive expressions of the range (e.g. "about" 10 percent) are announced. This expression is interpreted numerically as marking a range of ±50 basis points around the forecast.[11] The upper and lower bounds as well as the mean are recorded. Second, since the announcement is deliberately vague, some rounding errors in the announcement are inevitable. For example, even if the Bank of Japan predicts the growth rate to be "10.18% ± 0.48%," the Bank's announcement may say "about 10%." The same announcement, however, may reflect a slightly different target, such as "9.89% ± 0.46%." Third, in the official announcement forecasts and actual (realized) rates are described in terms of growth rates (in percent) over the last four quarters. Denoting the officially announced annual growth rate forecast by $g'(t)$, we can use past data (the previous four quarters) on the log level of M2 + CDs, $m(t-4)$, to derive the implied (log) level forecast of the money supply in the current quarter, $f(t)$:

$$g'(t) = 100[f(t) - m(t-4)]. \tag{3.1}$$

Although a potential seasonality problem is avoided in this definition, the actual money growth in three out of four quarters covered in this forecast formula is already known. When three quarters of a forecast have already been realized, it is perhaps not surprising that the forecasting record illustrated in table 3.3 appears to be very good.[12]

Quarter-to-quarter values for the official money projections would provide a better indication of the accuracy of these forecasts. These values can be calculated straightforwardly, since the actual growth rate for the last quarter is announced at the same time as the "forecast" for this quarter. Quarter-to-quarter forecasts, denoted $g(t)$, are given by

$$g(t) = 400[f(t) - m(t-1)]. \tag{3.2}$$

The rate of change is multiplied by 400 in order to annualize the growth rate. This conversion is applied separately to the ceiling, the mean, and the floor of the forecast statistics. The actual rate of monetary growth is also converted to a quarter-to-quarter basis. Table 3.4 shows the track record in terms of these quarter-to-quarter growth rates.

Comparing table 3.3 (announced, $g'(t)$, four-quarter growth rate) with table 3.4 (implied, $g(t)$, quarter-to-quarter growth rate) makes it clear that the "true" forecast errors are much larger than unadjusted official figures would suggest. The average mean absolute error of the official (unadjusted) forecasts is 0.46 percentage points during the 1978–1991 period, while the implied errors are almost four times larger (1.7 percentage points). Moreover, the implied quarter-to-quarter money-growth projections are much more variable than the official figures. The standard deviation of the adjusted values is 1.73, compared to a standard deviation for the official values of 0.47. As a result, the official and adjusted values at times provide different signals about the rate of monetary growth.

Accuracy of the Bank of Japan's forecasts

Ito (1989a) and Hutchison and Judd (1992) investigated whether the announced forecasts predicted the money supply without systematic bias and whether they incorporated all the publicly available information available at the time of the forecast. Ito tested forecast bias, whereas Hutchison and Judd tested forecast efficiency.

Consider a forecast, $f(t)$, made at period $t - 1$ for the money supply at period t. An unbiased predictor of *ex post* realized values of $m(t)$ can be tested by the equation

$$m(t) - m(t - 1) = a + b[f(t) - m(t - 1)] + e(t), \tag{3.3}$$

where $e(t)$ is a disturbance term and where the unbiasedness property implies that $a = 0$ and $b = 1$. In addition, if the forecasts are efficient, the forecast errors are not correlated with any information available at the time of prediction. The efficiency property implies that $a = 0$ and $b = 0$ in the equation

$$m(t) - f(t) = a + bx(t) + e(t), \tag{3.4}$$

where $x(t)$ includes information available at time $t - 1$. A weak-form test includes only lagged forecast errors in the information set $x(t)$. A semi-strong test includes all publicly available information.

The unbiasedness test is presented in table 3.5 in terms of growth rates in line with the form in which the Bank of Japan's forecasts are announced. The joint test of unbiasedness ($a = 0$ and $b = 1$) is not rejected at the 5 percent significance level. The Bank of Japan forecasts, calculated on a one-quarter-ahead quarterly basis, are unbiased conditional estimates of money growth. This result is also found in Hutchison and Judd 1992.

Ito (1989a) and Hutchison and Judd (1992) investigate various forms of the efficiency property. Although mixed results are found for the efficiency tests, the overall conclusion is that the efficiency property cannot be rejected at conventional levels of significance. This indicates that the forecasts are efficient to the extent that the "information set," $x(t - 1)$, is not correlated with the forecast errors.

"Inside" information in the Bank of Japan's forecasts

The forecasts might contain "inside" information known to the Bank of Japan about future policy actions but not yet made public. A direct test of inside information is to check for the "information content" of the

Table 3.4
"Forecast" and actual M2 + CDs growth rate: implied quarter-to-quarter rate. ("Shocks": actual minus mean. "Large shocks": outside range.)

	Forecast					
	Floor	Mean	Ceiling	Actual	Shocks	Large shocks
78:3	8.87	11.63	14.39	13.06	1.43	
78:4	9.52	11.35	13.18	10.25	−1.10	
79:1	8.94	10.76	12.59	9.93	−0.83	
79:2	12.76	14.60	16.44	13.84	−0.76	
79:3	10.14	11.98	13.81	10.91	−1.06	
79:4	5.80	7.63	9.47	8.33	0.70	
80:1	4.62	5.54	6.46	7.93	2.39	+1.47
80:2	11.42	13.29	15.16	11.80	−1.49	
80:3	8.67	9.60	10.53	4.42	−5.18	−4.25
80:4	6.03	6.97	7.92	6.13	−0.84	
81:1	4.05	4.99	5.94	7.11	2.11	+1.17
81:2	9.66	11.57	13.49	13.07	1.50	
81:3	8.57	10.45	12.32	10.76	0.31	
81:4	7.67	9.53	11.38	9.78	0.25	
82:1	6.86	8.70	10.54	7.21	−1.49	
82:2	8.98	10.85	12.71	7.75	−3.09	−1.23
82:3	8.23	10.11	11.99	10.25	0.14	
82:4	4.01	5.89	7.76	6.14	0.27	
83:1	3.18	5.07	6.95	5.31	0.24	
83:2	5.61	7.51	9.40	7.90	0.39	
83:3	6.04	7.95	9.86	8.21	0.26	
83:4	3.99	5.89	7.78	6.62	0.74	
84:1	4.57	6.46	8.36	8.16	1.70	
84:2	6.20	8.09	9.98	6.44	−1.65	
84:3	7.96	9.86	11.76	9.23	−0.63	
84:4	5.37	7.25	9.14	6.78	−0.47	
85:1	6.74	8.64	10.53	8.32	−0.31	
85:2	4.87	6.76	8.64	7.99	1.23	
85:3	6.11	7.99	9.88	8.96	0.97	
85:4	5.82	7.70	9.58	9.54	1.84	
86:1	6.49	8.36	10.23	8.38	0.16	
86:2	4.23	7.03	9.84	5.97	−1.07	
86:3	7.21	9.09	10.98	10.34	1.24	
86:4	6.42	8.30	10.18	7.71	−0.60	
87:1	5.20	7.09	8.97	10.13	3.04	+1.15
87:2	4.82	6.69	8.55	10.46	3.77	+1.91

Table 3.4
(continued)

	Forecast					
	Floor	Mean	Ceiling	Actual	Shocks	Large shocks
87:3	8.43	10.30	12.16	13.27	2.98	+1.11
87:4	8.45	10.29	12.13	11.47	1.18	
88:1	8.95	10.78	12.61	10.97	0.19	
88:2	8.44	10.27	12.10	7.74	−2.53	−0.70
88:3	8.42	10.27	12.13	11.76	1.49	
88:4	8.15	10.00	11.86	10.33	0.33	
89:1	8.78	10.64	12.50	9.79	−0.85	
89:2	6.74	8.59	10.43	5.52	−3.07	−1.18
89:3	9.23	11.11	12.98	11.77	0.66	
89:4	7.80	9.67	11.54	11.63	1.96	+0.09
90:1	5.98	7.84	9.70	15.90	8.06	+6.20
90:2	3.11	4.92	6.74	10.35	5.42	+2.61
90:3	8.15	9.97	11.79	8.26	−1.71	
90:4	6.00	7.84	9.68	4.30	−3.54	−1.70
91:1	6.31	8.20	10.09	0.65	−7.55	−5.66
91:2	0.66	2.60	4.53	1.51	−1.09	
91:3	5.43	7.39	9.36	4.56	−2.83	−0.87
91:4	1.23	3.20	5.16	1.87	−1.32	
92:1	0.01	1.97	3.93	−1.07	−3.04	−1.08
92:2	0.62	2.60	4.57	−0.56	−3.16	+1.18
92:3	1.76	3.76	5.76	−0.26	−4.02	−2.02
92:4	−0.12	1.89	3.90	−0.29	−2.18	−0.17
93:1	−0.90	1.11	3.11	0.37	−0.73	
93:2	0.17	2.17	4.17	4.74	2.57	+0.57
93:3	−0.82	1.16	3.14	2.04	0.88	
93:4	−1.16	0.80	2.77	−0.87	−1.67	
94:1	−1.89	0.08	2.05	0.79	0.71	
94:2	2.03	4.02	6.01	5.11	1.09	
94:3	−1.01	0.96	2.94	3.22	2.26	0.28
94:4	−1.15	0.81	2.76	1.50	0.69	
95:1	0.10	2.05	4.00	4.01	1.96	0.01
95:2	3.14	5.10	7.06	4.10	−1.00	
95:3	0.31	2.26	4.22	1.69	−0.47	
95:4	−1.84	0.11	2.06	2.51	2.39	0.44
96:1	1.61	3.57	5.53	3.54	−0.03	

Table 3.5
Tests of unbiasedness property $m(t) - m(t-1) = a + b[f(t) - m(t-1)]$: estimates and standard errors for sample period 1978:4–1986:4. Hypothesis: $f(t) = m(t)$ or H_0: $(a,b) = (0,1)$. $F(2,31) = 0.385$. Significance = 0.683.

a	b	
−0.133	0.922	$R^2 = 0.699$
(0.266)	(0.106)	DW = 1.60

forecasts when publicly available information, $x(t-1)$, is added to a simple forecasting model. Hutchison and Judd (1992) construct a simple VAR model with lagged values of money growth, income growth, percentage change in interest rates, and percentage change in exchange rates—information available when the Bank of Japan announced its forecasts—and obtain forecast errors roughly similar to those of the Bank's forecasts. The forecasts are out-of-sample forecasts. The forecasting equation is estimated, using a "rolling regression" technique, only with information known at the time of the forecast. The root mean square errors (RMSEs) of the VAR and Bank of Japan forecasts are 2.7 percent and 2.2 percent, respectively, while the analogous mean forecast errors are 0.3 percent and –0.7 percent. Moreover, the VAR model forecasts pass the weak-form efficiency test in that forecast errors are not autocorrelated.

This suggests that the private sector, by using simple forecasting techniques, could do just about as well in forecasting money growth as by relying solely on Bank of Japan forecasts. But do the announced money forecasts improve the VAR model forecasts and hence provide some inside information about the Bank's future actions? One simple way to check for the information value of Bank of Japan forecasts is to estimate an equation predicting money growth with and without the forecasts ($g(t)$) included. If the inclusion of the Bank of Japan forecast contributes significantly to the predictive power of the estimated equation, it gives some support to the inside-information hypothesis. The coefficient from this regression—i.e., the coefficient on $g(t)$ in the regression of $m(t)$ on the information set $x(t)$ and $g(t)$—will be large (on a scale from zero to unity) if the information value of the announced Bank of Japan forecast is high and significantly contributes to the formation of expectations on the part of the public.

As is evident from table 3.6, the Bank of Japan's forecast does not appear to add significantly to the explanatory power of the forecast equation. That is, the coefficient on $g(t)$ is not significant at the 90 percent level of confidence, and the standard error of the equation is reduced only

Table 3.6
Information value of Bank of Japan forecasts (sample period: 1978:3–1988:1), with t statistics in parentheses. Source: Hutchison and Judd 1992.

Dependent variable: Growth in M2 + CDs	Without Bank of Japan projections	With Bank of Japan projections
Constant	2.79 (1.60)	2.70 (1.57)
M_{t-1}	0.27 (1.37)	0.19 (0.96)
M_{t-2}	0.22 (1.13)	0.16 (0.79)
M_{t-3}	0.30 (1.57)	0.27 (1.44)
M_{t-4}	−0.13 (−0.65)	−0.23 (−1.06)
I_{t-1}	−0.92 (−2.09)	−0.86 (−1.99)
I_{t-2}	0.28 (0.65)	0.20 (0.46)
I_{t-3}	−0.44 (−1.03)	−0.39 (−0.92)
I_{t-4}	0.45 (1.22)	0.43 (1.18)
Y_{t-1}	−0.03 (0.86)	0.05 (1.22)
Y_{t-2}	0.01 (0.15)	−0.01 (−0.21)
E_{t-1}	0.00 (0.23)	0.00 (0.06)
E_{t-2}	0.20 (1.40)	0.01 (0.68)
E_{t-3}	−0.01 (−0.77)	−0.00 (−0.29)
E_{t-4}	−0.02 (−1.61)	−0.02 (−1.35)
g_t	—	0.25 (1.31)
$\overline{R}^2$	0.40	0.42
SEE	1.53	1.50
Q	17.13	14.70

marginally. Moreover, if one measures the overall "information value" as the reduction in the forecast standard error from adding the announced Bank of Japan money projections to the VAR model, it is only 0.4 percent. It appears that the Bank of Japan's forecasts provide relatively little new information to the public.[13]

Test for a monetarist rule

The "forecasts" announced by the Bank of Japan may also provide a powerful test of a monetarist rule. In particular, the Bank's reactions to its forecast errors reveal how monetary policy is conducted. Suppose there is a positive forecast error—that is, the money supply grew faster than was forecast. The monetarist $k\%$ rule would prescribe a compensating decrease in the next quarter in response to the positive forecast error in order to keep a $k\%$ growth rate in the target period (say, a year). An accommodative monetary policy, on the other hand, would not offset higher-than-forecast growth in the money supply.

Moreover, a strict monetarist or non-activist approach to monetary policy eschews "fine tuning" of the economy. This would suggest that the monetary target is independent of economic conditions. If money-supply management follows fine tuning as advocated by traditional Keynesians, the money-supply target will react to economic conditions. Ito (1989a) tests these hypotheses by means of the equation

$$f(t) - f(t-1) = k + a[m(t-1) - f(t-1)] + bz(t-1) + e(t), \tag{3.5}$$

where $z(t-1)$ represents economic conditions and k represents the value of the monetarist $k\%$ rule. Economic conditions are represented by inflation and real GNP growth. A non-activist policy would lead to a zero vector of coefficients on $z(t-1)$. A rigid monetarism rule implies that a positive jump in the money supply should be compensated by a subsequent negative movement to maintain the long-run target. In terms of equation 3.5, this implies $a = -1$. Monetarism with "rebasing" may be implied by $a = 0$. That is, the jump in the money supply is allowed to occur, and perhaps it is interpreted as a one-time idiosyncratic event, but future money-supply growth is not affected after rebasing. A fully accommodative policy implies a significantly positive a coefficient in equation 3.5. That is, an unanticipated rise in money growth is allowed to continue.

The results are presented in table 3.7. The coefficient on the lagged forecast error, a, is estimated to be significantly positive at the 1 percent level of significance. The positive sign implies that a recent "surprise" increase in the actual money supply causes the Bank of Japan to increase its next "forecast" by more than what has already occurred.

The evidence rejects the hypothesis that the Bank of Japan practiced a monetarist rule. The estimated coefficient, a, implies that any increase or decrease in the level of money supply is accommodated. When the actual money supply deviated from the target, there was no effort (expressed in forming the next target) to correct the deviation. A jump in the money supply not only affected the level of the money supply but also prompted a further jump in the same direction for the future target. However, neither inflation nor the GNP growth rate affected the change in the money-supply target; this indicates that a simple activist approach was not followed.

One might wonder what made monetarism (or the rhetoric of monetarism) gain popularity in the mid 1970s in both the United States and Japan, and why the theory is not completely dismissed by the central banks. The answer could be political rather than economic. By high-

Table 3.7
Determinants of targets using quarter-to-quarter growth rates. Estimates and (in parentheses) standard errors of $f(t) - f(t-1) = k + a[m(t-1) - f(t-1)] + b\, z(t-1) + e(t)$ for the sample period 1978:4–1986:4. Values in brackets indicate statistical significance.

Constant	a	Quarterly inflation	Quarterly growth		Null: $a = 0$	Null: $a = 1$
−0.05	0.69	NA	NA	$R^2 = .13$	$F = 1.11$	$F = 0.02$
(0.44)	(0.29)			DW = 2.63	[0.30]	[0.02]
0.13	0.69	−0.06	NA	$R^2 = 0.10$	$F = 1.12$	$F = 5.39$
(0.62)	(0.30)	(0.14)		DW = 2.60	[0.30]	[0.03]
−1.55	0.69	NA	0.43	$R^2 = 0.23$	$F = 1.29$	$F = 6.29$
(0.79)	(0.27)		(0.19)	DW = 2.43	[0.27]	[0.02]
			[0.03]			
−1.44	0.69	−0.03	0.42	$R^2 = 0.20$	$F = 1.27$	$F = 6.02$
(0.93)	(0.28)	(0.13)	(0.19)	DW = 2.41	[0.27]	[0.02]
		[0.82]	[0.03]			

lighting the money supply as an intermediate target, it gives the central bank a convenient, and perhaps justified, argument when its tight monetary policy is opposed by other branches of the government.

Monetary Policy and Financial Liberalization

The emphasis on operating instruments and the transmission process of monetary policy also changed around this time in response to two major changes in the Bank of Japan's operating environment. First, the balance-of-payments and exchange-rate constraints were formally relaxed after 1973 with the end of the Bretton Woods system, allowing the Bank of Japan to pursue the new "money-focused" monetary policy and focus its attention more on price inflation. External considerations still played an important role in policy decisions, but they were not paramount. Second, the financial system began a transition from a regulated and administratively controlled structure to one that permitted market forces to play a more prominent role in the allocation of credit.[14] Financial liberalization had at least three important implications for the Bank of Japan: the increased market sensitivity of interest rates and portfolio decisions increased the complexity of the process of transmitting monetary policy, the increased financial assets and services made it more difficult to measure the money supply, and liberalization in general rendered the demand and supply of money more unstable and thus made a money-focused policy more difficult to implement.

Liberalization, however, did not result in a sharp shift in operating tactics or instruments used by the Bank of Japan. The transition of the Bank's policy to incorporate a more liberated financial environment has been gradual and is still in progress. The interbank rate remains a key policy target and indicator of monetary policy (Fukui 1986), and in fact the interbank rate played the same role as the federal funds rate in the United States in the conduct and implementation of monetary policy after 1975 (Dotsey 1986). Market-sensitive interest rates in Japan have enhanced the interest-rate-expenditure channel of monetary policy and reduced the credit-allocation channel that was so prominent before 1975; however, quantitative controls and interest-rate ceilings have been removed slowly. (The Bank of Japan did not officially end the policy of window guidance until July 1991.) Figure 3.3 presents a schematic outline of the process of transmitting monetary policy after liberalization.

Japan's Ministry of Finance has traditionally maintained extensive controls on interest rates. Before the wave of liberalization started in the 1980s, deposit interest-rate ceilings loosely linked to the official discount rate were legally binding and lending interest rates were effectively regulated through setting the "prime" lending rates in relation to the official discount rates. Thus, the Bank of Japan's official discount rate was the key rate in the regulated structure. The regulated interest rate on three-month deposit accounts, for example, was typically set 1.5 percentage points below the discount rate. The "yield curve" on time deposits was constrained to slope upward; for example, two-year deposit rates were typically set 2.25 percentage points above three-month deposits.

The reform strategy adopted by the Ministry of Finance in the late 1970s was to gradually deregulate interest rates on some instruments and incrementally reduce minimum purchase amounts and/or maturity restrictions, allowing households and small firms greater access. The basic elaborate regulated structure was maintained, but with the "free" instruments existing side by side with regulated instruments (Takeda and Turner 1992).

Several developments had especially important implications for the interpretation of monetary aggregates by the central bank. In May 1979, negotiable certificates of deposits (CDs) were introduced, with a minimum amount of ¥500 million ($3 million at the time). The CD interest rate was freely negotiated between the issuing institution and the buyer,

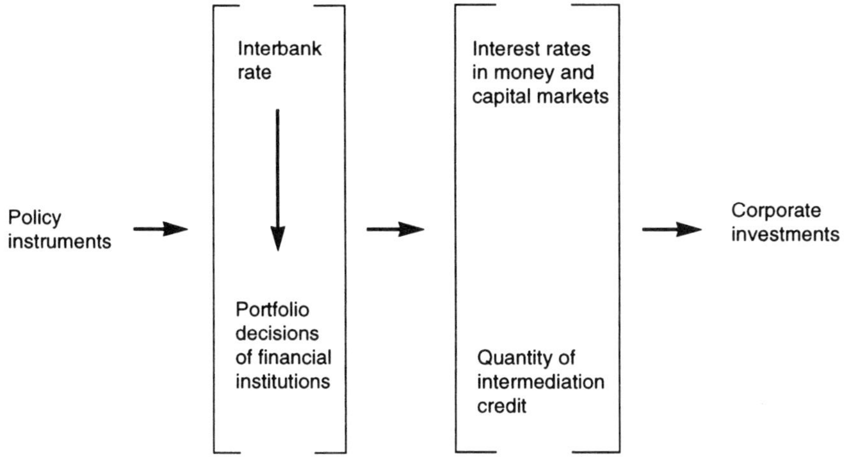

Figure 3.3
Post-liberalization transmission of monetary policy. Source: Cargill and Hutchison 1988, p. 239.

and there was no regulation on the interest rate determined in the primary or the secondary market. However, the initially large minimum amount for CDs was only gradually reduced (from ¥500 million to ¥300 million in 1984, ¥100 million in 1985, and, in 1988, to ¥50 million with terms ranging from two weeks to two years).

At the beginning of 1985, CDs were virtually the only bank-issued instrument with an unregulated interest rate, but even then the minimum amount was high enough to exclude most households and small and medium-size firms. And CD maturities other than 3–6 months were explicitly prohibited.

Two additional types of deposits with market-determined interest rates were introduced in 1985: the money-market certificate (MMC), with a minimum amount of ¥50 million, and large-amount time deposits (LTD), with the initial minimum amount set at ¥1 billion. The MMC interest rate was initially determined as the CD rate minus 0.75 percentage point, and the LTD interest rate is freely determined in negotiations between the bank and the depositor. In the beginning most LTD depositors were large corporate customers, but the appeal of LTDs to smaller enterprises and individuals increased with the successive reductions in minimum purchase amounts. In particular, LTDs became very popular when the minimum deposit amount was lowered to ¥100 million in October 1987. The minimum amounts for CDs and MMCs were also lowered repeatedly during the second half of the 1980s and the early 1990s.

Table 3.8
Market-rate deposits as a share of all bank deposits, 1980–1993 (end-of-period percentages). Source: Bank of Japan information, adopted from p. 8 of Choy 1994.

	Time deposits	MMCs	Small MMCs	Nonresident yen deposits	Foreign currency	CDs
1980	0.0	0.0	0.0	0.7	4.3	1.3
1985	2.0	2.2	0.0	1.0	7.8	3.5
1986	6.5	3.2	0.0	0.7	7.5	3.4
1987	15.3	5.3	0.0	0.7	8.0	3.2
1988	23.7	7.3	0.0	0.7	6.5	4.5
1989	37.6	2.8	4.8	0.5	6.3	5.0
1990	44.1	0.1	12.3	0.5	7.7	4.2
1991	45.4	0.0	7.4	0.4	7.1	3.9
1992	49.7	0.0	0.0	0.4	5.6	4.0
1993	56.4	0.0	0.0	0.2	5.1	4.5

In June 1993 regulations on the interest rates of time deposits were completely deregulated, and in October 1994 all other regulations on deposit interest rates (including those on demand or ordinary deposits) were eliminated. The shares of various market rate instruments (market interest-bearing accounts) in total bank deposits from 1980 to 1993 are shown in table 3.8. In 1980 only a little over 6 percent of deposits were associated with market interest rates. This jumped to over 16 percent in 1985 and climbed steadily. In terms of the share in the broad money aggregate (M2 + CDs), already by the end of 1990 40 percent was held in LTDs and 15 percent in (new-type) MMCs.[15] The growth of "liberalized interest rate" deposits against "regulated interest rate" deposits in the late 1980s was an interesting, but necessarily temporary, phenomenon. After 1993 the distinction is meaningless since all deposit rates have been deregulated.

The End of Window Guidance

Window guidance was used to restrain commercial banks' loans to corporations. As a direct quantitative control, however, window guidance came to be viewed as inconsistent with a more open and flexible financial system. Starting in the mid 1970s, the Bank of Japan evolved an operating strategy more in line with a liberalized financial environment; as a result, window guidance was deemphasized as a policy instrument during the years 1975–1985. In fact, there was active debate over the de-

Table 3.9
The development of window guidance, 1957–1991. Source: Bank of Japan, Institute of Monetary and Economic Studies, with some changes in wording.

	Objectives	Measures
Mar. 1957–June 1958 Dec. 1959–Aug. 1960 July 1961–Oct. 1962	City banks	Regulations over volume of loans on a monthly basis for each bank
Jan.–Dec. 1963	City banks Long-term credit banks Trust banks (banking account) Major regional banks	Amendment from monthly to quarterly basis Restraint set over the total volume of increase in lending expressed in percent of decrease from the same quarter of the previous year for each institutional category, the lending then to be distributed to each bank according to the bank's outstanding loans
Sep. 1966–Sep. 1967	Major mutual loan and savings banks (added)	
Oct. 1967–Dec. 1971	City banks Long-term credit banks	Bank of Japan guided banks to hold a sound reserve position for both monetary restraint and relaxation and not to increase excessively their loans (reserve position guidance)
Jan. 1972–June 1976	City banks Long-term credit banks Trust banks (banking and trust accounts) Regional banks Mutual loan and savings banks Major credit associations	Restriction on increase in lending on a quarterly basis for each bank (When necessary, the original lending limit can be arranged during the term.)
July 1976–Sep. 1979	same as above	Direction of each bank on its lending plans began to be respected *as much as possible*
Oct. 1979–Dec. 1980	same as above	Banks listed in Jan. 1972–June 1976 measure
Jan.–Dec. 1981	same as above	Direction of each bank on its lending plans should be respected *in principle*
Jan. 1982–	same as above	Direction of each bank on its lending plans should be respected *completely*
July 1991		Window guidance officially ends

sirability of abolishing window guidance as early as 1982; however, the Bank of Japan was concerned that an acceleration of bank lending might require a more aggressive and direct approach. Window guidance was officially abandoned in July 1991. Adoption of the Basle capital requirements[16] for Japanese banks was one of the reasons the Bank of Japan felt that banks would not increase lending excessively.

The Outcome of the New Policy (Was It a "Monetarist" Policy?)

The effect of the new policy regime during the period 1975–1986 was to significantly reduce the rate of monetary growth around a fairly predictable medium-term trend (figure 3.2). There is little doubt that the significant shift in the strategy of monetary policy and in its design helped achieve greater price stability than in the pre-1975 period (Pigott 1980; Suzuki 1986).

Perhaps the high-water mark of the Bank of Japan's success in fighting inflation under the new regime was its response to the 1979 oil-price shock. Interbank interest rates were increased by more than 800 basis points over a 12-month period in an effort to quickly avert inflationary pressures and to curb a rise in inflationary expectations. The results are shown in table 3.10. Japan avoided both significant inflation and recession, achieving a degree of macroeconomic stability not seen in the other large industrial countries.

The Bank of Japan's quarterly forecasts, the success in reducing the inflation rate in a short period, and the absence of inflation since 1975 have attracted a great deal of attention. Some academics have argued that the money forecasts have reduced monetary uncertainty and contributed to a more stable real economy. (See, e.g., Meltzer 1985.) Others have suggested that the monetary forecasts have helped the Bank of Japan follow a more consistent and predictable policy than the Federal Reserve (Friedman 1983, 1985). More generally, analysis of the forecasts helps to shed light on the rules-versus-discretion debate over the conduct of monetary policy.

What has been the role of monetary forecasts within the general framework of Japanese monetary policy? It is clear from the evidence presented above that the forecasts have not served as implicit intermediate targets for monetary control. When the actual rate of monetary growth deviated from the rate forecast, the next period's forecast was most likely to be adjusted toward the actual growth rate. That is, if the actual growth rate was higher than the forecast rate in quarter t, the fore-

Table 3.10
Macroeconomic performances after 1978–1980 oil shock. Source: International Monetary Fund. *World Economic Outlook*, April 1987.

	1979	1980	1981	1982
Real GNP (annual change, in percent)				
Japan	5.3	4.3	3.7	3.1
United States	2.5	−0.2	1.9	−2.5
Germany	4.0	1.5	—	−1.0
All industrial countries	3.4	1.3	1.4	−0.4
Unemployment rates (percent of labor force)				
Japan	2.1	2.0	2.2	2.4
United States	5.9	7.2	7.6	9.7
Germany	3.3	3.4	4.9	6.8
All industrial countries	5.1	5.8	6.7	8.2
Inflation: GNP deflator (annual change, in percent)				
Japan	3.0	3.8	3.2	1.9
United States	8.8	9.1	9.6	6.5
Germany	4.0	4.8	4.0	4.4
Inflation: consumer prices (annual change, in percent)				
Japan	3.7	7.7	4.9	2.7
United States	11.3	13.5	10.4	6.1
Germany	4.1	5.4	6.3	5.3
All industrial countries	9.1	11.7	9.9	7.4

cast rate of quarter $t + 1$ was higher than the forecast rate in quarter t. Hence, it was more than just base drift. The forecasts followed actual monetary growth developments and did not serve as targets. Moreover, the officially announced forecasts were shown not to significantly reduce economic uncertainty by helping to improve the private sector's predictions of future monetary growth.

These results are clearly not consistent with a simple $k\%$ monetarist rule. If the $k\%$ rule were to be taken seriously, the target rate for quarter $t + 1$ should move in the opposite direction of the deviation, so that $k\%$ growth in the money stock could be maintained in the long run. That is, if the actual rate were higher than the target rate in quarter t, then the target of the quarter $t + 1$ should be lower than the target rate in quarter t, in order to compensate for the unexpected increase.

The years 1975–1986 may be termed the period of "eclectic gradualism," a position between Keynesian fine tuning and a monetarist

$k\%$-growth rule (Suzuki 1985). Little evidence of traditional monetarism is evident, however, despite the pronouncements of some monetarists.[17]

The debate, however, is often confused by ambiguity over the meaning of monetarism. The Bank of Japan's operations are no more monetarist than those of the US Federal Reserve; it focuses on interest rates and does not adhere to a $k\%$ rule. At the same time, the Bank of Japan is a price-stabilizing central bank with few equals in the past two decades, and price stability cannot be maintained over long periods of time without attention to the long-run growth of the money supply. Much of the debate about the monetarist or monetary experiment of the Bank of Japan focuses on technical operating issues; however, the ultimate objective of price stability can be achieved through either interest-rate policies or money-focused policies, though technical considerations will favor one approach over the other. In the broader sense, the Bank of Japan has achieved the objective of price stability by nonmonetarist means.

3.5 1985–1996: Asset Inflation, Asset Deflation, and Monetary Policy

The first five years of this phase were characterized by high economic growth, yen appreciation, continued financial liberalization, and low CPI inflation. In the background, however, a financial bubble in the form of increasing stock and land prices appeared. The latter half of the period, in contrast, is characterized by the burst of the asset-price bubble when the Bank of Japan shifted toward tight monetary policy in 1989. The collapse of asset prices had a devastating effect on the real economy and on the financial system. As stock and land prices plummeted, the economy went into a recession. The subsequent problems for the financial system in the form of nonperforming loans (estimated to be about 10 percent of GNP) have created Japan's most severe financial crisis since 1950.

The Bank of Japan's policy played an important and controversial role in each of these periods. Monetary policy was expansionary during the first five years, and some observers criticize the Bank's willingness to accommodate asset inflation. The issues behind the expansionary monetary policy are complex, however.

The rapid growth in monetary aggregates in the second half of the 1980s concerned the Bank of Japan, but there was initially some doubt about its inflationary consequences. The money supply conspicuously accelerated in 1987 and again in 1989, breaking the pattern of gradual reduction of the money supply (0.5 percent annually) of the period

1975–1986. The Bank of Japan, however, was apparently surprised at the jump in money growth. "Large shocks" of money growth outside the announced projection range occurred ten times between 1987 and 1991 (table 3.3), and only four times between 1978 and 1986.

Two important factors made the evaluation of the monetary stance highly problematic at the time. First, significant deregulation of financial markets and the introduction of new financial instruments had recently occurred. Deregulation of deposit interest rates proceeded in stages, so that the share of deposits with deregulated interest rates in the M2 aggregate rose from zero in 1985 to more than 50 percent in 1990. If the monetary increase was caused simply by portfolio shifts triggered by deregulation, then temporarily rapid money growth need not have had inflationary consequences. Second, there was no sign of general inflation, primarily because of the decline in import prices associated with yen appreciation. It may be questioned whether monetary restraints should have been applied in response to rapid land-price and stock-price increases when the wholesale-price index was *dropping* at annual rates ranging from 0.5 percent (1987) to 4.7 percent (1986) during the period 1985–1988. Moreover, this pattern was consistent with financial deregulation, which could have caused asset-price changes as well as an upward shift in money demand without inflationary consequences.

Financial Liberalization and Money Demand

Whether financial deregulation contributed to the surge in money growth after 1985 can be investigated by estimating money-demand functions and testing for structural stability. This is accomplished by first estimating the money-demand function with pre-1985 data (i.e., data from the period before the introduction of MMCs and LTDs) and then evaluating out-of-sample forecast errors. If the out-of-sample forecasts represent a hypothetical money supply that would have been the case if deregulation had not been implemented, the "surprising" rise in the money supply may be regarded as the part attributable to deregulation.

We estimate several formulations of the money-demand function and present the results in table 3.11,[18] reporting estimates based on a real-adjustment formulation and on a nominal-adjustment equation. The CPI price deflator is employed. For the interest rate, the difference between the interbank rate and the own (M2 + CDs) rate is used. Real GNP is used for the economic-activity variable. Equations are estimated over

Table 3.11
Money demand function estimates and deviations of actual M2 + CDs from projected M2 + CDs money from 1985:1 to 1991:1.

Adjustment specification[a]	Real	Nominal
Estimates for 76:2–84:4		
$M(t-1)/P(t-1)$	0.838 (10.92)	—
$M(t-1)/P(t)$	—	0.927 (15.27)
LGNP	0.182 (1.269)	0.086 (0.787)
Interest rate	−0.005 (−4.51)	−0.0025 (−2.86)
R^2	0.996	0.997
DW	2.194	2.666
Estimates for 85:1–91:1		
$M(t-1)/P(t-1)$	0.679 (3.20)	—
$M(t-1)/P(t)$	–	0.905 (5.13)
LGNP	0.300 (2.154)	0.249 (2.23)
Interest rate	−0.004 (0.58)	0.0068 (1.14)
R^2	0.993	0.996
DW	1.820	2.163
CHOW $F(8,44)$ significance	1.004 (0.446)	1.242 (0.297)
((Actual − Projected[b])/Actual) × 100		
85:1	1.6	1.8
86:1	2.7	3.1
87:1	3.5	4.4
88:1	3.2	6.9
89:1	3.7	9.1
90:1	6.4	13.8
91:1	2.7	13.5

a. In each equation, a constant, a trend, and seasonal dummies for second, third, and fourth quarters are used as exogenous variables. The left-hand side (dependent variable) of each equation is $\log(M(t)/P(t))$, where M is end-of-quarter M2 + CDs and P is CPI. Interest rate is the Tegata (interbank) rate minus the own interest rate of M2 + CDs. The right-hand-side (independent) variables are expressed in natural logarithms, except for the interest rate. LGNP is the log of GNP.
b. Projected values obtained from 76:2–84:4 estimated equation.

the pre-reform 1976:2–1984:4 period and the post-reform 1985:1–1991:1 period. The last panel shows the money-demand out-of-sample forecast errors (actual less forecast values) for the period 1985:1–1991:1 obtained from the parameters estimated for 1976–1984 (first panel).

Contrary to first impressions that liberalization accounted for the acceleration in monetary growth, the statistical tests cannot reject the null hypothesis of no structural break in 1985. Moreover, the magnitude of actual money over its projected path is only 3–14 percent, even after five years. These results are consistent with those of Yoshida (1990), who finds a stable money-demand function for Japan over the period 1968–1989 using an error-correction methodology to estimate money demand. Using a multivariate cointegration methodology, however, Yoshida and Rasche (1990) find that the money demand did shift upward in 1985 (though the income elasticity was unchanged). Other studies find similarly disparate results, depending on sample periods and econometric methodology.

Our results indicate that a shift in the stance of monetary policy, and not financial deregulation, was primarily responsible for rapid monetary growth during 1987–1989. Nonetheless, there is substantial uncertainty over this result in the statistical literature, probably indicating that an upward shift in money demand and an explicitly more expansionary monetary policy shared responsibility for rapid monetary growth during this period. Similarly, the Bank of Japan argues that a combination of factors—including low interest rates, high transaction demand associated with strong growth and a boom in asset markets, and financial deregulation (especially the increase in LTDs)—led to the jump in money growth in 1987.

Concluding Comment

Japan's monetary policy has changed dramatically since World War II, responding and adapting to swings in external conditions, external shocks, and financial liberalization. In this chapter we have discussed postwar monetary policy in terms of five monetary regimes or phases, each of which illustrates a special feature of the Bank of Japan's policy.

The first phase, 1945–1950, provided little flexibility for independent monetary policy. Monetary policy was dictated by government deficits. Excessive monetary growth, extremely high inflation rates, and government deficits were brought to an end by the programs initiated by the Dodge Plan. The beginning of the Korean War in June 1950 may have prevented the Japanese economy from experiencing a serious and prolonged recession from the Dodge Plan's disinflation policies.

The stable financial and macroeconomic environment set the stage for the second phase, 1950–1971, in which Japan achieved rapid economic growth with moderate inflation. The Bank of Japan's policy during this period should be judged as a success, since it achieved its primary objective of exchange-rate stability and at the same time limited the inflation rate to about 5 percent. The Bank's policy was constrained not only by an external policy target, but also by a rigidly controlled and administered financial system that limited policy instruments and limited the channels through which monetary policy influenced the economy. In this environment, the Bank's policy relied heavily on quantitative controls over credit and administrative guidance over bank lending.

The third phase, 1971–1975, was a short but turbulent period of transition. Aside from the inflationary monetary policy immediately after the war, the easy monetary policy of the early 1970s represents the first major policy failure of the Bank of Japan. Excessive concern with external conditions and accommodation to a political agenda led to the wild inflation (exacerbated by the 1973 oil-price shock) and subsequently to the need to impose a serious recession in order to break the inflationary process.

During the fourth phase, 1975–1985, the Bank of Japan adopted a more independent approach that permitted it to focus on domestic price stability. The shift to flexible exchange rates after 1973 gave the Bank of Japan more flexibility to avoid conflicts between internal and external objectives. The economic performance of the Japanese economy during this phase is impressive by any standard, especially in the light of major structural changes in the financial system, the 1979–80 oil-price shock, and the growing internationalization of the Japanese economy. The Bank of Japan's success at achieving price stability during this period drew attention from the rest of the world.

The fifth and last phase, covering 1985 to the present, is a period of considerable difficulty for the Japanese economy and for Bank of Japan policy. Financial liberalization cannot be held entirely responsible for the rapid growth in the monetary aggregates after 1986. It is difficult to identify a sizable upward shift in the demand for money, which could have been expected to reduce the impact of higher monetary growth on the economy. In the next chapter, we provide an overall evaluation of the Bank of Japan's role in the asset inflation and the subsequent deflation and recession.

4 Exchange Rates, Policy Coordination, and a Yen Currency Area

Economic policy in Japan in the immediate postwar period was mainly concerned with rebuilding the economy and fostering rapid growth. Providing adequate liquidity to support growth was the primary objective of monetary policy; there was less emphasis on the rate of inflation. The overriding constraints facing the Bank of Japan in achieving this objective, up until the end of the 1960s, were the balance of payments and the commitment under the Bretton Woods system to keep the international value of the yen fixed. The need to maintain fixed exchange rates limited the Bank of Japan's discretion in its conduct of monetary policy. Balance-of-payments deficits and downward pressure on the yen necessitated a contractionary policy and slower growth; surpluses and upward yen pressure required an expansionary policy.

Although rapid growth in productivity eased the balance-of-payments constraint in the 1960s, not until the end of the Bretton Woods era was the Bank of Japan entirely free to choose its own policy objectives. Indeed, the Bank's attempts to maintain the system with an undervalued exchange rate were an important factor in the monetary expansion and the "wild inflation" of the early 1970s. This experience gave the Bank of Japan a strong incentive to make domestic price stability its main policy objective once it was free of the exchange-rate constraint.

The immediate objective of the Bank of Japan in the mid 1970s was to reduce the high inflation rate. With this in mind, as was discussed in chapter 3, the Bank of Japan introduced a new approach to formulating and carrying out policy as well as a new way of announcing its policy intentions. The Bank's success in lowering inflation, and keeping it low since the late 1970s, has been attributed to this "money-focused" monetary policy (Suzuki 1985; Fukui 1986). The key element of the money-focused approach has been to increase the weight on price stability, and correspondingly reduce the weight on the state of the economy, exchange rates, and other factors, when determining the monetary-policy response to economic developments.

Nonetheless, the Bank of Japan has never focused solely on price stability, nor has it attempted to minimize deviations of any given money aggregate from targeted values (Bryant 1991; Hamada and Hayashi 1985; Hutchison and Judd 1992; Ito 1989a). Rather, the stated objective was to stabilize longer-term monetary growth around a declining trend, at least in the years 1975–1985. Short-term policy decisions took into account a variety of factors, depending on the concerns of the moment, such as the state of the business cycle, exchange rates, and asset-price inflation.

International factors, such as the exchange rate, the balance of payments, and efforts to coordinate policy internationally, have influenced the conduct and the control of Bank of Japan policy. Even after the breakup of the Bretton Woods system, but especially after the Plaza Agreement of 1985, the Bank of Japan remained very much concerned with external factors in formulating monetary policy despite the lack of formally binding exchange-rate and balance-of-payments constraints.

A policy designed to limit exchange-rate appreciation normally involves heavy intervention in the foreign-exchange market, which in turn provides liquidity to the banking system and stimulates monetary growth. The central bank may offset the rise in liquidity, for example, by drawing in credit extended to banks or by selling government bonds. If the interventions are sufficiently large, however, the exchange-rate objective may come into conflict with the objective of price stability. The potential for conflict has been particularly acute in Japan, since the yen has experienced recurring bouts of intense pressure to appreciate since the early 1970s, moving from 360 yen per dollar in 1971 to under 80 yen per dollar in early 1995 before climbing back above the level of 120 yen per dollar in late 1996. As figure 4.1 shows, the consequence has been a positive correlation between the accumulation of foreign-exchange reserves and yen appreciation.

In this chapter we investigate international aspects of Japan's monetary policy by examining the pattern of official intervention in the exchange market and the extent to which the Bank of Japan has been able to insulate domestic monetary control from exchange-rate considerations since the early 1970s. We explain sources of conflict between domestic monetary control and exchange-rate policy, highlighting periods

Figure 4.1
Dollar-to-yen exchange rate (1970:1 = 100) and international reserves (billions of dollars).

such as the latter 1980s when an expansionary policy stance contributed to the excesses of the "bubble economy." This stands in contrast with the 1993–1995 recession, where monetary stimulus was fully consistent with both internal (stimulating aggregate demand) and external (limiting yen appreciation) objectives but was not particularly effective. In this context, we also discuss moves toward international policy coordination (the Plaza Agreement, the Louvre Accord, and so on), which influenced exchange-rate policy and which at times heightened the conflict between internal and external policy. Finally, depreciation against the yen and high variability have undermined the dollar's usefulness as the main currency for international reserves and transactions. These two factors have led some analysts to predict that a yen currency block may emerge in East Asia.

4.1 Exchange Rates, Intervention, and Monetary Policy

There has been a close link between movements in the yen/dollar exchange rate and Japanese foreign reserves since the breakup of the Bretton Woods system in the early 1970s. With several notable exceptions, the Bank of Japan purchased international reserves (mainly US dollars) and sold yen in the foreign-exchange market during episodes of yen exchange-rate appreciation. During episodes of yen depreciation, the authorities tended to purchase yen and sell international reserves. This type of intervention in the foreign-exchange market is termed "leaning against the wind" because the objective of the authorities is usually to try to slow or reverse the movement in the exchange rate.

Central banks may be motivated to intervene in this manner because economic stability is often viewed as synonymous with exchange-rate stability, or out of concern that exchange markets are excessively volatile and prone to price bubbles (departures from fundamental determinants), or because of pressure from interest groups lobbying against either appreciation or depreciation.

Episodes of Appreciation

There were particularly large increases in reserves, reflecting dollar purchases and yen sales in the foreign-exchange market, when the yen was under heavy pressure to appreciate during the breakup of the Bretton Woods system (1971–1973), and during other periods when the dollar declined sharply (the late 1970s, the mid 1980s, and the early 1990s). Large declines in the stock of official reserves occurred after the two major oil-price hikes and consequent depreciations of the yen (1973–74 and 1978–79). The two periods of rapid money growth in Japan, one in the early 1970s and one in the late 1980s, both followed periods of rapid yen appreciation, substantial foreign-exchange intervention, and the accumulation of international reserves.[1]

Table 4.1 illustrates the most dramatic episodes of yen appreciation and reviews the most important economic circumstances around the time of each event. The first episode, discussed in detail in chapter 3, was perhaps the most dramatic event in Japan's postwar economic experience: the breakup of the Bretton Woods system. The yen appreciated from 360 to 260 per dollar between August 1971 and July 1973, and "wild inflation" followed. Attempts by the Bank of Japan to maintain existing exchange-rate parities despite enormous pressure to revalue led to a highly expansionary monetary policy. The pressure for monetary expansion was also political in nature: Prime Minister Tanaka pushed for a decline in the discount rate precisely when the Bank of Japan was planning to tighten monetary conditions. This episode resulted from the first major mistake in Japan's monetary policy since the Dodge Plan

Table 4.1
Episodes of appreciation (fall in yen-per-dollar rate).

	Episode 1	Episode 2	Episode 3	Episode 4
Dates	August 1971–July 1973 (24 months)	Jan 1976–Oct 1978 (33 months)	Feb 1985–Aug 1986 (18 months)	Apr 1990–Apr 1995 (5 years)
Yen	From 360 to 260 ¥/$ (−28%)	From 305 to 180 ¥/$ (−41%)	From 260 to 150 ¥/$ (−42%)	From 160 to 80 ¥/$ (−50%)
Evaluation of yen movement	Undervalued to equilibrium	Response to "dollar crisis"	Undervalued to overvalued	Undervalued to overvalued
How much sterilized?	Partially	Completely	Partially	Unclear
Growth, inflation, interest rate	"Overheating" evident; inflation rising to double digits, monetary expansion and interest rate declining until mid 1972.	Inflation on declining trend	Stable inflation, strong output growth; asset-price inflation	Deep recession from 1992; deflation, falling asset prices, bank crisis
Other observations	Chaos after big regime change—Japan was last major country to admit that Bretton Woods system had collapsed.	Dollar crisis; appreciation quickly reversed after the dollar defense package	At beginning of this phase, dollar was overvalued. Little action from Feb to Sept 1995. Yen appreciation initially encouraged, especially after Plaza Accord (Sept 1985); intervention policy reversed after March 1986, when appreciation was judged excessive, monetary expansion started.	At beginning of this phase, yen was probably undervalued. No net increase in reserves in first 3 years; massive and sustained BOJ action started around April 1993.
Evaluation	Mistake in causing wild inflation		Mistake in causing bubble	

brought stability to the economy in the early 1950s. Resisting yen revaluation led to rapid monetary growth—monetary-base growth, for example, began to accelerate sharply in 1972 and peaked at an annual rate exceeding 35 percent in early 1973. Loose monetary conditions were reflected in call money interest rate declines through most of 1971 and 1972. Inflation rose to double-digit levels at the beginning of 1973, and this, along with the dramatic oil-price hikes that began later in the year, led to the disastrous "wild inflation."

The second episode, January 1976–October 1978, may be characterized as a "dollar crisis." Yen appreciation was quickly reversed once a credible dollar defense package was introduced by the US government. Although foreign-exchange intervention by the Bank of Japan was heavy as the exchange rate moved from 305 to 180 yen per dollar, growth in the monetary aggregates continued to decline gradually in line with the "money-focused" policy orientation recently adopted by the Bank of Japan. No inflationary effects were associated with dollar-support intervention during this period.

Another major policy mistake by the Bank of Japan was the expansionary policy adopted during the third episode, February 1985–August 1986. Moderate yen appreciation in early 1985 was initially welcomed as a long-overdue correction to the overvalued dollar. The communiqué of the Plaza economic summit of the Group of Five in September 1985 (section 4.3 below) encouraged further dollar depreciation and announced a commitment to coordinated intervention operations by the major countries. Japan joined other countries in selling dollars from late September through the end of October, and tightened monetary conditions by raising interest rates.

Coordinated intervention proved only too successful—orderly dollar depreciation turned into a rout. Startled by the switch from yen undervaluation to overvaluation, the Bank of Japan changed from yen-support to dollar-support intervention, attempting to limit further yen appreciation by buying dollars and selling yen in the foreign exchanges. An expansionary policy stance was adopted: interbank rates declined, and monetary-base growth increased from 5 percent in 1986 to 15 percent in 1987. This did not result in a sharp rise in general price inflation, however, partly because yen appreciation kept import prices down.[2] But the Bank of Japan's expansionary stance contributed to and then accommodated the asset inflation of the second half of the 1980s. The subsequent "burst" of the bubble led to a deep recession and to banking problems whose effects are still felt in Japan.

The last episode detailed in table 4.1 is the movement of the yen from 160 per dollar in April 1990 to under 80 per dollar in April 1995. Similar to the initial stage of the appreciation starting in early 1985, the yen was regarded as undervalued in the middle of 1990, and no attempt was made to limit its rise.[3] The lack of response to yen appreciation also reflected the high level of economic activity in 1990 and early 1991, when high capacity utilization, low unemployment, and rapidly rising asset prices lessened concerns about the adverse impact of a strong yen on competitiveness. But continued yen appreciation was again eventually met with alarm, which was followed by heavy dollar-support intervention. Moreover, by the middle of 1991 it was clear the economy was slowing. Recession and collapsing asset prices, victims of the bursting bubble, contributed to sharp declines in the growth of the monetary base and in the growth of M2 + CDs. Dollar-support intervention operations were particularly heavy in 1994, having been coordinated with other central banks after the April meeting of the G7 countries' central banks and finance ministers.

Unlike previous episodes of yen appreciation, in this case yen sales (dollar purchases) in foreign-exchange markets were entirely consistent with domestic objectives against a background of recession, falling asset prices, and plummeting money growth. Indeed, the Bank of Japan lowered key short-term interest rates to stimulate money growth and the economy, as well as to support foreign-exchange-market intervention in the attempt to stem the rise of the yen. Nonetheless, the attempt at monetary expansion was in large part offset by the continuing deflationary effects of the collapse of the bubble economy and by worsening banking problems.

Episodes of Depreciation

Table 4.2 focuses on the two episodes of sharp yen depreciation, each associated with a large oil-price shock.[4] In both cases the monetary authorities sold foreign-exchange reserves and tightened monetary conditions to strengthen the yen. Within 10 months of the first oil-price shock, which occurred in October 1973, the yen had depreciated from 260 to 300 per dollar. Yen purchases at the time contributed to the fall in monetary-base growth, but a restrictive policy stance had already been adopted earlier in the year in response to building inflationary pressures. Money-market rates rose again after the oil shock, further tightening monetary conditions. Thus, foreign-exchange sales during this episode were

Table 4.2
Episodes of depreciation (rise in yen-per-dollar rate).

	Episode 1	Episode 2
Dates	Oct 1973–July 1974 (10 months)	Jan 1979–April 1980 (14 months)
Yen	from 260 to 300 ¥/$ (15%)	from 200 to 250 ¥/$ (25%)
Sterilized?	No	No
Growth, inflation, interest-rate movements	"Wild inflation" background and recession after oil shock; restrictive monetary policy	Sharp rise in interest rates; stable output growth; modest rise in inflation
Other observations	Aftermath of oil shock; large interventions only during first 4 months of depreciation episode	Oil shock in middle of episode; quick response by Bank of Japan to "extinguish" inflation pressure; Japan only major industrial country to avoid recession

unsterilized and contributed to the overall restrictive monetary-policy stance.[5]

Evaluation of the second depreciation episode, when the yen moved from 200 to 250 per dollar between January 1979 and April 1980, is complicated by the oil-price hike that occurred in the middle of the period (in the spring of 1979). The economic conditions at the outset, however, were much more favorable than at the time of the previous episode: inflationary pressure was not evident, money growth rates were fairly stable, and interest rates had been steady for some time. The Bank of Japan reacted very quickly at this point, selling dollars in support of the yen, and international reserves dropped sharply. Monetary-base growth declined substantially as the yen depreciated, reflecting unsterilized intervention operations and a sharp rise in short-term interest rates.

4.2 Linking Foreign-Exchange Intervention to Monetary Conditions

These episodes illustrate the links among exchange-rate management, intervention in the foreign-exchange market, and monetary policy. These links have some systematic element, mainly since intervention usually responds in a "leaning against the wind" manner to movements in the exchange rate. And during most episodes the Bank of Japan has attempted to "sterilize" its intervention operations (that is, to maintain the existing course of monetary policy). But the exceptions had far-reaching consequences. Indeed, the "systematic" components of the intervention and sterilization actions explain only a fraction of the actual policy measures taken. Not only was exchange-rate policy a key element in the "wild inflation" of the early 1970s; it also played a role in creating the bubble economy of the late 1980s.

Intervention Policy

The systematic elements of intervention and sterilization policy may be captured by estimating simple policy-reaction functions to account for intervention and sterilization actions. A simple function for a central bank's intervention would relate the magnitude of intervention to the percentage change in the exchange rate. Consider the equation[6]

$$I_t = \alpha + \beta \, \Delta \mathrm{XR}_t + \varepsilon_t, \tag{4.1}$$

where I_t is a measure of the amount of intervention and $\Delta\mathrm{XR}_t$ is the percentage change in the average monthly exchange rate (with an increase defined as an appreciation of the yen against the dollar).

A number of studies have estimated intervention policy equations based on equation 4.1 for Japan. Table 4.3 shows some of the results from a recent study by Glick and Hutchison (1994a). The dependent variable is changes in the dollar-denominated value of (net) official foreign asset holdings (I_t), expressed in percentage change form by scaling the level of foreign asset holdings at the end of time t.[7] Also reported are instrumental variable estimates that attempt to correct for the potential simultaneity bias arising from contemporaneous feedback from intervention to the exchange rate.[8]

Not surprisingly, the sign of the estimated coefficient of the exchange-rate variable is positive and statistically significant, indicating that the Bank of Japan tends to sell (buy) foreign exchange when the yen depreciates (appreciates). During the whole of the post-Bretton Woods period the Japanese authorities have responded, on average, to a 1 percent appreciation of the yen by increasing international reserves by about 0.5–1 percent. The lagged dependent variable is highly significant, indicating that the longer-run intervention response exceeds the initial impact effects. The low adjusted R^2 statistics indicate that substantial variation in international reserves is not systematic (about 70–80 percent is not explained by the model). That is, many factors apparently influence

Table 4.3
Response of official foreign-exchange reserves to exchange-rate appreciation. Estimation period: 1973:3–1990:12. Dependent variable is defined as monthly percentage change in foreign-exchange reserves (I_t). Series were seasonally adjusted. Exchange rate is defined as logarithmic change in average monthly exchange rate of dollar against yen; an increase in the exchange rate denotes an appreciation of the yen. Numbers in parentheses denote marginal significance levels. Q_{msl} refers to the marginal significance level of the Ljung-Box Q statistic for serial correlation. OLS: ordinary least-squares regression estimation. INST: instrumental-variables estimation. Source: Glick and Hutchison 1994a.

Exchange rate	Lagged dependent variable	Q_{msl}	Adj. R^2	OLS or INST
0.74	—	0.00	0.22	OLS
(0.00)	0.28	0.36	0.29	OLS
0.61	(0.00)	0.00	0.20	INST
(0.00)	—	0.37	0.28	INST
0.96	0.30			
(0.00)	(0.00)			
0.52				
(0.05)				

Exchange-rate appreciation	Exchange-rate depreciation	Lagged dependent variable	Q_{msl}	Adj. R^2
0.37	1.02	0.26	0.20	0.30
(0.01)	(0.00)	(0.00)		

intervention policy which are not captured by this simple empirical model, and the weight placed on each factor may also vary over time depending on political and economic circumstances.

We have already observed how intervention policy has changed over time, particularly the reaction to exchange-rate changes, and this is one reason for the low explanatory power of the intervention policy reaction functions reported in table 4. 3. Takagi (1991) and Glick and Hutchison (1994a), looking at this point more closely, estimate equation 4.1 with separate dependent variables for periods when the yen is appreciating and periods when it is depreciating.[9] The results, shown in the lower panel of table 4.3, indicate that the Japanese monetary authorities indeed tend to intervene more (roughly three times as much) in response to a yen exchange-rate depreciation than to an appreciation.[10,11] Asymmetric intervention policy by the Bank of Japan is also investigated by

Watanabe (1994), who divides the post-Bretton Woods period into five episodes. He finds that significant shifts have occurred in policy responses, with some periods characterized by asymmetric responses and others by more symmetry.[12]

At first glance it appears odd that a bias by policymakers toward foreign-exchange sales (against yen depreciation) is consistent with the large accumulation of foreign-exchange reserves by Japan over the last two decades. However, there is a simple explanation: Relatively high longer-term productivity growth and other factors have led to rising international competitiveness in Japan and to yen appreciation against the dollar over most of the managed-floating-rate period. Under these circumstances, a symmetric leaning-against-the-wind policy would have led to an even greater accumulation of foreign-exchange reserves and to subsequent problems for monetary control.[13] From this perspective, greater resistance to currency depreciation than to appreciation may be interpreted as an effort by the Bank of Japan to limit the potentially excessive monetary stimulus associated with the trend accumulation of foreign reserves.

Sterilization Policy

It is apparent from at least two episodes (the early 1970s and the second half of the 1980s) that an activist intervention policy has the potential to impede a central bank's ability to direct monetary targets toward achieving domestic policy objectives. However, the Bank of Japan has usually attempted to limit the monetary effects of exchange-market intervention by means of "sterilization." For example, when the foreign-exchange fund purchases dollars to limit yen appreciation, it pays for the transaction by crediting the reserves of commercial banks and liquidity in the banking system rises. In a sterilization operation, the Bank of Japan attempts to reduce this liquidity effect by selling debt instruments to commercial banks or by using other means to draw down bank reserves.

To clarify the systematic linkages between money growth and foreign-exchange intervention, let us express the change in the monetary base, ΔMB, as

$$\Delta MB_t = \Delta FA_t + \Delta DC_t, \tag{4.2}$$

where ΔFA and ΔDC denote the changes in the official foreign reserve and domestic credit components of the monetary base, respectively, valued in yen. If the authorities respond to a rise (fall) in foreign assets—

i.e. a foreign (domestic) currency support intervention operation—by decreasing (increasing) domestic credit, they are attempting to insulate the monetary base from the operation.

In general, a sterilization operation will be successful only if domestic bonds and foreign bonds are imperfect substitutes in investors' portfolios. If domestic and foreign bonds are perfect substitutes, then domestic interest rates are tied to the "world" level and sterilized intervention is not effective.[14]

When changes in domestic credit offset moves in foreign assets completely (one for one), the monetary base is completely insulated (complete sterilization). Estimating the response of domestic credit to changes in foreign reserves therefore provides some idea of the extent to which monetary policy has been affected by intervention in the foreign-exchange market.[15]

Table 4.4 presents the estimates over various periods for the contemporaneous and long-run effect of changes in foreign-asset holdings on domestic credit in the study by Glick and Hutchison (1994a).[16] The full managed-floating period, beginning in 1973, is reported, along with subperiods that correspond to possible policy-regime shifts by the Bank of Japan after the adoption of official monetary-growth projections (1978:7)[17] and after the Plaza Agreement by the G5 countries to coordinate intervention (1985:9). The estimates suggest that the immediate (contemporaneous) response by the Bank of Japan is to sterilize between 20 and 90 percent of the rise in foreign reserves; the wide range in estimates depends on the period investigated and the estimation method employed. The point estimates for "long-run" sterilization are always higher than the corresponding estimated contemporaneous effects; however, the long-run coefficients are typically imprecise, with large standard errors.

Taken as a whole, the results point to fairly strong efforts by the Bank of Japan to sterilize the effect of intervention operations on the monetary aggregates, especially over longer periods. Less-than-complete sterilization (coefficient smaller in absolute value than –1) was generally the rule; however, considerable variation was also observed during the subperiods. In particular, less sterilization was observed immediately after the collapse of the Bretton Woods system (1973:5–1978:8) and after the Plaza Agreement (1985:9–1990:12). This contributed to the "wild inflation" and the asset inflation in those respective periods. The generally greater sterilization during the "money-focused" episode (1978:7–1985:8) is consistent with the policy of decelerating monetary growth.

Table 4.4

Response of domestic credit to changes in foreign assets. All equations include contemporaneous and three lags of foreign asset changes, two lags of the dependent variable, a constant, and a time trend. Numbers in parentheses for the contemporaneous effect denote marginal significance levels of *t* statistic against −1; numbers in parentheses for the long-run multiplier effect denote marginal significance levels of F test against −1; Q_{msl} refers to the marginal significance level of the Ljung-Box *Q* statistic for serial correlation. Source: Glick and Hutchison 1994a.

Sample period	Contemporaneous	Long-run multiplier	Q_{msl}	Adj. R^2	Regression estimation technique
1973:5–	−0.75	−0.88	0.01	0.52	OLS
1990:12	(0.00)	(0.13)			
	−0.90	−1.02	0.01	0.50	INST
	(0.74)	(0.95)			
1973:5–	−0.47	−0.64	0.90	0.30	OLS
1978:6	(0.00)	(0.13)			
	−0.20	−0.35	0.96	0.23	INST
	(0.03)	(0.16)			
1978:7–	−0.85	−0.99	0.02	0.53	OLS
1985:8	(0.08)	(0.94)			
	−0.80	−0.95	0.01	0.53	INST
	(0.46)	(0.86)			
1985:9–	−0.76	−0.90	0.45	0.66	OLS
1990:12	(0.00)	(0.27)			
	−0.84	−0.95	0.48	0.65	INST
	(0.55)	(0.79)			
1978:7–	−0.79	−0.90	0.02	0.58	OLS
1990:12	(0.00)	(0.24)			
	−0.84	−0.95	0.02	0.57	INST
	(0.55)	(0.81)			

	Exchange-rate appreciation		Exchange-rate depreciation		
Sample period	Contemporaneous	Long-run multiplier	Contemporaneous	Long-run multiplier	Adj. R^2
1973:5–	−0.74	−0.96	−0.73	−0.78	0.53
1990:12	(0.00)	(0.75)	(0.00)	(0.04)	
1978:7–	−0.78	−0.95	−0.77	−0.83	0.58
1990:12	(0.02)	(0.69)	(0.00)	(0.14)	

Monetary Control

The sharp yen appreciation in 1971–1973 and in 1985–1987 suggests that the accumulation of foreign reserves did, in fact, contribute to rapid growth of the monetary base and of the broad money supply. Was money-supply growth "excessive" during these periods?

Figure 4.2 shows the cumulative percent differences between actual broad money (M2 + CDs) growth and forecasts of broad money growth during these two episodes. The forecasts are derived from out-of-sample dynamic predictions of a simple 24 lag autoregressive money-growth equation, with a constant and a time trend, estimated over the period 1971:1–1990:12. The horizontal scale in the figure measures the number of months after the beginning of each episode—dated as 1971:8 in the first case and 1985:9 in the second. Positive (negative) values indicate underprediction (overprediction) of actual money growth. This figure shows that in both episodes actual money growth was much more rapid than forecast: the cumulative forecast error was over 6 percent by early 1973 (during the first episode) and almost 4 percent in the middle of 1987 (during the second episode). Thus, relative to past patterns and trends in money growth, growth rates in both episodes of yen appreciation were unusually high. The fact that the second episode did not result in explosive consumer-price inflation, in contrast to the experience of the early 1970s, has been attributed in part to a favorable shift of money demand associated with financial liberalization that accommodated the excessive money growth.[18] In the preceding chapter, however, we found little evidence of a significant and sizable shift in money demand. Moreover, asset prices did rise rapidly after the Plaza Agreement and the switch to dollar-support intervention. The accumulation of foreign reserves at this time clearly created the potential for the additional inflation that eventually emerged in the late 1980s.

4.3 Policy Coordination, Intervention, and Excessive Money Growth

In the previous section we focused on instances of conflict between external and internal objectives in Japan—conflict that, at times, resulted in loss of monetary control. To what extent can efforts at international policy coordination, such as the Plaza Agreement of September 1985, be held responsible?

Attempts to maintain undervalued exchange rates in the early 1970s contributed to rapid monetary growth and high inflation in a number of

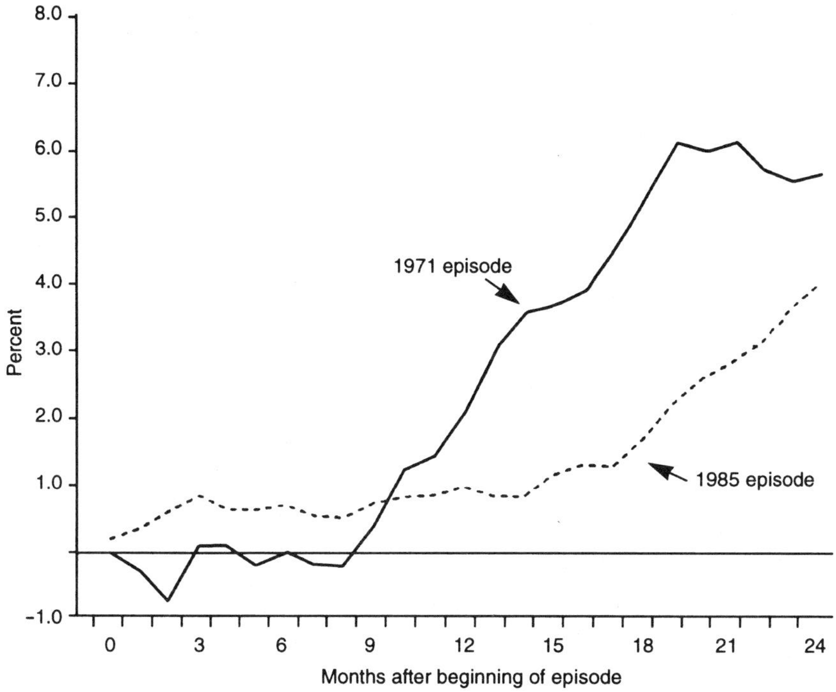

Figure 4.2
Cumulative errors in broad money forecasts in 1971 and 1985 episodes. Source: Glick and Hutchison 1994a.

industrial countries, including Japan. Since that time, countries have been able to choose exchange-rate arrangements more freely. Some have opted for formal arrangements, such as the European Monetary System; others have pursued policies without formal commitments. Austria, for example, maintained the most stable exchange-rate peg in Europe (Austrian schilling to German mark) even before joining the EMS in 1995. Other countries, of course, decided to pursue much more flexible exchange-rate arrangements; their choices of exchange-rate regimes generally depended on their degree of trade openness and on their dependence upon other countries, as well as on factor mobility.

Japan has pursued an active exchange-rate policy despite the relaxation of a formal obligation to intervene in foreign-exchange markets. This policy has been motivated partly by the view that excessive exchange-rate volatility is harmful to the economy (especially to international trade and financial relations) and partly by the concern at times that yen appreciation had gone too far and would hurt the export competitiveness of Japanese industry. Attempts at managing the exchange rate have influenced overall policy on several occasions since the "wild inflation" of the early 1970s, but not to the extent that price stability was seriously compromised. Japan's secular inflation remained low by international comparison and relative to the experience during the Bretton Woods period. At times, however, international concerns led to more expansionary policies than would have been justified on purely domestic grounds.

The Bonn Summit of 1978 initiated internationally coordinated macroeconomic and energy policies, but there was no attempt to reinstate a rule-based system. Japan agreed to stimulate demand by implementing public-spending measures if growth fell short of 7 percent (an ambitious target). These measures were subsequently implemented. Japan's intervention and monetary policies were not greatly affected by the Bonn Summit, mainly because the burden was shouldered by fiscal policy. The already-large budget deficits grew worse in 1978–79 because of the fiscal stimulus agreed to at Bonn.

The next serious attempt at international policy coordination involving Japan occurred in September 1985, when the finance ministers and central-bank governors of the G5 countries met at the Plaza Hotel in New York. In the Plaza Agreement, governments agreed to encourage continued depreciation of the dollar—if necessary, by coordinated intervention in foreign-exchange markets. The key sentence of the Plaza communiqué stated that the ministers and governors "stand ready to cooperate more closely to encourage this [further orderly appreciation of the main nondollar currencies] when to do so would be helpful."[19] By signing the Plaza Agreement the United States shifted its policy position closer to those of Japan and Europe, "[on] the view that recent shifts in fundamental economic conditions among their countries, together with policy commitments in the future, have not been reflected fully in exchange markets."[20]

The Plaza Agreement was noteworthy in that Japan now coordinated its intervention policy with the United States (and Europe), rather than going it alone in pursuing an exchange-rate objective. Large sales of dollars in the exchange markets by the Bank of Japan and other G5 central banks, including the Federal Reserve, continued the downward pressure on the dollar after the Plaza Agreement (Ito 1987).[21] It was reported by the Federal Reserve Bank of New York that total intervention by the G10 central banks between the Plaza Agreement and the end of October amounted to $10 billion, with US sales amounting to more than $3 billion, other G5 members' sales at $5 billion, and the remaining G10 members' sales at $2 billion (Federal Reserve Bank of New York 1985–86, p. 47). A senior Japanese official stated that Japan had sold $3 billion from late September to early November (ibid., p. 46), and Japan's published exchange-rate reserves dropped nearly $1 billion during September alone.

In light of all the discussion at the Plaza about intervention in the foreign-exchange market, it is perhaps surprising that the participants did not fully agree to monetary-policy coordination. In the Agreement, Japan alone specifically linked monetary policy to the exchange rate when it committed to the "flexible management of monetary policy with due attention to the yen exchange rate." Heavy dollar sales, if not completely sterilized, would raise Japanese interests rates and tighten money markets. It is reported that the Bank of Japan was directed by the top levels of the Ministry of Finance not to sterilize intervention operations, in order to have the largest possible effect on the exchange rate, but reportedly did so anyway (Funabashi 1988). In any event, monetary conditions did tighten as the Bank of Japan raised short-term interest rates in late October, though it kept the discount rate at the 5 percent level throughout 1985.[22]

The desired effect of coordinated intervention more than met the expectations envisioned by the signatories of the Plaza Agreement and, as a consequence, forced a quick policy reversal. Dollar depreciation, which started in February 1985, quickened after the agreement, and only a few months later, in spring 1986, the Bank of Japan switched from trying to push the dollar lower to trying to support the dollar. The actions taken to push the dollar down didn't have much impact on monetary conditions. There was only modest monetary tightening immediately after the Plaza Agreement—declining foreign-exchange reserves, slightly higher interest rates, and somewhat slower monetary-base and broad money growth.

In contrast, the subsequent dollar-support intervention operations by Japan were clearly associated with an expansionary monetary policy. During the period 1986–1988 Japan's foreign-exchange reserves jumped more than fourfold, from $22 billion to $90 billion. This jump was accompanied by an increase in monetary-base growth from 5 percent to nearly 15 percent. The discount rate was lowered several times during 1986 and again in February 1987. The 2.5 percent discount rate set in February 1987 was then maintained until the middle of 1989.

In what is often interpreted as a quiet target-zone policy, the subsequent moves to coordinate policy focused on stabilizing exchange rates around existing levels. The Baker-Miyazawa Joint Communiqué, issued in October 1986, when the yen-dollar rate stood at about 160, announced that "the exchange rate . . . is now broadly consistent with the present underlying fundamentals." Japanese Finance Minister Miyazawa and US Treasury Secretary Baker reaffirmed their "willingness to cooperate on exchange market issues." A second Baker-Miyazawa meeting in January 1987 made an almost identical statement on the exchange rate. A month later the participants at the G7's Louvre meeting[23] agreed that their currencies were "within ranges broadly consistent with underlying economic fundamentals."

The market interpreted the Louvre Accord as setting the target zone at 150–160 yen per dollar (*Nihon Keizai Shinbun*, February 23, 1987). According to confidential personal interviews conducted by Yoichi Funabashi (1988), the target midpoint ranges for dollar, mark, and yen exchange rates agreed at the Louvre meeting, though not publicly disclosed, were 1.825 DM to $1 and ¥153.5 to $1. Voluntary exchange-market intervention was apparently agreed upon for exchange-rate fluctuations within a 2.5 percent band around the midpoint, but intervention was expected to intensify outside this range, with consultation on policy adjustments obligatory if a 5 percent band was exceeded.

The Japanese reportedly favored "massive interventions" to support the target ranges, while the American representatives were reluctant to make such a large commitment. The Europeans argued that the scale did not matter, only the impact on the market (Funabashi 1988; p. 187). Presumably they hoped that modest but coordinated intervention would convey to the market information about policy intentions and thereby have a large impact on the exchange rate. In the published communiqué, only Japan agreed to follow monetary and fiscal policies to expand domestic demand, announcing a cut in the discount rate at the same time.[24]

In any event, the dollar came under downward pressure in early January 1987, when the yen appreciated from the high 150s to the low 150s very quickly. It was reported that the Bank of Japan bought about $8 billion during the first two weeks of January (*Nihon Keizai Shinbun*, January 15, 1987). During the first five weeks after the Louvre meeting, however, the dollar was quite stable against the yen, and it was stronger against the European currencies (prompting operations to support the mark). After the middle of March, however, renewed pressure on the dollar prompted large-scale dollar purchases in the foreign-exchange market by Japan.[25] The 5 percent baseline was breached nonetheless, and subsequent attempts at stabilizing rates at even lower target levels also met with limited success. The target-zone experiment was abandoned, or at least temporarily shelved, soon after the Black Monday stock-market collapse of October 19, 1987. In subsequent G7 meetings, Japan continued to push for renewed attempts at currency stabilization but usually was disappointed (Ostrom 1994a). Exceptions include a short period after the April 1994 G7 meeting when the exchange rate approached 100 yen per dollar. US Secretary of the Treasury Lloyd Bentsen said at the time that the exchange rate had gone beyond the level justified by fundamentals, and shortly thereafter the United States joined 15 other countries in a bout of coordinated dollar purchases in the exchange markets (Ostrom 1994b). For the most part, however, Japan has continued active intervention in exchange markets on a unilateral basis.

Did efforts at international policy coordination lead Japan to adopt expansionary policies, resulting in an economic boom and a rise in inflation in the years 1986–1990?[26] The focus of the Plaza Agreement, of course, was on pushing the dollar lower which would tend to have contractionary monetary effects. That agreement marked a breakthrough only in that a general consensus was reached on the desirability of coordinated intervention when exchange markets did not properly reflect fundamentals. Nonetheless, the Plaza Agreement sowed the seeds of a more aggressive intervention policy with monetary effects when the Japanese government committed to a "flexible" approach to monetary policy in light of exchange-rate developments. When the yen broke the (then) post-Bretton Woods record of 178 yen per dollar in March 1986, the Bank of Japan reversed its direction of intervention from selling to buying dollars. This intention was reinforced in subsequent forums, particularly with the Baker-Miyazawa agreement of October 1986 and the Louvre Accord of February 1987.

Glick and Hutchison (1994a) show that sensitivity of intervention to exchange-rate changes—which had been declining (in absolute value) for several years—rose after the Plaza Agreement. The more activist exchange-rate policy was reflected by a rapid increase in international reserves after 1985 (figure 4.1). In this sense, the efforts at coordinated intervention brought a multilateral dimension to intervention operations and a more activist policy stance by the Bank of Japan to combat further yen appreciation. Table 4.4 also indicates that there was less sterilization after the Plaza Agreement, which essentially allowed some monetary effects of intervention (as the official communiqué suggested).[27]

The Plaza Agreement marked a radical shift in the United States' intervention policy (earlier in the Reagan administration one of "benign neglect"), bringing it more into line with the "activist" exchange-rate-management policy long advocated by Japan. As Funabashi (1988, p. 18) notes, the Europeans were not enthusiastic about the Plaza strategy, thinking that the "overvalued dollar" was a problem between Japan and the United States. In negotiations at the Plaza over the proportion of intervention responsibilities (the preparation of the "nonpaper" on intervention strategy, which was not made public), the Europeans were consistently pushing for a smaller role (ibid., p. 20).

Whatever the proximate cause, however, monetary policy was expansionary in the latter part of the 1980s, and it was commonly associated with an attempt to stem yen appreciation and prop up the dollar. Inflation rose with the bubble economy, peaking at nearly 4 percent (CPI year-over-year change) in January 1991, but did not skyrocket to the 25 percent rate recorded in late 1974. Rather, the main policy concern was about the bubble in asset prices, notably stock and land prices.

4.4 A Yen Currency Bloc and Optimal Currency Areas

The volatility of the dollar exchange rate, as well as its trend depreciation against the yen and the mark, have undermined its role as the world's main currency for trade and financial transactions and store of value. Japan's and other industrial countries' efforts to stabilize the dollar exchange rate have obviously met with quite limited success. The response in Europe was to develop measures to limit intra-European exchange-rate volatility, usually centered around the mark as the key currency. This began with the "snake in the tunnel" exchange-rate arrangements in the early 1970s and developed into the European Monetary System in 1978. If the Maastricht Treaty is fully implemented, a core of European countries may have a common currency (the "Euro") by the end of the 1990s. European efforts have addressed exchange-rate stability and a common currency in tandem with further development of a single integrated market for the free movement of goods, services, and capital with the European Union. A similar process of regional economic integration, though not monetary union, has occurred with the North American Free Trade Area agreement.

As regional economic and financial integration proceeds in Europe and North America, many wonder whether a similar economic bloc may form in Asia with Japan as the anchor. The term "yen bloc" used in this context has several interpretations. One interpretation of "yen bloc" is an area where the yen is used extensively in transactions outside Japan as an invoice or vehicle currency. The larger the number of international transactions denominated in yen, the greater the political incentive to form a currency area in which other currencies are pegged to the yen. In this context, a yen bloc typically means an Asian version of the European Monetary System with the yen playing the role of the mark as the anchor currency. A broader interpretation takes "yen bloc" to mean an economic bloc, such as free-trade zone or a tariff union, where intraregional transactions are preferentially treated in terms of inspections, tariffs, and quotas. The yen bloc in this context more closely resembles an Asian trading bloc, similar to the EC or the North American Free Trade Area, with Japan as the economic and political leader.

The Yen as an International Currency

The uses of a currency in international and financial markets closely parallel the roles of domestic money as a unit of account, as a means of payment, and as a store of value. An international currency should fulfill the medium-of-exchange function as a vehicle currency for the private sector and an intervention currency for the official (government) sector, the unit-of-account function as an invoice currency for the private sector and as a currency peg for the official sector, and the store-of-value function as a portfolio asset for the private sector and as a reserve currency for the official sector. By all these criteria, the dollar has maintained its special role as the key international currency. However, the importance of the yen has expanded in tandem with the Japanese economy.

As table 4.5 shows, the role of the yen as an invoice currency for Japan's exports and imports has been increasing. The yen-invoiced proportion of total Japanese exports increased from 1 percent in 1970 to almost 30 percent in 1980 and around 40 percent in the early 1990s. The yen-invoiced proportion of imports has increased more slowly, rising from nearly zero in 1970 to about 15 percent in 1990.

The proportions of Japan's exports and imports invoiced in yen, though growing, remain lower than the national currency proportions of other advanced countries' international trade. Using 1987 trade data for the six major industrial countries (the United States, Japan, Germany,

Table 4.5
Invoice currencies (in percent) of Japan's exports and imports, 1970–1991. Imports for 1985 and 1986 are figures for fiscal year (April–March). Source for exports and imports invoicing: Kawai 1992. Original sources: exports until 1982, Bank of Japan; after 1983, *yushutsu kakunin* statistics and *yunyu hokoku* statistics, 1991; imports until 1980, ibid., 1985 Ministry of Finance; after 1986, *yushutsu kakunin* statistics and *yunyu hokoku* statistics, 1991. Source for import ratios: Ministry of Finance, Foreign Trade Statistics.

	Exports		Imports	
	Yen-denominated	Dollar-denominated	Yen-denominated	Dollar-denominated
1970	0.9	90.4	0.3	80.0
1975	17.5	78.0	0.9	89.9
1980	28.9	66.3	2.4	93.1
1981	31.8	62.8	na	na
1982	33.8	60.9	na	na
1983	42.0	50.2	3.0	na
1984	39.5	53.1	na	na
1985	39.3	52.2	7.3	na
1986	36.5	53.5	9.7	na
1987	33.4	55.2	10.6	81.7
1988	34.3	53.2	13.3	78.5
1989	34.7	52.4	14.1	77.3
1990	37.5	48.8	14.5	75.5
1991	39.4	46.7	15.6	75.4

France, the United Kingdom, and Italy), Black (1991) shows that the United States predominantly uses dollars for both its imports (80 percent) and its exports (94 percent). The other countries tend to use their national currencies for the major share of their exports but much less so for their imports. The mark, for example, is used as the invoice currency for 52 percent of Germany's imports and 82 percent of the exports in 1987. The corresponding figures for Japan are the lowest in the group, at only 11 and 33 percent respectively. The yen is also the lowest in the group as an invoice currency in other industrial countries' trade.

The literature usually points to two reasons for the relatively low degree of yen invoicing in Japan (see Ito 1994; Kawai 1992; Taguchi 1994). First, given that the United States uses the dollar for its imports, a country that exports to the United States extensively, like Japan, will have a lower export yen-invoicing ratio. The United States was the destination for 30 percent of Japanese exports in 1991, higher than all of Asia (29 percent) or the European Community (19 percent). Seventeen percent of the exports to the United States were invoiced in yen, compared to 42 percent for the EC and 51 percent for Asia (Ito 1994). Second, the dollar is the transaction currency in international commodity markets, such as for crude oil and metals. Since Japan imports a large quantity of raw materials (36 percent of total imports in 1991), it will tend to record a higher proportion of dollar invoicing. Reflecting this pattern, 24 percent of Japan's manufactured-goods imports were invoiced in yen in 1991, compared to only 2 percent for raw materials.

Ito (1994) notes, however, that neither the concentration of trade with the United States nor even the relatively high ratio of raw-materials imports can explain the low national currency ratio of invoicing of Japan compared with that of the major European countries. Even half of Japan's exports to Asia (presumably the natural yen-bloc area) are denominated in dollars, a third-country currency. There appears to be little evidence that a currency bloc based on the use of the yen as an invoice currency is emerging in Asia.

The yen as a banking and reserve currency has not evolved much more than its role as an invoice currency. Table 4.6 shows the currency denominations of foreign-exchange transactions in the three largest foreign-exchange markets in 1986, 1989, and 1992. In the Tokyo market, yen-dollar exchanges were the predominant transactions in all three years. In New York, about one-third of the transactions were mark-dollar exchanges and one-fourth were yen-dollar exchanges. In the United Kingdom in 1992, pound-dollar transactions accounted for less than 20 percent of the London market, while mark-dollar transactions accounted for 23 percent and yen-dollar transactions for only 13 percent. Although cross-currency trades (nondollar-to-nondollar transactions) did grow substantially between 1989 and 1992, mark-yen transactions still amounted to only 3 percent in London and New York and 4 percent in Tokyo. Thus, yen-involved transactions outside Japan are dominated by other currencies.

Table 4.7 shows official foreign-reserve holdings by central banks around the world and in selected Asian countries, broken down by currency denomination. In 1990, yen-denominated reserves accounted for less than 10 percent of total international reserves held by central banks in the world and 17 percent in Asia. This is much less than the share in foreign-exchange-market transactions. Although there was a jump in the yen-denominated assets of central banks in 1985, this is attributable to passive capital gains associated with the sharp yen appreciations against the dollar. Yen-denominated assets accounted for as much as 30 percent of Asian central banks' international reserves in 1987. However, it is remarkable that Asian central banks seem to have decreased their

Table 4.6
Currency composition (in percent) of transactions on foreign-exchange market, including interbank, customers, futures, and options transactions. In Tokyo, interbank transactions represent three-fourths of total transactions. "Cross" means exchange between non-dollar currencies, "*/$" means other currencies and dollar. Source: Bank of Japan, *Bank of Japan Monthly Bulletin* (in Japanese), December 1992.

	London	New York	Tokyo
April 1986			
Transactions/day	$90.0 billion	$58.5 billion	$48.0 billion
	UK/$ 30.0	DM/$ 34.2	Yen/$ 81.6
	DM/$ 28.0	Yen/$ 23.0	DM/$ 7.7
	Yen/$ 14.0	UK/$ 18.6	UK/$ 2.6
	SFr/$ 9.0	SFr/$ 9.7	SFr/$ 4.0
	*/$ 16.0	*/$ 14.5	*/$ 2.6
	Cross 3.0	Cross na	Cross 1.5
April 1989			
Transactions/day	$187.0 billion	$128.9 billion	$115.2 billion
	UK/$ 27.0	DM/$ 32.9	Yen/$ 72.3
	DM/$ 22.0	Yen/$ 25.2	DM/$ 9.7
	Yen/$ 15.0	UK/$ 14.6	UK/$ 4.3
	SFr/$ 10.0	SFr/$ 11.8	SFr/$ 4.3
	FFr/$ 2.0	Can/$ 4.0	
	*/$ 15.0	*/$ 11.5	*/$ 3.3
	Cross 9.0	Cross 3.6	Cross 6.1
	DM/yen 2.0	DM/yen na	DM/yen 1.0
April 1992			
Transactions/day	$303.0 billion	$192.3 billion	$128.0 billion
	DM/$ 23.0	DM/$ 33.7	Yen/$ 67.3
	UK/$ 19.0	Yen/$ 22.8	DM/$ 14.1
	Yen/$ 13.0	UK/$ 9.3	UK/$ 3.8
	SFr/$ 6.0	SFr/$ 7.9	SFr/$ 1.7
	*/$ 22.0	*/$ 15.0	*/$ 5.3
	Cross 17.0	Cross 11.3	Cross 7.8
	DM/yen 3.0	DM/yen 2.8	DM/yen 3.9

yen-denominated assets from 1987 to 1990, offsetting almost all their capital gains in yen from 1984 to 1987. Again, we have little evidence of the yen's becoming an international reserve currency.

Other statistics cited by Tavlas and Ozeki (1992) show that the share of yen-denominated debt increased significantly in most Asian countries (most notably Indonesia, Thailand, and Malaysia) during the 1980s. These countries are recipients of Japan's yen-denominated loans (as part

Table 4.7
Official foreign reserves. Source: Tavlas and Ozeki 1992, table 25.

	1980	1981	1982	1983	1984	1985	1986	1987	1988	1989	1990
Percentage of all countries' official reserves											
Yen	4.4	4.2	4.7	5.0	5.8	8.0	7.9	7.5	7.7	7.9	9.1
US$	68.6	71.5	70.5	71.4	70.1	64.9	67.1	67.2	64.9	60.2	56.4
UK£	2.9	2.1	2.3	2.5	2.9	3.0	2.6	2.4	2.8	2.7	3.2
DM	14.9	12.3	12.4	11.8	12.7	15.2	14.6	14.4	15.7	19.3	19.7
FFr	1.7	1.3	1.0	0.8	0.8	0.9	0.8	0.8	1.0	1.3	2.1
SFr	3.2	2.7	2.7	2.4	2.0	2.3	2.0	2.0	1.9	1.7	1.5
NGu	1.3	1.1	1.1	0.8	0.7	1.0	1.1	1.2	1.1	1.1	1.2
Percentage of selected Asian countries' official reserves											
Yen	13.9	15.5	17.6	15.5	16.3	26.9	22.8	30.0	26.7	17.5	17.1
USD	48.6	54.4	53.2	55.7	58.2	44.8	48.4	41.2	46.7	56.4	62.7
UK £	3.0	2.5	2.7	2.9	3.5	4.1	3.6	3.9	4.2	6.4	4.9
DM	20.6	18.9	17.6	16.7	14.6	16.4	16.7	16.7	17.4	15.2	14.2
FFr	0.6	0.6	0.7	0.8	0.6	0.9	1.1	1.0	0.5	0.5	0.2
SFr	10.6	5.1	5.6	6.6	4.9	4.93	5.1	5.7	3.4	3.0	0.5
NGu	2.8	3.1	2.6	1.8	1.9	2.1	2.2	1.5	1.0	0.9	0.5

of official assistance). Even though some of the increases were due to yen appreciation, foreign borrowing from Japan by Asian countries seems to have outpaced borrowing in dollars (Ito 1994).

Exchange-Rate Co-Movements

The extent to which countries peg their currencies against the yen may also provide evidence of the international importance of the yen. Many Asian countries have adopted a "basket" currency system in which the exchange rate is determined as a weighted average of the values of other currencies. However, the particular currencies in the basket or their weights are usually not announced by policymakers. Although the weights are not announced, it is theoretically possible to infer this basket from historical data (if its contents are not changed too often).

Frankel and Wei (1994) examined the weekly exchange-rate movements of nine Asian currencies: the Korean won, the Singapore dollar, the Hong Kong dollar, the Taiwan dollar, the Malaysian ringgit, the Indonesian rupiah, the Philippine peso, the Thai baht, and the Chinese yuan. The weekly changes in these Asian currencies (in terms of the Swiss franc) were regressed on changes of the US dollar, the Japanese yen, the German mark, the Australian dollar, and the New Zealand dollar (all in terms of the Swiss franc) for the sample period from January 1979 to May 1992 and several subperiods. Frankel and Wei found high weights (from 0.90 to 1.00) on the US dollar for all nine currencies for the full period and for all subsamples. In general, the yen did not have a statistically significant effect on the Asian currencies. The exception was the Singapore dollar, which showed statistically significant coefficients for the yen in all subperiods. However, the weight of the yen was less than 0.15, while the weight on the dollar was about 0.80. Thus, most Asian countries implicitly limit the movements of their currencies against the US dollar; there is not much evidence that they peg against the yen.

Trade and Capital Flows

The idea of an East Asian economic group (EAEG), with Japan in a leadership position, has been discussed widely.[28] This movement is partly a defensive reaction to the development or strengthening of trading blocs in North America and Europe and partly a response to the difficulties of reaching multilateral trade agreements through the General Agreement on Tariffs and Trade (GATT).

As is evident from table 4.8, there has been a significant increase in Japan's exports to other Asian countries since the mid 1980s. In 1991 the value of Japan's exports to Asian countries, broadly defined, surpassed that of Japan's exports to the United States. Although Japan also increased its imports from Asia, this increase was similar to the increase in imports from other regions. The net effect has been a sharp rise in Japan's trade surplus with the rest of Asia.

It is not clear whether Japan's greater concentration of trade in Asia is due to a regional bias (in the sense of Asian countries' tending to trade with one another rather than with non-Asian countries) or simply to a confluence of factors including rapid regional growth and greater restrictions on Japan's exports to the United States and Europe. Frankel (1993) formally tests the regional-bias hypothesis by regressing trade flows for a cross-section of countries against variables such as output growth, relative incomes, distance, and regional dummy variables for the EC, the Western Hemisphere, and Asia. He found East Asia to have a regional trade bias, but he did not find the intra-Asia trade bias to be centered around Japan. Moreover, the intraregional trade bias of ASEAN countries diminished during the 1980s, in contrast to the EC

Table 4.8
Japan's trade, in millions of dollars, by region.

	1981	1986	1991
Exports			
United States	38,609	80,456	91,538
Canada	3,399	5,526	7,251
Western Europe	23,748	37,483	59,158
Southeast Asia	34,426	41,788	96,176
Korea	5,658	10,475	20,068
Taiwan	5,405	7,852	18,255
Hong Kong	5,311	7,161	16,315
Singapore	4,468	4,577	12,213
Thailand	2,251	2,030	9,431
Malaysia	2,424	1,708	7,635
Philippines	1,928	1,088	2,659
Indonesia	4,123	2,662	5,612
China	5,095	9,856	8,593
Total (world)	152,030	209,151	314,525
Imports			
United States	25,297	29,054	53,317
Canada	4,464	4,895	7,698
Western Europe	11,541	18,118	39,209
Southeast Asia	31,930	29,489	58,810
Korea	3,389	5,292	12,339
Taiwan	2,523	4,691	9,493
Hong Kong	669	1,073	2,064
Singapore	1,944	1,463	3,415
Thailand	1,061	1,391	5,252
Malaysia	2,927	3,846	6,471
Philippines	1,731	1,221	2,351
Indonesia	13,305	7,311	12,770
China	5,292	5,652	14,216
Total (world)	143,290	126,408	236,737

and Western Hemisphere groups. East Asian countries, contrary to popular belief, have tended to open up more for trade outside the region.

Japan's direct investment in Asian countries grew at a much slower rate than Japan's direct investment in the United States during the first half of the 1980s, and only slightly faster during the second half. The share of Asian countries in Japan's foreign investment was not substantially larger in the early 1990s than the early 1980s (Ito 1994). Asia does not appear to be the primary target of Japan's direct investment. Nonetheless, Japanese direct investment is a larger proportion of its total direct investment in most other Asian countries today than it was in 1980.

A Yen Bloc?

The evidence presented does not suggest that a yen bloc is forming in Asia. Regional trade concentration in Asia is weakening. Asian exchange rates are not generally linked to the yen, and use of the yen as an invoice, vehicle, or reserve currency in the Asian region is very limited. The financial crisis in Japan has also led Japanese banks to proceed more cautiously in their international activities, partly reversing their rapid expansion abroad (which started in the early 1980s).

Given this evidence, can we conclude that a strong yen bloc is not in place? It is too early to tell. There is some evidence that Japan's interest-rate movements are now influencing interest rates around the world (Hutchison and Singh, forthcoming), and particularly in East Asia (Glick and Hutchison 1990; Chinn and Frankel 1994). Moreover, to judge by comovements in stock prices, Asian countries are subject to common shocks (Ito 1994). Financial integration of this nature and a high degree of common shocks may suggest that East Asia is an "optimal currency area." This could exert economic pressure toward greater financial and monetary integration between Japan and other East Asian countries, including an arrangement limiting exchange-rate volatility, despite limited progress to date.

Conclusion

Japan continued to follow an active policy of foreign-exchange intervention even after the collapse of the Bretton Woods system, driven in large part by a desire to dampen exchange-rate fluctuations against the US dollar ("leaning against the wind"). Partly in conflict with this policy, however, there was strong pressure for yen appreciation over most of the period 1981–1996 as the yen/dollar rate moved from 360 in 1971 to (briefly) around 80 in early 1995 before recovering to 120 by the end of 1996. The trend appreciation of the yen in real terms was related to Japan's high (by international standards) productivity growth and its recurring large current-account surpluses. At times Japanese officials attempted to resist yen appreciation and target the level of the exchange rate, but these efforts met with very limited success and were soon replaced by more modest efforts to dampen exchange-rate fluctuations.

The Bank of Japan has attempted to offset a large part of the monetary effects of foreign-exchange intervention operations, not always successfully. The two major mistakes of monetary policy—the "wild inflation" that followed the breakup of the Bretton Woods system and the bubble economy of the second half of the 1980s—were both partly attributable to the attempt to limit yen appreciation. Intervention against the rise in the yen undoubtedly contributed to the expansion of the monetary aggregates during these episodes.

Some of the monetary effects of the Bank of Japan's activist "leaning against the wind" policy, which would be expected to lead to excessive money growth when "real" fundamentals cause trend yen appreciation, were moderated by an asymmetric intervention policy. That is, foreign-exchange intervention in response to a given change in the yen is somewhat larger during episodes of depreciation than appreciation. Consistent with this attempt to limit monetary effects, there has generally been less sterilization during episodes of yen depreciation when the Bank of Japan is losing foreign-exchange reserves. This has tended to dampen monetary-base growth and tighten monetary conditions precisely when the yen weakens. Resisting yen depreciation more vigorously than yen appreciation, and allowing foreign-exchange sales to have a larger impact on the monetary base than foreign-exchange purchases, helps limit the overall accumulation of international reserves and dampens upward pressure on monetary-base growth.

Attempts to coordinate macroeconomic policies internationally also contributed to excessive monetary ease and to the rise of the bubble economy in the second half of the 1980s. The massive intervention that followed the Plaza Agreement did not represent a reversal of established Japanese policy; however, the Bank of Japan was prompted to take an even more activist stance, and this was further exacerbated by the sharp exchange-rate movement. The Plaza Agreement signaled an even more fundamental shift in US intervention policy. The United States finally came around to the Japanese and European position that exchange markets at the time did not properly reflect "fundamentals" and agreed to intervene in markets in a substantial and coordinated fashion.

The dollar's instability has undermined its desirability as an international transactions and reserve currency. With the European Monetary System, Europe has moved to a system of pegged rates, largely centered around the mark rather than the dollar. Similar concerns, and the failure of activist intervention policies to limit the dollar's volatility, have led some to consider the possibility of a yen bloc in Asia, in line with the growing importance of Japanese finance in the world economy. However, there is little indication to date of a yen bloc forming in Asia, and relative to Japan's economic importance the yen continues to be a relatively "underrepresented" currency in international trade and finance.

5 The Bubble Economy and Its Collapse

The Japanese economy of the second half of the 1980s is commonly characterized as the "bubble economy." Starting in 1986, the prices of assets (ranging from stock and land to paintings and country club memberships) doubled and then tripled within a few years. The Nikkei 225 index, for example, increased from the 13,000s in December 1985 to the 39,000s in December 1989. Similarly, the price index for commercial land in six metropolitan cities tripled between March 1986 and March 1990.

The burst of the bubble came in the first half of the 1990s. Stock prices declined by 60 percent between 1990 and August 1992, and they continued to decline until the Nikkei index began to rebound after June 1995. Even though the Nikkei increased significantly in percentage terms during the following year, the 21,000 level reached by late 1996 was still only slightly more than half of its peak value. Representative land prices in metropolitan areas also declined by half from 1991 to 1995, and they continued to decline through early 1996.

In retrospect, the rise and fall of asset prices from 1985 to 1995 appears to be a classic financial bubble,[1] rivaling some of the most spectacular in history.[2] Debate at the time, however, focused on whether the asset-price increases were based on fundamentals, on whether monetary policy played a role in stimulating the asset-inflation phase, and on whether monetary policy should have targeted asset prices rather than more traditional price indices (such as the consumer-price index).

The Bank of Japan has been criticized for playing a role in starting the asset-price bubble and for not moving sooner to stop asset prices from increasing further. This chapter focuses on the causes of the asset-price inflation and on the role played by the Bank of Japan.

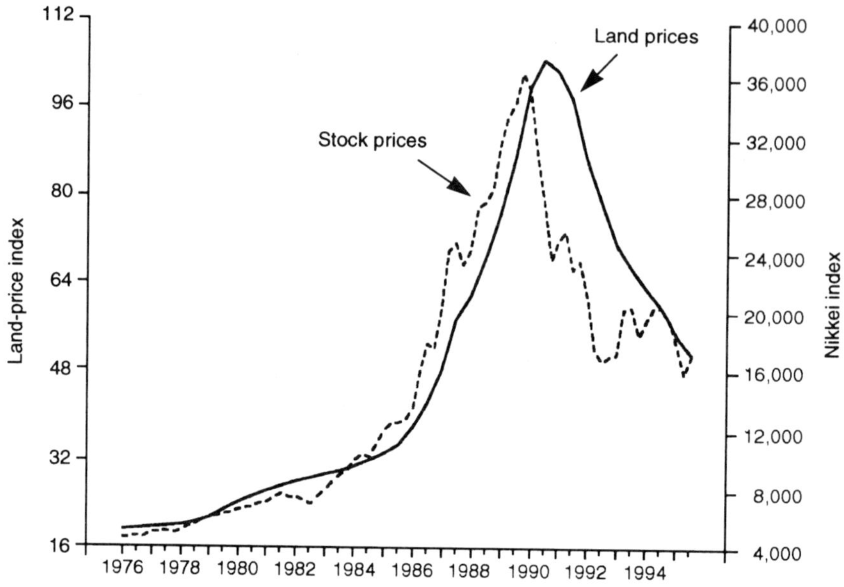

Figure 5.1
Land prices versus stock prices.

5.1 Movements of Financial and Macroeconomic Variables

Figure 5.1 describes the movement of the land and stock prices from 1976 to 1995.[3] Two features of this figure stand out immediately. First, land-price and stock-price movements are highly correlated. Second, the sharp rise in asset prices from 1985 to 1990 is a sharp deviation from the previous trend and, judging by the sharp decline in the early 1990s, does not appear consistent with longer-term equilibrium values. The long-term trend shows a steady rise from the mid 1970s to the mid 1980s and a sharp acceleration around 1985. The duration and the magnitude of the decline were also remarkable. By 1995 the level had returned to roughly the point that would have been attained had the steady trend established from the mid 1970s to the mid 1980s continued unabated.

Figures 5.2 and 5.3, respectively, plot the growth of Japan's nominal GDP and real GDP against quarterly stock returns.[4] To judge from these figures, there is only a weak correspondence between changes in stock prices and the growth of either nominal or real GDP. Real GDP grew at a higher rate in the second half of the 1980s, when stock returns were high, than in the first half of the 1990s, when stock returns turned nega-

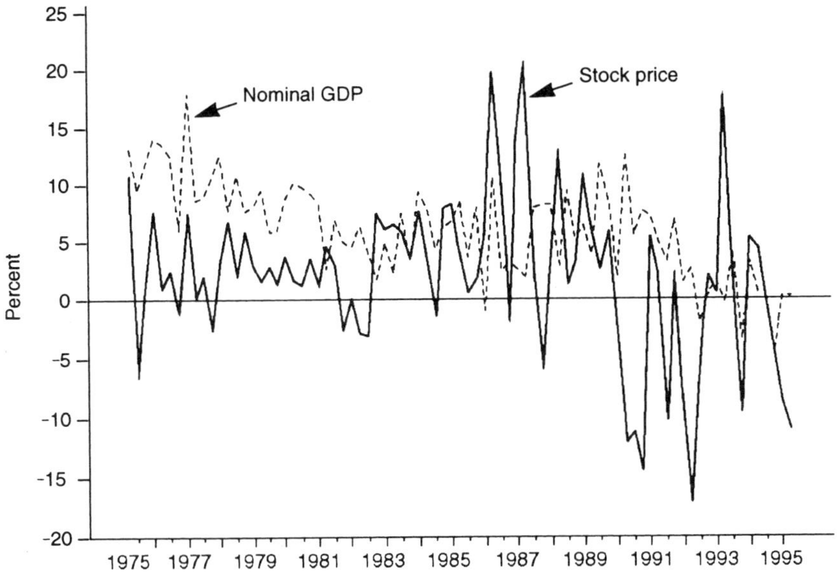

Figure 5.2
Growth rates of nominal GDP and stock prices.

tive. However, the statistical correlation between real-GDP growth and stock returns is very weak.

Figure 5.4 shows movements in interest rates: the government bond rate, the call rate, and the official discount rate. Interest rates declined from the fourth quarter of 1985 to the first quarter of 1987, when the runup in asset prices began. The rapid decline in interest rates was motivated in part by concern over yen appreciation from February 1985 to the summer 1986.

The behavior of real interest rates and the real money supply are other indicators of monetary policy that may have some bearing on asset prices. Figure 5.5 illustrates movements in the real call rate (nominal call rate less CPI inflation rate) and the real M2 + CDs growth rate. Both the real interest rate and the rate of real monetary growth were stable between 1982 and 1985. The beginning of the asset-inflation period (1985:3–1987:2), however, is characterized by increased monetary growth and a declining real interest rate. The monetary tightening from the second quarter of 1989 to the middle of 1990 is reflected by the sharp increase in the real interest rate, but not by the monetary aggregates (whose growth slowed only after the middle of 1990).

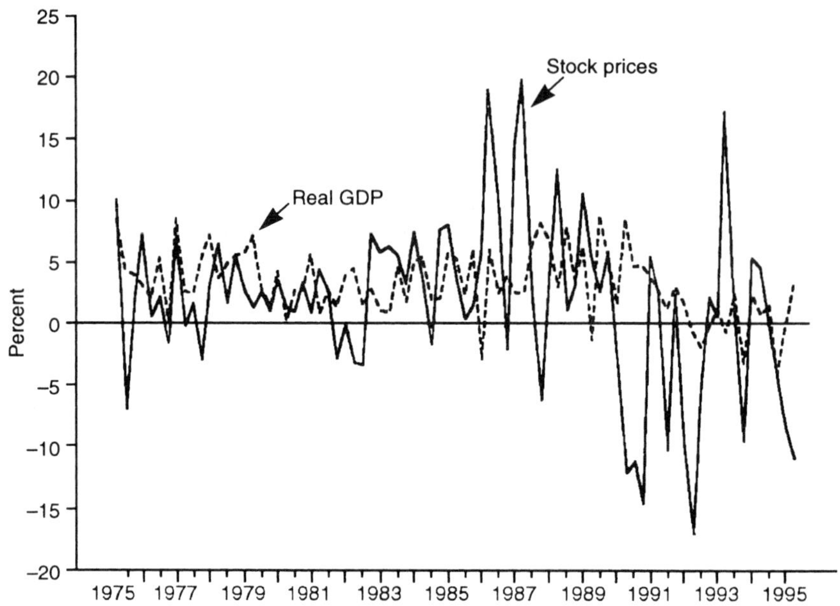

Figure 5.3
Growth rates of real GDP and stock prices.

After the fall in asset prices, the shift to a more expansionary monetary stance is suggested by the decline in interest rates beginning in early 1991. By early 1993, real interest rates had fallen below 2 percent. Despite lower interest rates, however, monetary growth continued to decline until the end of 1992. Indeed, the main monetary aggregate (nominal and real M2 + CDs) fell during 1992, creating widespread fears of general price deflation and even deeper recession. This raises the issue of whether monetary policy was sufficiently stimulative at the time, especially since Japan experienced almost no output growth during the four years that followed the asset-price collapse.

5.2 Was There an Asset-Price Bubble in Japan?

Whether the sharp rise and fall in Japanese asset prices should be characterized as a speculative bubble has attracted a great deal of academic and policy interest.[5] In order to judge whether asset-price movements reflect a bubble, however, it is necessary to develop some measure of a "normal" level.[6]

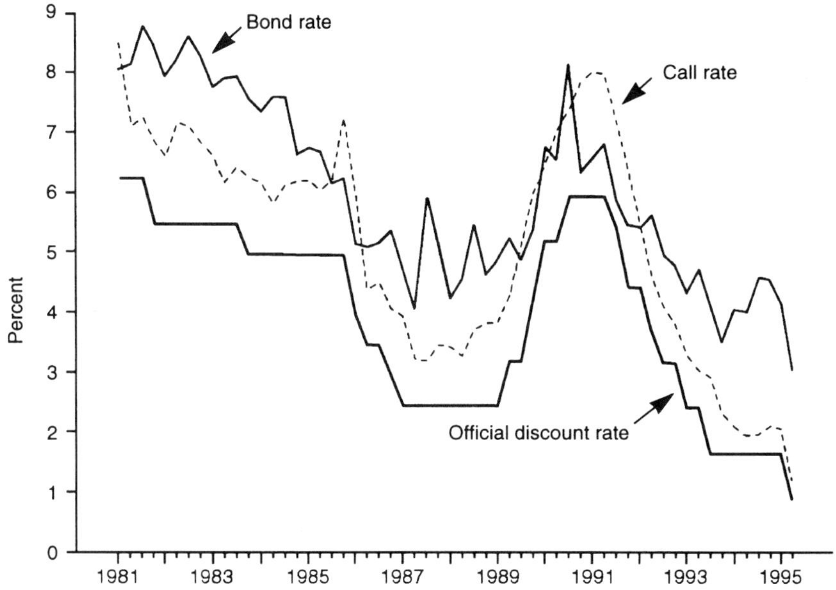

Figure 5.4
Nominal interest rate for government bonds, call rate, and official discount rate.

A Framework for Asset Pricing

Investors hold an asset to earn a stream of earnings—dividends in the case of stocks and rents in the case of land. In this regard, the fundamental value of an asset may be thought of as the discounted future stream of earnings derived from the asset. According to this standard definition, asset prices change when expectations about future earnings change or when the discount factor (the future path of the interest rate or risk premium) changes. Assuming a constant discount factor and constant growth rate of earnings factor, we can write the current fundamental value of an asset as

$$P_t = \frac{D_t}{r - g} \tag{5.1}$$

where D denotes earnings (dividend or rent), r the discount factor (interest rate), g the growth rate of earnings, and P the price of the asset. This expression assumes an infinite stream of earnings; however, investors may be interested in holding assets for finite periods.

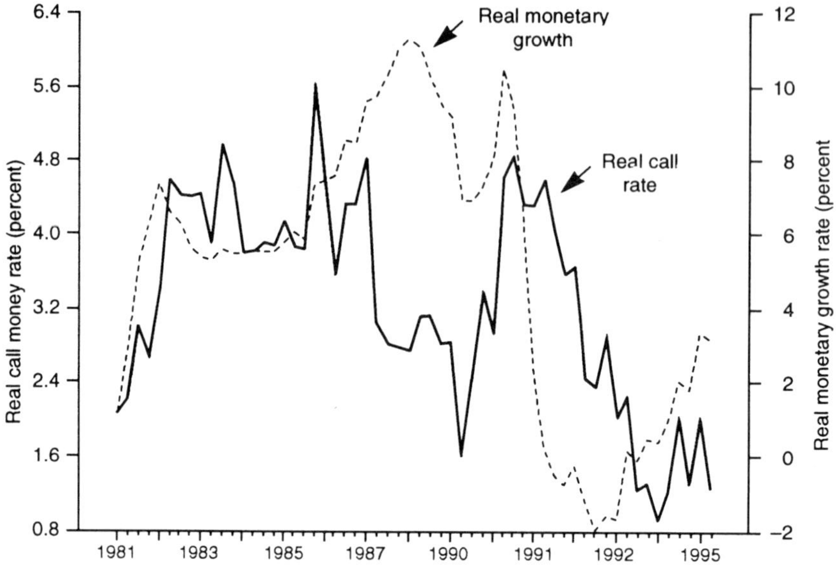

Figure 5.5
Real call rate and real monetary growth.

The total return from holding an asset for one period is the sum of direct earnings (dividend or rent) and the expected market value of the asset at the end of the year. The rate of return (that is, the total return divided by the current price) should equal a comparable asset for investment with similar risk such as corporate bond. This may be expressed as

$$P_t = \frac{D_t + P_{t+1}}{1 + r_t} \tag{5.2}$$

or, equivalently,

$$r_t = \frac{D_t + (P_{t+1} - P_t)}{P_t} \tag{5.3}$$

where P_{t+1} is the expected asset price one year from today at time t and the r_t is the (rate of return) interest rate from t to $t + 1$. This definition reveals the potential for "speculation"—a bet on the pure price movement without a significant change in fundamental value. If many (if not all) investors suddenly think that the next-period price would rise more than before, a change in the resale value one period from now will change the current valuation of this asset (with a discount factor). Even without a change in direct earnings, pure (wishful) expectation of a rise in the resale value can change the current value of the asset. Higher expected capital gains ($P_{t+1} - P_t$) will push up the current price P_t until the expected rate of return equals the interest rate (or the rate of return of similar assets).

What would prompt such a sudden change in the expected future price? Such a change could reflect the belief that earnings will increase in the future (after one year but before the second year) and/or that the resale value of the asset in the second year will rise. This chain of thought can be extended to the infinite future. As long as expectations are optimistic and investors believe that higher capital gains will continue into the future, the current price will be higher. This is a classic bubble, with higher current prices due simply to the expectation of higher prices in the future.

Among the various types of bubbles, a stochastic bubble process may also be useful in understanding the Japanese experience. During a stochastic bubble process, the price level deviates (in fact, increasingly deviates) from the fundamental value for some time and then, at some point, abruptly collapses back to the fundamental value. The expected return (calculated from the weighted average of the next-period price level with weights of probabilities of two different outcomes) should be consistent with expected return of comparable assets. As long as the bubble path continues, *ex post* excess returns continue to be observed (positive autocorrelation), apparently violating the efficient-market hypothesis.[7]

The Role of Fundamentals

The above framework sheds some light on whether the increase in Japanese asset prices may be attributed to underlying fundamentals. This judgment relies, however, on the appropriateness of the theoretical framework, and on our measures of the fundamental determinants (since bubbles are inferred from residuals of the model).

As equation 5.1 indicates, the higher the expected dividend (rent) growth rate, the higher the stock (land) price, and the lower the interest rate, the higher the stock (land) price. Although it is difficult to estimate the growth rate of expected future dividends (rent), there are at least three reasons to believe that expectations about future returns of stock and land assets became more optimistic in the second half of the 1980s.

Table 5.1
Simulation of asset prices with alternative values of interest rates (r) and dividend growth rates (g). P/D: ratio of price to earnings.

r	g	$1/(r-g) = P/D$
5%	4%	100
4%	3%	100
5%	3%	50
6%	3%	33.3

First, financial liberalization in Japan created a boom in the financial services and banking industry; it also attracted a large number of foreign financial institutions, which in turn contributed to the high demand for commercial properties in Tokyo. This is supported by detailed analysis of land-price movements in the Tokyo area. Land-price movements reveal that the prices of land for commercial use led the general increase in land prices, which first rose in central Tokyo, and then spilled over to neighboring land (first tier suburbs, and then other parts of Japan).[8]

Second, economic growth rates rose in the second half of the 1980s relative to the first half (figure 5.3). Expectations of future economic growth, whether *ex post* realized or not, likely became more optimistic, creating higher expectations about future dividends.

Third, monetary policy eased significantly in 1986 and 1987. In February 1987 the official discount rate was lowered to 2.5 percent, a record low at the time, where it remained until May 1989. Market rates also stayed at low levels. Lower interest rates, according to equation 5.1, increase the fundamental value of an asset.

The simple calculations presented in table 5.1 illustrate this point. When the required rate of return is 6 percent and the dividend growth is 3 percent, the P/D ratio is 33. If the required rate of return (interest rate) were to decline from 6 percent to 5 percent (with g held constant at 3 percent), however, the P/D ratio would increase to 50. A further decline from 5 percent to 4 percent (with g held constant at 3 percent) would increase the P/D ratio to 100. The same result would be obtained if r were held at 5 percent but g increased from 3 to 4 percent. Table 5.2 shows the actual levels of r and g in Japan in the second half of the 1980s. Indeed, the long-term bank interest rate[9] went down by 1.7 percentage points from 1985 to 1988, while the growth rate went up by 1.3 percentage points from 1986 to 1988. These changes, if at the time they were ex-

Table 5.2
Interest rates and growth rates: official discount rate (ODR) in December of year, long-term-loan bank rate (r) for year, and real GDP growth rate (g) for year. Source: Toyo Keizai Statistical Annual (original sources: Bank of Japan and Economic Planning Agency).

	1985	1986	1987	1988	1989	1990
ODR	5.0	3.0	2.5	2.5	4.25	6.0
r	7.5	7.0	6.1	5.8	5.8	6.8
g	4.9	2.6	4.1	6.2	4.7	4.8

pected to be permanent, could explain the rise in Japanese asset prices in the late 1980s.

The Role of Bubbles

Even in the late 1980s, many economists argued that asset inflation could not be explained by fundamental factors alone and was better characterized as a speculative bubble. Several arguments support this point of view.

First, the levels of asset prices in the late 1980s were not supported by any reasonable calculations of the fundamentals relationship. Direct returns (dividends in the case of stocks, rents in the case of real estate) were far too low to justify investment—unless capital gains were expected. This is especially so since dividend yields were generally much lower in Japan than in the United States or Europe. Ueda (1990) concluded that Japan's price-dividend ratio and that of the United States were more or less comparable through the 1960s, that they started to diverge during the 1970s, and that in the 1980s Japan's price-dividend ratio skyrocketed.[10] Ito and Hirono (1993) compiled the rents and purchase prices of high-rise condominiums (rather homogeneous housings with active transactions) in the Tokyo metropolitan area. Using hedonic price methods, they calculated the standardized prices and rents, controlling for such factors as the floor space of the unit and the commuting time (walking time to rail station and rail time to the core of Tokyo). Table 5.3 shows the prices and rents of such a standardized unit. If one purchased such a unit for investment purposes, the direct yield was below 0.5 percent. During the asset-inflation period, the yield declined to only 0.26 percent. Most of the gains must be expected in the form of asset-price increases. In fact, the most salient feature of the Japanese land and housing problem is not high real-estate values relative to other

Table 5.3
Standardized hedonic price and rents in Tokyo (units for prices and rents: 10,000 yen). Prices and rents are estimated from the hedonic price (rent) equations for a 60-square-meter condominium unit, built in 1980, at a location a 5-minute walk from the Mitaka station (18 minutes from the Shinjuku station), on a second floor or above, facing south, with no parking lot. Rents are in annual payments. Source: Ito and Hirono 1993.

	1981	1982	1983	1984	1985	1986
Price	3628.9	3532.0	3063.0	3167.7	3176.4	3210.9
Rent	12.072	11.337	11.290	13.797	15.115	15.093
Yield	0.33%	0.32%	0.37%	0.44%	0.48%	0.47%
	1987	1988	1989	1990	1991	1992
Price	4863.9	6487.4	6323.0	6712.5	6949.1	6101.5
Rent	15.940	17.201	16.705	18.425	18.425	19.045
Yield	0.33%	0.27%	0.26%	0.27%	0.27%	0.31%

advanced countries; it is the low direct yield (the high ratio of price to earnings). This aspect can be readily used as evidence of a bubble. The asset inflation merely aggravated what had always been the low yield of Japanese real estate.

Second, by international and historical standards, the increase in the value of real estate in the second half of the 1980s was remarkable. In 1990 the market value of all the land in Japan, according to several estimates, was four times the land value of the United States, which is 25 times Japan's size. Even with much higher growth prospects for Japan, it would be difficult to justify a 100:1 differential in the relative price of land between the two countries.

Third, although the direction of asset prices is consistent with the direction of the fundamentals, the magnitude of the response was exaggerated. For example, the appreciation of total Japanese land values exceeded Japan's GNP in 1987. By analogy, a typical household would have experienced an appreciation in its holdings of stocks and real estate exceeding its salary income for that year. At a more theoretical level, even though the interest rate was lowered in 1986 and 1987, the lower interest rate could not have been expected to last forever (which is the basis for deriving equation 5.1). Thus, the impact of the lower interest rate on the asset price should have been much smaller than what was observed. Ito and Iwaisako (1996) make this point using simple simulations based on equation 5.1 and relaxing the assumptions. Their results are shown in table 5.4. The simulation is based on the following thought experiment: How much would P/D change when, with g assumed to be 3 percent, r changes from 6 percent to either 5 percent or 4 percent only for K periods (and then returns to its previous level)? When K is less than 10 years, even a 2-percentage-point decrease, which would triple the asset price if it were expected to be permanent, should result in only a 20 percent increase in the asset price. This is a powerful argument against the fundamentalists view.

Fourth, once the process of asset inflation starts, expectations may become self-fulfilling. In the Japanese case, this self-fulfilling process is more complicated because of the close connections among real-estate, corporations, the stock market, and financial institutions. Since many corporations own land, rising land prices increase corporate liquidation values. This is usually not reflected on corporate balance sheets, but nonetheless it will generally increase stock prices. Corporations also can benefit from enhanced borrowing potential, since more highly valued land may be used as additional collateral. Furthermore, Japanese banks

Table 5.4
Change in price-dividend ratio (P/D) with r changing from 6 percent to either 5 percent or 4 percent, with g assumed to be 3 percent. Source: Ito and Iwaisako 1996.

	Change in P/D	
K	$r = 5\%$	$r = 4\%$
0	33.33	— (no decrease)
3 months	33.51 (0.54%)	33.59 (0.78%)
6 months	33.59 (0.78%)	33.75 (1.26%)
1 year	33.74 (1.23%)	34.06 (2.19%)
2 years	34.06 (2.19%)	34.70 (4.11%)
3 years	34.37 (3.12%)	35.33 (6.0%)
5 years	34.97 (4.92%)	36.56 (9.69%)
10 years	36.38 (9.15%)	39.55 (18.7%)
∞[a]	50.00 (50.0%)	100.00 (200%)

a. $K = \infty$ implies a once-and-for-all permanent change, and corresponds to table 5.1.

hold a significant amount of equity in nonfinancial corporations, and when equity prices rise their capital base increases and allows an expansion of lending. These links among land prices, corporate value, the stock market, and bank lending create a strong co-movement between land prices and stock prices in Japan. This co-movement, illustrated in figure 5.1, is statistically significant (Ito and Iwaisako 1996).

Fifth, empirical studies attempting to relate movements in land and stock prices to fundamentals in Japan have not been very successful. Hutchison (1994), for example, examines the nature of fundamental disturbances that have accounted for fluctuations in Japanese nominal and real land prices during the postwar period. The disturbances are characterized into three groups: macroeconomic supply disturbances, macroeconomic demand disturbances, and a residual (which may include speculative pressures).[11] Hutchison finds that aggregate demand disturbances, a category that includes shifts in monetary policy, have played a relatively minor role in fluctuations of real land prices. Aggregate supply shocks (e.g., productivity changes, technology developments, and changes in expectations of future economic growth) are important, but by far most of the variation in land prices is unexplained. This large residual is partly attributable to nonmacroeconomic factors specific to the land market (such as changes in tax-code provisions and financial liberalization) that increased the demand for Japanese real estate. The large unexplained movements in land prices (residuals from the estimated model), however, suggest that speculative bubbles may also have played a role.

The Role of Financial Liberalization

Before drawing judgments on the relative role of fundamentals versus bubbles, one should recognize that in the second half of the 1980s asset inflation—though not of the same order of magnitude as in Japan—was evident in many countries. Indices of real asset prices for 13 industrialized countries, consisting of equity, residential-real-estate, and commercial-real-estate components, illustrate a broad-based process of asset inflation in the second half of the 1980s (Borio et al. 1994).

The international character of asset inflation suggests common explanatory factors. The coincidence of financial liberalization and asset inflation and deflation has led a number of observers to argue that liberalization played a major role in the financial disruptions of the 1980s and in the problems that the 1990s inherited from the boom-and-bust period. This view is rooted in the traditional argument that unregulated and competitive banking is inherently unstable in the absence of government supervision. In the context of liberalization in the 1980s, the removal of binding portfolio constraints permitted banks and other depositories to adopt riskier investment and loan portfolios, including the adoption of high loan-to-value ratios.

Borio et al. (1994) conclude that the broad-based asset inflation was accounted for by relaxation and removal of various constraints on portfolio activity, especially for depository institutions, rather than by general macroeconomic policy.[12] Nakajima and Taguchi (1995) also place responsibility for the asset inflation on financial liberalization and on the incentives for banks to adopt riskier loan and investment portfolios. They argue that banks, directly or indirectly, provided imprudent levels of credit to the real-estate and equity markets in an effort to offset declining profit margins and declining market shares and to maintain the franchise value of commercial bank charters (supported in the past by a regulated and administratively controlled financial environment).

Views that trace the bubble economy to financial liberalization can point to a number of special features of the Japanese financial system in the mid 1980s that made asset inflation more probable in the context of a newly liberated financial structure and a more accommodating monetary policy.

Table 5.5
Lending to real estate and nonbank companies, in trillions of yen. (Data are for all banks, and include trust accounts. Numbers in parentheses denote percentage of total lending.) Source: Bank of Japan, *Economics Statistics Annual.*

	1984	1985	1986	1987	1988	1989
Total lending outstanding	299.3 (100%)	249.6 (100%)	273.3 (100%)	297.6 (100%)	322.3 (100%)	356.8 (100%)
To real estate	17.4 (7.5%)	22.2 (8.9%)	30.2 (11.1%)	33.5 (11.3%)	37.3 (11.7%)	43.3 (12.1%)
To nonbank companies	23.2 (10.2%)	29.6 (11.9%)	36.9 (13.5%)	45.1 (15.2%)	50.9 (15.8%)	59.6 (16.7%)

First, market participants had more portfolio flexibility than they had ever had in the past. This is especially true for small depositories: like American savings-and-loan institutions during the 1980s, small Japanese credit-union-type depositories aggressively pursued lending in speculative real-estate ventures during the bubble phase, and, like their US counterparts, they did so without oversight.

Second, the shift to slower growth after the 1973 oil-price shock reduced the corporate sector's reliance on bank credit and services. As a result, banks sought out new markets outside traditional corporate finance and were willing to assume new and often higher risks with which they had little previous experience. Table 5.5 illustrates the increased bank lending to real estate during the bubble phase; figure 5.6 illustrates the distribution of funds into real-estate lending as of June 1991.

Third, the main-bank system of industrial organization began to unravel in response to financial liberalization, which in the past had served as an effective system to evaluate and monitor risk. No widely available financial-disclosure framework was available to replace the main-bank system.

Fourth, despite a common perception that Japanese banks were subject to a Glass-Steagall-type rule, they in fact had considerable authority to directly purchase and hold equities, and this allowed bank credit to flow easily into equity markets. In addition, "hidden reserves" of banks were tied directly to the fortunes of the stock market (table 5.6).

Fifth, the regulatory monitoring system lagged behind market developments, and "administrative guidance" could not keep pace with the fast-changing financial environment.

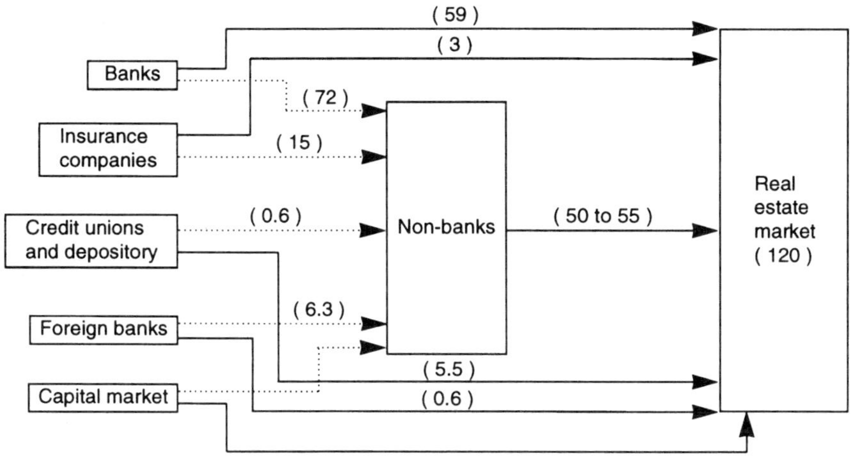

Figure 5.6
Flow of funds to real estate market, June 1991 (trillions of yen, as of June 1991). Dotted lines represent indirect lending activities. Source: Ministry of Finance.

Table 5.6
Estimated unrealized capital gains on share holdings of 21 major banks at selected values of Nikkei 225 Index, as of March 1995, in millions of yen (source: banks' financial statements), with data on Japan's life insurance companies given for comparison.

	Nikkei index				
	18,000	16,000	14,000	12,000	10,000
City banks	8.66	5.17	1.67	−1.82	−5.12
Long-term credit banks	2.32	1.36	0.41	−0.54	−1.49
Trust banks	2.60	1.68	0.76	−0.16	−1.08
Total, 21 major banks	13.58	8.21	2.84	−2.52	−7.69
Eight largest ins. cos.	8.05	4.19	0.33	−3.54	−7.4
Total, 20 life ins. cos.	10.31	5.65	0.99	−3.67	−8.33

Sixth, complete deposit guarantees encouraged risk taking at the very time the Bank of Japan provided the liquidity and financial liberalization provided the asset-diversification powers.

The risk-incentive nature of government deposit guarantees (i.e., the "moral hazard" problem) also helps to explain the coincidence of asset inflation and financial liberalization in Japan and elsewhere.[13] The liberalization process in the 1980s in most cases failed to change the existing system of government deposit guarantees, which had been designed for a more regulated and administratively controlled financial environment. As a result, government deposit guarantees provided incentives to assume risk, while regulatory and market innovations permitted depositories to manage and assume more risk. In addition, the regulatory authorities responsible for administering the government deposit guarantee system were subject to perverse incentives in how they dealt with troubled institutions that, in turn, encouraged greater risk taking on the part of depository institutions.

The empirical verification of the risk incentives of deposit guarantees and agency problems have been documented in the greatest detail for the United States because the failure of deposit insurance has been more transparent there than elsewhere and because detailed microeconomic data on depository behavior is more generally available.[14] The risk-incentive and agency problems of deposit guarantees have not been empirically investigated in Japan, with the notable exception of the work of Fries et al. (1993), nor does it appear likely that sufficient data is publicly available to allow extensive empirical testing of the risk incentives generated by deposit guarantees. At the same time, there is no evidence that Japan's financial system is special, or that it responds differently to incentives than other systems. Nor is there any reason to doubt that the type of agency problems that accounted for regulatory inertia in dealing with the American S&L crisis are not fully operable in Japan.

Fundamentals or Bubbles?

Table 5.7 summarizes the set of factors that generated the asset-price bubble and the consequent problem of nonperforming loans. In view of the available evidence, the asset-inflation phase of the second half of the 1980s can be characterized in the following terms: The initial jump in stock and land prices during 1985–86 was most likely related to changes in fundamentals. Aggregate productivity gains in Japan were very strong at the time. Demand for real estate, particularly in the Tokyo area, increased significantly. Expansionary monetary policy pushed interest rates to very low levels.

Financial deregulation, changes in the flows of funds, and the increased risk-taking activity of banks also figured in the beginning of the runup in asset prices, but whether these factors should be characterized as fundamental determinants or speculative activities is somewhat problematic. On the one hand, this activity is rational from the viewpoint of financial institutions in the sense that they aggressively

Table 5.7
Special features of the bubble and burst of the bubble economy contributing to the problem of nonperforming loans.

Factor	Outcome
Financial liberalization starting in middle of 1970s	Increased asset-diversification powers for bank and nonbank depositories; increased ability to manage and assume risk
Downward shift in potential GDP growth path after 1973 oil-price shock reduced corporate dependence on banking system (as rate of investment fell)	Banks sought out new markets, aggressively moving into real-estate lending, and competing with *jusen* (housing-loan) companies in 1980s.
Decline of main-bank system and overall reduced role of banks in enterprise groups	Reduced ability of banks to monitor risk
Japanese banks were permitted to hold equities in nonfinancial businesses as part of the enterprise-group framework. Banks could apply 45 percent of appreciation of equity holdings to "hidden" or "latent" capital.	Capital position of banks depended on equity market, so during equity-price increases banks would expand loans and investments and during equity-price declines banks would contract loans and investments.
Reliance by regulatory authorities on "administrative guidance" to monitor bank and nonbank depositories	Regulatory authorities were less able to monitor risk as bank and nonbank depositories engaged in greater asset diversification than in past. Bank and nonbank depositories had few incentives to limit risk.
Pervasive system of government deposit guarantees	Reduced oversight powers and enhanced asset-diversification powers; as a result, depositories became more sensitive to risk incentives embedded in deposit-guarantee system.
Monetary ease in 1987 and 1988 as Bank of Japan placed greater emphasis on exchange-rate objectives than domestic considerations	Bank of Japan provided liquidity that supported asset inflation.
Incentives for regulatory authorities to adopt forbearance and forgiveness in dealing with troubled institutions	Incentives to assume risk

expanded into the real-estate business because of expanded asset-allocation powers, changes in traditional business relationships, and so on. On the other hand, financial liberalization combined with lax supervision clearly allowed more lending into real estate on a speculative basis.

Indeed, at some point, probably in late 1986 or 1987, asset inflation appeared to become a speculative bubble with little restraint either from financial institutions or the regulatory authorities. Expectations of asset-price increases fed upon themselves, and price/dividend and price/rent ratios increasingly deviated from fundamental values until the crash in the early 1990s. Speculators during the asset inflation typically thought that, even though the "levels" of stock and land prices were abnormally high and would eventually fall, further investment was warranted as long as other investors thought prices would continue to rise. Many felt that they would be among the first to sell their asset holdings, realizing large capital gains, when the market started to fall. This kind of behavior has been variously characterized as stochastic bubbles, herd instincts, momentum trading, and bandwagon behavior. The literature on various models of stock-price and foreign-exchange-rate bubbles has gained a large academic following in recent years.

5.3 The Burst of the Bubble (1990–1995)

Asset prices declined rapidly in 1990–91. The Nikkei 225 stock-price index reached 38,915 on the last business day of 1989 and then tumbled. By October 1, 1990, the Nikkei stood barely above 20,000, having declined almost 50 percent in 9 months. The Nikkei 225 index fell below 15,000 by summer 1992, and only broke the 20,000 point again in early 1996. Land prices began to fall in late 1991, and by 1995 prices were generally only half their peak values. At that time, the typical land price was similar to that prevailing 10 years earlier.

Sources of Decline

A combination of policy actions and the self-correcting mechanism of the speculative process (deflating the bubble) were responsible for the asset-price decline from 1990 to 1992. By the middle of 1989, the monetary authorities were fully aware of, and concerned about, asset inflation. From May 31, 1989, discount rates were increased in steps from the then historic low of 2.5 percent (table 5.8). By the end of 1989, the official

Table 5.8
Official discount rates, 1983–1995.

1983	1986				1987	1989			1990	
Oct 22	Jan 30	Mar 10	Apr 21	Nov 1	Feb 23	May 31	Oct 11	Dec 25	Mar 20	Aug 30
5.0	4.5	4.0	3.5	3.0	2.5	3.25	3.75	4.25	5.25	6.0

1990	1991			1992		1993		1995	
Aug 30	July 1	Nov 14	Dec 30	Apr 1	Jul 27	Feb 4	Sep 21	Apr 14	Sep 8
6.0	5.5	5.0	4.5	3.75	3.25	2.5	1.75	1.0	0.5

discount rate was 4.25 percent. The official discount rate was also raised twice in 1990.

The Ministry of Finance also introduced several measures to slow land-price rises. Controls over banks' real-estate lending were introduced in April 1990. Lending to the real-estate sector was identified as one of the sources of asset inflation: banks' lending to real estate and to non-banks specializing in real-estate lending increased at around 20 percent per year during the second half of the 1980s, while total bank lending grew at only 9 percent (table 5.5). These controls were not immediately effective, however, since lending to the real-estate sector continued through nonbanks, such as housing-loan companies (*jusen*) and leasing companies.

In an attempt to prevent speculation, the Ministry of Finance raised the capital-gains tax on land transactions, which are taxed separately in Japan. The Ministry of Finance also changed inheritance taxes with respect to land holdings. In Japan land has been used as a device for reducing inheritance taxes.[15] The value of land is assessed significantly less than market value, while loans are fully deductible in inheritance taxation. Thus, individuals with wealth who plan to leave inheritances to their children have an incentive to borrow and purchase real estate. This was an important factor in the increase in demand for land during the asset-inflation phase.

In order to reduce the inheritance demand for land, the Ministry of Finance slightly increased the assessment ratio (to market value) for inheritance taxes and changed the rules so that land purchased within 3 years of the purchaser's death was assessed at its actual purchase value.

The Ministry of Finance also attempted to slow the corporate demand for land. Corporate demand for land had also increased during the asset-inflation phase as development projects, both commercial and residential, flourished. Hoarding of land for future use was also prevalent.

Many economists in Japan pointed out that real-estate taxes were low while capital gains taxes were high, so that owners tend to be locked into particular real-estate holdings. A new national land tax was proposed and introduced, and large-lot land holding was made subject to this tax so as to reduce corporate demand for land.

Beyond policy factors, Iraq's invasion of Kuwait (August 2, 1990) further weakened the outlook, lowering expectations of economic growth and making oil supplies uncertain. Measures of business and consumer confidence declined precipitously (Hutchison 1992). Soon after the invasion, the Bank of Japan raised the interest rate to 6 percent as further evidence of the Bank's concern over the Middle Eastern situation and its potential effect on prices.

Furthermore, once the sharp decline in asset prices had begun, banks had an incentive to reduce lending for real-estate and other purposes. When the Basle risk-based capital ratio was negotiated in 1988 as an international minimum standard for banks with international businesses, Japanese banks were allowed to count 45 percent of their equity holdings as part of their tier II capital. Japanese banks hold significant amounts of stocks as part of the *keiretsu* (enterprise group) relationship. But as the value of these equities was devoted to meeting capital-asset requirements, the cost of capital increased, reducing the incentive of banks to make loans.

But the most important reason for the collapse of asset prices was the self-correcting mechanism inherent in stochastic speculative processes. Expectations of further price drops generated selling, which in turn led to price declines. During the spring of 1990, for example, the Nikkei futures tended to lead the decline in cash markets. In fact, this was responsible for the view that futures transactions were making the stock market too volatile, and it led to tightening of margin requirements in the Nikkei futures market in Osaka in 1991.[16]

Implications for the Real Economy

Asset deflation slowly but surely affected the real side of the economy. Growth of real GDP stayed below 1 percent for four straight years (1992–1995). Such a long period of low growth is unprecedented since the beginning of reindustrialization in postwar Japan. Although the discount rate was lowered repeatedly in 1991 and 1992, it did not stimulate the economy. In February 1993, the official discount rate was lowered to 2.5

percent, which was the historically low level from 1987 to 1989. There was a concern that the low interest rate might lead to another round of asset inflation; however, low discount rates hardly moved the stagnant economy. The yen appreciation in the first half of 1993, from 125 to below 110, dashing hopes of a quick recovery. And yen appreciation in the first four months of 1995, from 100 to the low 80s, worsened further the outlook for a strong economic rebound.

The Bank of Japan countered the yen appreciation and the slow recovery by lowering the official discount rate again in 1995. The discount rate was eventually lowered in steps to 0.5 percent, a historic low for Japan and low by any standard. After some yen depreciation, the economy started to show signs of recovery by the end of 1995. By early 1996, recovery appeared to be underway.

5.4 A Critical Review of the Bank of Japan's Policy

The rise and fall of asset prices appears, in retrospect, to have been in large part a classic bubble process. Could macroeconomic policy (especially monetary policy) have acted sooner to prevent the bubble, or at least to contain it before it reached such proportions?

Critics of the Bank of Japan's monetary-policy stance during the period of asset inflation and deflation usually emphasize two points regarding discount-rate changes. First, monetary easing in 1986–87 may have been excessive in terms of the number and size of the discount-rate cuts, especially the discount-rate cuts on November 1, 1986 and February 23, 1987. Second, monetary tightening, starting with the discount-rate increase on May 31, 1989, may have been delayed too long. Many economists argued that the discount rate should have been raised sometime in 1988 because the economy was growing quickly, especially since Germany and the United States had already raised their official discount rates. Japan could have raised its interest rate in 1988 in concert with Germany and the United States without fearing further yen appreciation, critics argue.

The trough of the small "yen-appreciation-induced recession" occurred during the fall of 1986, and thereafter growth rebounded. Despite the optimistic outlook for the real side of the economy, the official discount rate was cut twice (table 5.8). These two discount-rate cuts are often blamed for the asset-price speculation that followed. During the summer of 1987, the United States and Germany started to raise their

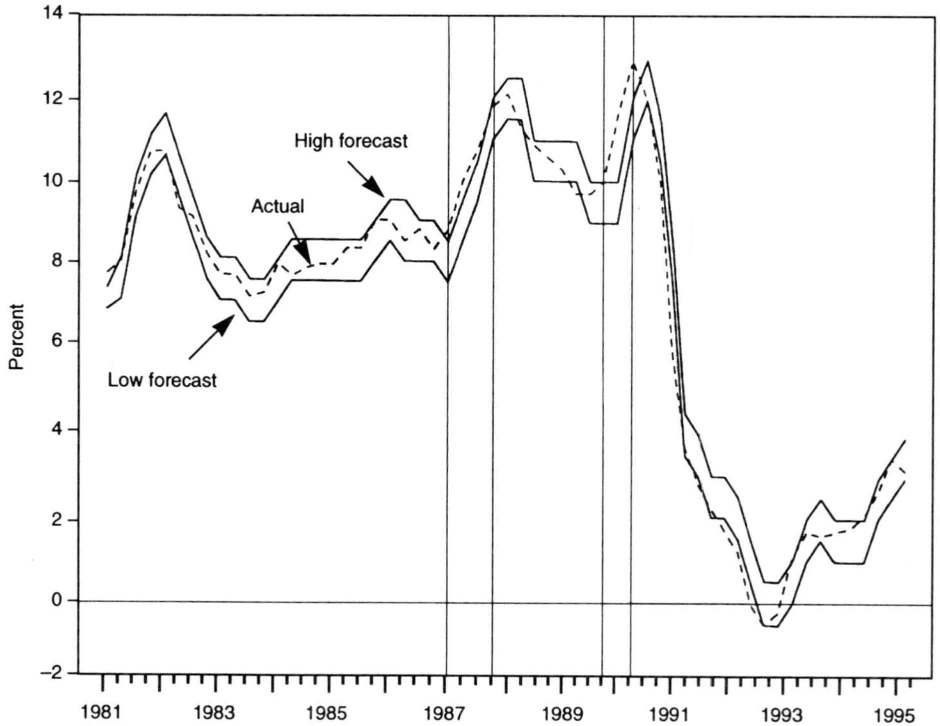

Figure 5.7
Money growth: high forecast, actual, and low forecast.

interest rates. However, worldwide stock-price declines triggered by the sharp decline of the New York Stock Exchange on October 19, 1987, reversed the course of monetary policies in many industrial countries.

Monetary easing was also evident in the growth of the money supply (M2 + CDs). In 1987 actual monetary growth accelerated from 8 percent to 12 percent, exceeding the Bank of Japan's own "forecast" for the first three quarters (figure 5.7). This was unusual in view of the wide band of the forecast.[17] The years 1987 and 1990 stand out in that the actual M2 + CDs growth rates exceeded the band, suggesting that monetary growth was unexpectedly fast during this period. An acceleration in monetary growth was also reflected in faster growth in bank lending and deposit growth.

Rapid monetary growth may also have fueled expectations of asset inflation. More-than-sufficient liquidity with very low interest rates encouraged risky investment. In an environment of financial liberalization and extensive government deposit guarantees, the excessive growth in liquidity increased the overall amount of risk taking.

A desire to limit yen appreciation and the attempts at international policy coordination that followed the Plaza Agreement and the Louvre Accord also contributed to the decision to pursue an expansionary monetary policy in the latter 1980s. Monetary policy in 1986 and 1987 was driven by a desire to "stabilize" (that is, slow down and stop) yen appreciation. The Louvre Accord of February 1987 stated that the G7 countries' monetary authorities would cooperate to keep the exchange rates at "current" levels. In order to fend off yen-appreciation pressure, monetary ease was maintained and interest rates were kept low. By targeting the exchange rate, monetary policy cannot be directed toward domestic objectives. Of course, the decision to target the exchange rate was designed to help domestic industry, and especially the export sector, but other domestic objectives became secondary.

Critics of the Bank of Japan's monetary-policy stance at the time, however, have more credibility after the fact. Indeed, in the midst of asset inflation it was not clear that Japan's monetary policy was deliberately expansionary. Consumer-price-index inflation, for example, stayed below 1 percent from 1986 to 1988, and monetary tightening started (with the increase in the discount rate May 1989) when it became clear that inflation was rising. This behavior is consistent with past actions in which the Bank, following standard central-bank practice, focused on general price inflation as the primary objective of policy. There is little theoretical justification for targeting asset prices instead of broadly defined consumer prices.

Moreover, the financial liberalization process in the second half of the 1980s made it difficult under any circumstances to measure a central bank's policy stance from monetary growth. The increase in monetary aggregates in 1987, shown in figure 5.7, reflects the introduction of new financial instruments categorized in the money-supply statistics (see table 3.8). Portfolio shifts prompted by interest-rate liberalization brought some funds into deposits in M2 + CDs from other financial products. In this context, even small shifts in money "demand" reduce the usefulness of monetary growth as an indicator of policy.

Because of the policy decision to prevent further yen appreciation and fiscal consolidation (reducing deficits by not expanding expenditures), monetary policy was not fully under the control of the central bank during 1986–1988. To the extent that this policy was expansionary, it was not a technical or policy mistake by the central bank so much as a failure of the broader economic policy set by the government.

Monetary Policy in the Asset-Deflation Period

Monetary policy remained tight until the middle of 1992, despite sharp declines in stock and land prices. A restrictive policy stance was generally supported by those who had been alarmed by the jump in asset prices. However, concern quickly shifted to the accompanying recession. Whether monetary policy was sufficiently stimulative in 1993 and 1994 became a new controversy. As real-GDP growth remained stagnant, critics argued that monetary policy could have been more expansionary, lowering interest rates faster and increasing monetary aggregates more in 1993 and 1994. Instead, fiscal policy became expansionary in 1994 and 1995 as a result of a mid-year budget revision in each of those years. Moreover, slower monetary growth was partly demand-driven, reflecting the reluctance of major firms to borrow at any interest rate because of overcapacity and slow sales. Yen appreciation in 1994 and 1995 also encouraged firms to invest less domestically and to shift production facilities and investments abroad. In this environment, lower interest rates did not translate into robust investment demand.

In 1995, the yen appreciated from 100 per dollar at the beginning of the year to 80 per dollar in April 1995. Business conditions deteriorated quickly, and there was fear of price deflation. Businesses and households found it difficult to repay debts contracted in nominal terms. The government prepared economic-stimulus packages, mainly involving more fiscal spending, twice during the year to support the economy. On

Table 5.9
Forecasts and actual values of real GDP growth rates for fiscal year (April 1–March 30). Consensus forecasts are obtained from various issues of Toyo Keizai, *Economic Statistics Annual*.

	Government forecast as of January	Consensus forecasts as of January–March	Actual
1992	3.5	2.71	0.4
1993	3.3	2.14	0.5
1994	2.6	0.79	0.7
1995	0.8	1.58	2.4

the monetary side, the Bank of Japan lowered the discount rate to 1.0 percent on April 14 and to 0.5 percent (a record low) on September 8.[18]

As table 5.8 shows, the discount rate was cut nine times from 1991 to 1995. Especially after 1992, discount-rate cuts were criticized as too slow in coming because the recession continued despite four years of monetary stimulus. However, occasional signs of recovery surfaced between 1993 and 1995, and it was not clear at the time that additional stimulus was needed. Table 5.9 summarizes the government forecasts and consensus forecasts of growth rates for the coming fiscal year by research institutions before the fiscal year begins, and the *ex post* actual rate. Optimistic forecasts at the beginning of each year were not realized, and mid-year downward revisions were made each time. Despite these over-optimistic forecasts, it is not clear that even more stimulative policies would have avoided the long recession without undesirable side effects.

Concluding Remarks

In this chapter we have reviewed Japan's period of asset-price inflation and deflation and evaluated whether it is better characterized as reflecting economic fundamentals or as a speculative bubble. We have argued that asset-price hikes were initially consistent with fundamentals. These fundamentals, including rapid productivity growth and strong GNP growth, were accompanied by an expansionary monetary policy that pushed interest rates to very low levels. Consumer and producer prices were stable, and the Bank of Japan was concerned with the high value of the yen exchange rate. A stimulative monetary policy was pursued, and a low priority was attached to asset inflation.

Against this economic backdrop, Japan had a newly liberalized financial system, and fundamental changes had been made in the flow of funds. Banks now had the ability and the incentive to lend aggressively to the real-estate market and to other markets, either directly or indirectly, and thus they accommodated asset-price hikes. And neither the built-in controls of the financial system for limiting risk-taking activity nor the regulatory authorities effectively limited pure speculative activity.

The later stages of the asset inflation fit the classic pattern of a speculative bubble, with expectations of future rises continuing to push prices up. Peak values of stocks (1989) and land prices (1991) were inconsistent with underlying fundamentals and out of line with historical trends and international counterparts.

Asset deflation was initiated by sharp monetary tightening in 1989 and 1990 and by a number of measures by the Ministry of Finance to stop land-price speculation. But the most important reason for the collapse was the inherent correction mechanism behind the speculative bubble. The only justification for abnormally high prices was the expectation of further asset inflation. When expectations turned pessimistic, the bubble collapsed to values closer in line with fundamental determinants.

Monetary policy may have moved sooner to limit the speculative bubble in asset prices. Perhaps the Bank of Japan should have been more concerned with asset inflation and its undesirable consequences. Low general price inflation and concern over the high value of the yen took precedence. If a substantially more restrictive monetary policy stance had been followed, asset inflation may have been contained. But there would have been a tradeoff in terms of an even more highly valued exchange rate and greater downward pressure on the aggregate price level.

6 Asset-Price Deflation: Nonperforming Loans, *Jusen* Companies, and Regulatory Inertia

The asset-price deflation of the early 1990s dramatically affected the profitability of Japan's financial institutions, leading to serious concerns over the stability of the country's entire financial system. Deterioration in the quality of loans to the real-estate sector—the primary problem—was compounded by a drop in the value of banks' large equity holdings and by worsening loan problems associated with a prolonged recession.[1]

The Ministry of Finance, the primary regulatory agency, was slow in reacting to the nonperforming-loan problem that was confronting financial institutions. After the initial sharp decline of stock and land prices in 1991–92, the Ministry of Finance first adopted a "forbearance policy," allowing banks to hold nonperforming loans without special writeoffs in the hope that the economy and the real-estate market would recover quickly.[2] However, smaller financial institutions with large real-estate exposure began showing signs of distress in 1993, and this was soon followed by even larger problems for the *jusen* companies (nonbank subsidiaries of financial institutions specializing in housing loans). The Ministry of Finance arranged a ten-year "rehabilitation" plan for the *jusen* companies. Rather than recognizing loan losses, however, the plan was predicated on a recovery of land prices. When land prices failed to recover, and with nonperforming loans growing in size and number, the rehabilitation plan was quickly abandoned.

As the financial crisis unfolded, Japan's regulatory authorities took a new approach to these problems in 1994 and 1995. The Ministry of Finance closed some of the lowest-quality institutions, created the Tokyo Kyodo Bank as a bridge bank that would receive the remaining assets of failed smaller institutions, allowed (or encouraged) massive writeoffs by some banks, and made a decision to close down the *jusen* companies.

An infusion of public funds, proposed for the first time in the 1996–97 budget, was earmarked to cover the costs of closing seven *jusen* companies, and a variety of other measures were enacted in the wake of the problems with nonperforming loans and *jusen* companies.

6.1 The Magnitude of the Problem

The problem of nonperforming loans is large in magnitude. On the basis of official statistics, nonperforming loans by all depository institutions at the end of September 1995 amounted to about 46 trillion yen (table 6.1). Such loans amount to about 10 percent of Japan's GDP and 6 percent of all the loans held by Japan's depository institutions. This estimate is substantially larger than the ¥38 trillion estimate publicized by the Ministry of Finance in December 1995. The difference results from including loans to *jusen* companies from agricultural cooperatives (¥4,900 billion) and the nonperforming loans at three failed banks which occurred in July and August 1995 (¥3,000 billion, of which ¥1,900 billion is attributable to the Kizu Credit Cooperatives, ¥380 billion to the Cosmo Bank, and ¥1500 billion to the Hyogo Bank). Loans from agricultural cooperatives to the *jusen* companies were restructured in 1993 at a reduced interest rate of 4.5 percent (concessionary terms). Although this does not fit the Ministry of Finance's narrow technical definition of nonperforming loans, which requires that the concessionary interest rate be below the official discount rate, these loans are an important part of the problem.

Clearly, some of the ¥46 trillion in nonperforming loans is recoverable from underlying collateral, and the estimated loss to the banks should be reduced correspondingly. The net losses can be estimated as follows:

Of the ¥24.7 trillion in loans to bankrupt borrowers, ¥15.7 trillion is estimated to be unrecoverable. Ministry of Finance documents give a lower figure, ¥8.6 trillion, but this is after subtracting ¥7 trillion in reserves.

Of the ¥18.3 trillion in restructured loans, ¥10 trillion (including ¥7.7 trillion from the *jusen* companies), is estimated to be unrecoverable.

The losses at the three failed institutions are not estimated by the Ministry of Finance but, by extending the cover ratio assumed for the other calculations, may be around ¥1.9 trillion.

The sum of these three components suggest that net losses to banks will be around ¥27 trillion.

Table 6.1
Nonperforming loans as of September 1995 (billions of yen). Source: Ministry of Finance, December 1995, with the noted modification below. (N.B.: This table differs from the official table available from the Ministry of Finance as explained in the notes below.)

	Bankrupt borrowers and overdue (1)	Restructured *Jusen* (a)	Others (b)	Total (2) = a+b	Total (1) + (2) = (3)
City banks	8,102	1,434	4,021	5,455	13,557
Long-term credit	2,116	1,502	353	1,855	3,970
Trust banks	2,797	2,068	1,437	3,505	6,301
Regional banks	3,348	851	777	1,628	4,976
Second-tier regional banks	2,202	257	364	621	2,822
Smaller institutions[a]	6,124	4,918[c]	335	5,253	11,377
Total	24,688	11,030	7,286	18,316	43,003
Three failed banks	3,070[b]			*	3,070
Grand total	27,758	11,030[d]	7,286	18,316	46,073

a. This category includes *Shinkin* banks, credit cooperatives (*Shin-yo kumiai*), labor credit Associations (*Rodo kinko*), *Shokokumiai chiokinko*, *Norinchuokinko*, and agricultural cooperative federations (*Ken Shin ren*).
b. The Kizu and Cosmo Credit Cooperatives and the Hyogo Bank failed in July and August of 1995. Their nonperforming loans are not included in the published table, but are noted below it. The Ministry of Finance estimates nonperforming loans at these institutions to be, respectively, ¥1,190 billion, ¥380 billion, and ¥1,500 billion. Hence, the amount of nonperforming loans in this table, ¥46,073 billion, is the sum of the Ministry of Finance's announced amount of nonperforming loans (¥38,086 billion), loans to *jusen* from agricultural cooperatives (*) (¥4,918 billion), and the nonperforming loans at the three failed banks (¥3,070).
c. In 1993 loans from agricultural cooperatives to *jusen* companies were restructured at a reduced interest rate (4.5%). However, this does not fit the Ministry of Finance's narrow technical definition of nonperforming loans, that requires the reduced interest rate should be below the official discount rate.
d. The *jusen* exposure of insurance companies (*Sei son po*) is ¥2.5 trillion; total nonperforming loans to the *jusen* companies are ¥13.5 trillion.

These estimates may be low, however. Other types of nonperforming loans are not included in the Ministry of Finance's definition for technical or definitional reasons. Published estimates of nonperforming loans from private sources typically range between ¥50 trillion and ¥60 trillion, and several estimates are almost twice the official estimate. Much of this uncertainty comes from the fact that few market transactions in land and property exist by which to properly evaluate the market value of many of the loans. These higher estimates of nonperforming loan often include loans overdue between 60 and 180 days (beyond 180 days they are counted in the Ministry of Finance's definition of nonperforming loan); loans sold to the Cooperative Credit Purchasing Company and discounted to the value at the time of the sale, although the eventual realized losses from sales by the Company may be much larger and will remain the responsibility of the original bank; restructured loans that carry interest rates lower than the original rate but higher than the official discount rate at the time of restructuring; and loans that are serviced by additional loans.

Japan's banks, once regarded as among the most financially secure in the world, have been continually downgraded by credit rating agencies. In August 1995 Moody's Investor Service released a new rating system for the major Japanese banks that does not incorporate the government support they enjoyed. The new rating system is designed to rate banks on a "stand alone" basis, without government support, and is a "measure of the likelihood that a bank will require assistance from third parties such as its owners, its industry group, or official institutions." According to the new Moody's rating system, no Japanese bank received a rating of A (exceptional intrinsic financial strength) or B (intrinsic financial strength), and the top 50 Japanese banks received an average rating of D (adequate financial strength limited by a variety of factors). In January 1996 Moody's cut its debt ratings of three large Japanese banks and that of the Yamaiachi Securities Company.[3]

Table 6.1 is based on information available as of September 1995. Some progress has been made by banks in setting aside reserves to write off bad loans, and three liquidation agencies have been established since 1993 to dispose of bad loans, but as of late 1996 the magnitude of the loan problem has not changed significantly. The Ministry of Finance's estimates are still regarded as conservative, and a number of banks and other depository institutions that are market insolvent (or close to it) are benefiting from the ministry's forbearance.

As of late 1995, the aggregate amount of loss (nonperforming loans minus recoverable collateral values) to be borne by the financial institutions is on the order of ¥27 trillion. More than one-fourth of these unrecoverable losses, about ¥7.6 trillion, are concentrated in seven *jusen* companies.

The Problem of the **Jusen** *Companies*

The *jusen* companies were created in the mid 1970s as subsidiaries of banks, securities firms, and life insurance companies. At that time, banks were concentrating on corporate lending and were not generally interested in expanding their operations to household lending, either for mortgage or consumer credit. The *jusen* companies initially expanded to provide consumer credit. Much like consumer finance companies in the United States, they borrowed from other institutions since they were not permitted to accept deposits. As the corporate sector reduced its dependence on bank credit after 1975, however, banks began to turn to consumer finance, and in the 1980s they became aggressive lenders to individuals. In response to the aggressive bank competition for individual loans, *jusen* companies turned to real-estate lending in the second half of the 1980s to substitute for the lost consumer lending business.

In April 1990 the Ministry of Finance introduced guidelines to banks to limit total lending to the real-estate sector; however, lending by *jusen* companies was exempted from this regulation. During 1990 and 1991, *jusen* lending increased rapidly as a result of funds provided by agricultural cooperatives and their prefectural federations. Concerns over the quality of assets held by the *jusen* companies were raised as early as 1992, and a 10-year rehabilitation plan was arranged for the seven *jusen* companies[4] in the spring of 1993. Lending to *jusen* companies was restructured so that "parent" banks (major shareholders in the *jusen* companies) were required to reduce the interest rate on outstanding loans to zero, other banks (nonparent banks lending to the *jusen* companies) were required to reduce the interest rate on outstanding loans to 1.5 percent, and agricultural cooperatives (and their prefectural federations) were to receive 4.5 percent interest income from *jusen* companies.

The arrangements were designed to provide liquidity to *jusen* companies until the expected future recovery in land prices made it possible to pay off the outstanding loans in 10 years. Land prices, however, continued to fall, and nonperforming loans held by *jusen* companies rose dramatically. For all practical purposes, the rehabilitation plan itself became bankrupt.

The full magnitude of the *Jusen* problem

The problem of the *jusen* companies became the focus of an intense policy debate in 1995 and even overshadowed the problem of banks' nonperforming loans. In August 1995 the Ministry of Finance conducted a special examination of the *jusen* problem. Of the total ¥13 trillion of *jusen* assets, nonperforming loans were estimated at ¥9.6 trillion, of which ¥6.4 trillion was considered unrecoverable and ¥1.2 trillion was considered a possible loss (table 6.2). This is more than one-fourth of all losses incurred by financial institutions to date.

Table 6.2
Jusen sources of funds, asset quality, and losses assumed by various institutions (trillions of yen) at time of *Jusen* resolution.

	Jusen sources of funds	Amount of *Jusen* losses assumed or loss sharing
City banks	1.45	1.17
Long-term-credit banks	1.48	1.05
Trust banks	2.10	1.49
Regional banks	0.85	0.67
Tier II regional banks	0.26	0.23
Life insurance companies	0.8	0.42
Agricultural cooperatives	5.5	0.53
Others	0.6	0.17
Total	13.04	5.73
Classification of *Jusen* assets		
Normal asset	3.5 (assumed by *Jusen* Resolution Corp.)	
Nonperforming but Recoverable	2.0 (assumed by *Jusen* Resolution Corp.)	
Possible loss	1.2 (secondary loss or intermediate solution)	
Definite loss	6.4 (primary loss or writeoff at this time)	
Total assets[a]	13.0	

a. Total many not agree with sum due to rounding.

The Ministry of Finance and the suppliers of funds to *jusen* companies agreed to dissolve the seven housing-loan companies, and in July 1996 the *Jusen* Resolution Corporation, now known as the Housing Loan Administration Corporation, assumed the ¥6.4 trillion of unrecoverable loans extended to failed *jusen* companies.

Table 6.2 gives the sources of funding of the seven *jusen* companies as of 1995. The majority of funding came from the 21 major banks and agricultural credit cooperatives, each providing about the same levels of funding (¥5.0 trillion for the 21 banks and ¥5.5 trillion for the cooperatives). Other funding sources were regional banks (¥1.1 trillion), life insurance companies (¥0.8 trillion), and others (¥0.6 trillion). Agricultural cooperatives' being the largest supplier of funds posed a major policy issue. If the potential loss of ¥7.6 trillion is divided in proportion to the outstanding loans to the *jusen* companies, the agricultural cooperatives would have been required to write off more than ¥3 trillion in losses. This was not possible, however, since these cooperatives operated with a small capital base. The lack of correspondence between the distribution of lending to the *jusen* companies and the ability of lenders to absorb the debt raised a serious policy issue in resolving the *jusen* problem.

In the summer of 1995, financial markets became increasingly concerned about the sharing of the burden of *jusen* losses among banks and other financial institutions, which further reduced the creditworthiness of Japan's banks. Politicians and Ministry of Finance officials suggested that banks should shoulder a more than *pro rata* share of *jusen* losses. The precedent for this approach had already been set when banks were required to provide a more than *pro rata* share in schemes for dealing with failing institutions (the Cosmo Credit Cooperatives, the Kizu Credit Cooperatives, and the Hyogo Bank) in July and August 1995. Banks not related to these institutions were asked to contribute to the loss-sharing scheme by contributing capital or by making below-market-rate loans to banks that assumed the assets of the insolvent institutions. The argument made to justify these requests was based on the public-good characteristic of the financial system and on the need to maintain stability. The policy of requiring unrelated banks to contribute directly to bailout schemes was referred to as the "all-Japan" rescue scheme.

Uncertainty over future bank losses because of uncertainty over the specific *jusen* resolution scheme and degree of the "all-Japan" component, however, led to a downgrading of Japanese banks' creditworthiness. The perception of increased risk in Japan's banks at large resulted in a "Japan premium" in the Eurodollar market—a premium over the London interbank interest rate required of Japan's banks. The Japan premium appeared in late July 1995, and it persisted for several months even though the Ministry of Finance attempted to assure the market by announcing a complete guarantee of its deposits.

Despite the assurances of the Ministry of Finance, the situation worsened in that the premium increased. The Japan premium increased further when the Daiwa Bank was discovered to have covered up derivative losses, amounting to at least $1 billion, resulting from a "rogue" trader in New York. The problem associated with the Daiwa Bank became even worse when the Ministry of Finance failed to properly inform US regulatory authorities[5] in a timely manner.

The *jusen* problem also reflects problems of smaller institutions in Japan, such as agricultural credit cooperatives. Several observers, including Cargill (1993b), Ostrom (1992), and Kane (1993), draw parallels between the credit cooperatives and the American savings-and-loans:

> Credit cooperatives have diversified significantly away from their traditional specialization on loans to farmers related to agricultural operations.

Some credit cooperatives have strong ties to the local community and to local politicians.

Credit cooperatives hold significant amounts of real-estate-related loans.

Credit cooperatives are not regulated and supervised by the Ministry of Finance or by the Bank of Japan, and local regulation and supervision are uneven in extent and sophistication. Significant risk resides in these small institutions because of the substantial uncertainty as to where they stand in Japan's deposit-guarantee system.

Thus, by the end of 1995 the *jusen* problem, the problem of nonperforming bank loans, and the risk exposure of large numbers of small financial institutions were seen as major and unprecedented policy issues. The financial debacle in Japan is as least as great as the collapse of the savings-and-loan industry and the related banking problems in the United States.

The Regulatory Response to the Problem of Nonperforming Loans

The first official responses to the problem of nonperforming loans were a series of specific uncoordinated actions predicated on a short recession and a rapid recovery of asset prices.

On August 18, 1992, the government announced a temporary rule change that allowed corporations to defer reporting stock-portfolio losses until the end of the fiscal year (March 1993), permitted other accounting innovations that delayed or concealed the impact of stock-price and land-price declines on reported assets, allowed banks (in special cases where a loan default would have adverse social effects) not to report interest concessions as taxable income (Packer 1994), directed the Postal Life Insurance System to support the stock market via funds provided to trust banks, postponed sales of government-held shares of Nippon Telegraph and Telephone and Japan National Railways, used administrative guidance to encourage institutional purchases of equities and discourage institutional sales of equities, and provided less-than-candid estimates of the magnitude of the problem of nonperforming loans.[6]

However, these actions had little impact on the downward trend in asset prices or on the deterioration of the financial system. The more specific and aggressive actions that followed will be considered below.

The Cooperative Credit Purchasing Company

The Cooperative Credit Purchasing Company (CCPC) was the first visible effort to deal with the problem of nonperforming loans. The CCPC was established in late 1992 and commenced operations in January 1993. The CCPC consists of the pooled funds of 162 banks and cooperatives, with the active encouragement and involvement of the Ministry of Finance. The CCPC purchases a real-estate loan (at a price determined by a panel of experts) from a financial institution, and the same financial institution provides the financing. The CCPC then sells the collateralizing real estate, and any difference between what the CCPC paid for the loan and the selling price is charged to the financial institution that originally sold the loan.

From the beginning, the CCPC was viewed with skepticism (Choy 1992; Salomon Brothers 1992). There were concerns that the planned loan purchases would represent only a small percentage of the nonperforming loans, that self-financing requirement limited access to only the strongest banks, that only the best of the nonperforming loans would be sold to the CCPC and would delay the inevitable adjustment, and that (since property management was retained by the original borrower) the incentives to cooperate were not clear.

These concerns remain. After two years of operation, the CCPC had purchased ¥8.7 trillion of loans at face value. To indicate how much bank assets have deteriorated, table 6.3 indicates the amount paid by the CCPC. The average loss ratio from March 1993 to May 1995 is 55.4 percent. The critical question, however, are these: To what purpose have the loans been purchased? How does the CCPC plan to dispose of these loans?

Packer (1994) investigated both questions. The CCPC now appears to have been set up primarily to provide accelerated tax benefits to the large banks without requiring the banks to directly write off losses and acknowledge the losses in their public reports. Sales of CCPC loans have been only a fraction of total holdings, and there is concern that revenues from loan sales and rental income from properties will not be sufficient to repay interest to the funding banks at market rates.

The Resolution and Collection Bank

The Tokyo Kyodo Bank was established in March 1995 to assume the assets of several failed credit cooperatives. This bank was reorganized

Table 6.3
Activity of CCPC, March 1993–May 1995 (billions of yen). Source: Cooperative Credit Purchasing Company.

	Number of transactions	(A) Book value of the assets	(B) Amount paid by the Cooperative	(C) Losses = (A) − (B)	(D) Loss ratio = (C)/(A)
1993					
Mar.	229	6,817	4,521	2,296	33.7%
Jun.	12	243	176	67	27.6%
Sep.	414	9,547	4,857	4,690	49.1%
Dec.	116	2,312	1,050	1,262	54.6%
1994					
Mar.	901	16,628	7,089	9,539	57.4%
Apr.	24	651	229	422	64.8%
May	12	155	45	110	70.9%
Jun.	33	712	251	461	64.7%
Jul.	138	1,471	521	950	64.6%
Aug.	280	2,999	1,219	1,780	59.4%
Sep.	1,123	13,940	6,090	7,850	56.3%
Oct.	85	1,839	773	1,066	58.0%
Nov.	34	510	170	340	66.7%
Dec.	81	1,260	480	780	61.9%
1995					
Jan.	94	1,313	423	890	67.8%
Feb.	240	3,283	1,131	2,152	65.5%
Mar.	933	12,247	4,578	7,669	62.6%
Apr.	99	1,132	429	703	62.1%
May	16	216	68	148	68.5%
Total	5,312	86,928	38,717	48,211	55.4%

in September 1996 into the Resolution and Collection Bank (RCB), which was loosely modeled after the US Resolution and Trust Corporation (set up in 1989 to liquidate assets of failed S&Ls).

The track record of the CCPC suggests that the RCB will have a difficult time liquidating bad loans. Many of these loans are tied to a real-estate market that remains depressed as of late 1996. As of this writing, the CCPC has sold only of fraction of the loans it has assumed. This is unimpressive, since the CCPC purchased the best of the nonperforming loans. The depressed real-estate market, the slow pace of economic recovery, and the lack of well-developed foreclosure and bankruptcy procedures make it difficult to dispose of nonperforming loans.

There is concern that the CCPC, the Housing Loan Administration Corporation, and the RCB will end up being a form of forbearance—merely new warehouses for bad loans, when the Ministry of Finance really needs to hold a garage sale.

The Banks' Response to the Problem of Nonperforming Loans

Japan's banks have taken several steps to reduce the size of the problem in addition to participating in the CCPC. The close relationship between private banks and regulatory authorities in Japan suggests that actions taken by the banks have the implicit if not the explicit approval of the Ministry of Finance and, hence, may be interpreted as a type of regulatory response.

Japan's banks have been increasingly setting aside funds in special accounts to eventually write off losses. Special provisioning by 21 banks increased from ¥1.9 trillion in March 1993 to ¥3.0 trillion in March 1994, and to ¥4.3 trillion in March 1995. The Sumitomo Bank took a more drastic step, charging losses of ¥826 billion to write off bad loans, and showed losses in its annual report for the period ending in March 1995.

Despite varying degrees of problems with nonperforming loans, Japan's banks continue to pay dividends. Dividends per share paid by major banks did not change between 1991 and 1995. The 21 leading banks paid out ¥317 billion in dividends while all banks paid out ¥433 billion yen for the year ending in March 1995. Dividends per earnings actually increased when the decline in earnings (adjusted for potential losses from nonperforming loans) was taken into account. This is not consistent with a strategy of writing off bad debts quickly, and it does not reflect the underlying fundamentals of the bank's operation.

The banks could pursue more aggressive remedies. More aggressive organizational restructuring, such as selling assets and subsidiaries (branches or foreign operations) or cutting personnel costs, could reduce operational costs.[7]

Assisted Mergers and the Deposit Insurance Corporation

In 1991, the regulatory authorities, for the first time in the postwar period, officially assisted mergers of insolvent depository institutions with stronger institutions, using the resources of the Deposit Insurance Corporation (DIC), the larger of Japan's two deposit-insurance agencies.[8] The DIC was established July 1971 with membership mandatory for city banks, regional banks, member banks of the second association of regional banks,[9] trust banks, long-term credit banks, *shinkin* banks, credit cooperatives, and labor banks. Before 1991, the DIC had never needed to pay depositors, though there are claims the Ministry of Finance arranged several unpublicized "rescue mergers" without DIC assistance.

Since 1991, however, the DIC has publicly assisted a small number of problem institutions, and two of the more recently assisted institutions have exhausted the reserves of the DIC.[10] Table 6.4 presents some specific information on the DIC's role in eleven assisted mergers from 1991 to 1995 that exhausted the DIC's funds. Several more assisted mergers took place in 1996, and even more are likely to take place in the next few years. The details of the assisted mergers reveal a disturbing pattern about the ability of Japan's regulatory authorities to effectively administer deposit guarantees and limit "moral hazard."

- The DIC for the first time in 1991 assisted the merger of the insolvent Toho Sogo Bank with the Iyo Bank, a regional bank. The decision to assist the merger was made in April 1991 and carried out in October 1991. Assistance was in the form of subsidized loans to the Iyo Bank of ¥8 billion over 5 years with an interest rate set 5 percentage points below the long-term government bond rate. The Iyo Bank was referred to as a "white knight" bank because of its willingness to take over the failed Toho Sogo Bank. The Toho Sogo Bank's shareholders retained ownership rights in that six shares of Toho Sogo equity were exchanged for one share of Iyo Bank equity.
- The Toyo Shinkin Bank in Osaka failed as a result of issuing fraudulent certificates of deposits. In October 1992 the DIC provided a cash payment of ¥20 billion to the Sanwa Bank, a large city bank, to help it acquire the Toyo Shinkin Bank. Again, shareholders of the failed institution retained ownership rights. One and a half shares of Toyo equity were exchanged for one share of Sanwa equity.
- The Kamaishi Shinkin Bank was acquired by the Iwate Bank in June 1993, with ¥26 billion contributed by the DIC to compensate for the fact that the Kamaishi Shinkin Bank was insolvent. Instead of adopting an assisted merger, the Kamaishi Shinkin Bank was liquidated, and its shareholders were not compensated; however, the regional federation of *shinkin* banks compensated the shareholders for the book value of the Kamaishi Shinkin Bank's equities.
- The DIC made a financial contribution to Osaka Koyo to absorb Osaka Fumin on March 1994. In contrast with the first three cases, Osaka

Table 6.4
Assistance by Deposit Insurance Corporation up to August 1995.

Dates of decision and (execution)	Amount of financial assistance (billion yen)	Failed bank (assets, in billion yen)	White knight (assets, in billion yen)	Comments
10/28/91 (4/1/92)	2[a]	Toho Sogo Bank (213.1)	Iyo Bank (2,890.7)	Merger
6/1/92 (10/1/92)	20	Toyo Shinkin Bank (304.2)	Sanwa Bank (35,349.7)	Most of branches were sold to other Shinkin banks before merged to Sanwa.
6/24/93 (10/1/93)	26	Kamaishi Shinkin Bank (44.7)	Iwate Bank (1,601.7)	Bad assets were shifted to another company. Other assets were sold to three banks and three Shinkin banks. Kamaishi Shinkin was liquidated.
7/28/93[b] (11/1/93)	19.9[b]	Osaka Fumin Credit Coop. (123.2)	Credit Coop. Osaka Koyo (234.5)	Merger after bad assets were shifted to another company. Assistance from Osaka government.
11/25/94 (3/13/95)	2.5	Credit Coop. Gifu Shogin (13.6)	Credit Coop. Kansai Kogin (1,136.5)	Merger after bad assets were shifted to another company.
2/9/95 (3/20/95)	40	Tokyo Kyowa Credit Coop (110) and Anzen Credit Coop (106.9)	Newly est. Tokyo Kyodo Bank	Assets liquidated and merged into a newly created bank. The new bank received capital infusion from the Bank of Japan, and shed the bad assets.
(7/31/95)	2.8	Yuai Credit Coop	Kanagawa Labor Bank	Merger
7/31/95	100	Cosmo Credit Coop	Tokyo Kyodo Bank	Funds also provided by Sanwa Bank, largest creditor to Cosmo, and others.

Table 6.4
(continued)

Dates of decision and (execution)	Amount of financial assistance (billion yen)	Failed bank (assets, in billion yen)	White knight (assets, in billion yen)	Comments
8/29–9/95	100	Hyogo Bank (3,400) and Kizu Credit Coop (1,200)	Hyogo Bank operated as new entity and Kizu moved to Tokyo Kyodo Bank.	These two failures exhausted the reserves of DIC. DIC is insolvent.

a. Subsidized lending of ¥8 billion (equivalent to ¥2 billion financial subsidy).
b. The decision of assistance was amended on October 28, to the effect that the amount of the assistance increased by $0.9 billion to reflect the worsening condition of the failed institution.

Fumin was a credit cooperative (Shinyo Kumiani). In exchange for assuming the debts, Osaka Koyo was given ¥19.9 billion. Again, shareholders of the failed institution were compensated for the book value of their holdings.

• In March 1995 the Credit Cooperative Gifu Shogin was merged with another credit cooperative, Kansai Kogin. The assets of the failed credit cooperative were shifted to another company, and Kansai Kogin was provided with a ¥2.5 billion yen payment.

• The failures of two credit cooperatives, Tokyo Kyowa and Anzen, were handled by establishing a new bank, Tokyo Kyodo Bank in March 1995. The new bank received an infusion of capital from the Bank of Japan. There are several distinct features of this case. First, all "shareholders" of the two credit cooperatives were asked to forfeit their position in the institution. While many would regard this as normal, it represents a departure from previous cases where the DIC or some other group compensated shareholders for their book value. Second, in addition to the ¥40 billion provided by the DIC, the Bank of Japan and a group of private banks each provided ¥20 billion of new equity funding. This represents a departure from the previous cases where the DIC provided the funds to accomplish the merger or liquidation. Apparently the DIC's funding resources were not adequate to fill the gap between market-value assets and market-value liabilities. In addition, Tokyo's metropolitan government was asked to provide subsidized loans. This rescue plan was heavily criticized for several reasons. First, the top managements of the two failed institutions had engaged in fraudulent behavior by lending to themselves through their own real-estate companies. The use of government funds to rescue an institution that had failed because of fraud was questioned, even though management was purged and prosecuted. No similar criticism of government intervention was raised when the DIC assisted the earlier mergers. The "public money" aspect is in fact a problem of transparency. DIC financial assistance also represents a use of public money, but it was not questioned in the media. It was revealed that the insolvency had already been discovered by examination of the institutions as early as spring 1993, almost a year and a half before the merger. During this regulatory delay, deposits and high-risk loans increased significantly, as did the cost of the bailout as the institutions attempted to aggressively work their way out of the problem with depositors' funds. Moreover, the large depositors taking advantage of the high interest rates offered by these troubled institutions escaped penalties, even though their deposits exceeded the threshold covered by deposit insurance (¥10 million). Some institutional depositors held deposits up to ¥800 million.

- The failure of the Yuai Credit Cooperative and its being merged with the Kanagawa Labor Bank on July 31 was a much less publicized case because of the institution's small size. The DIC's financial assistance to the Kanagawa Labor Bank was ¥2.8 billion.

- The Cosmo Credit Corporation collapsed in August 1995 in the wake of a classic run on deposits, after which the Ministry of Finance moved to place restrictions on fund withdrawals. Unlike the Tokyo Kyowa Credit Association and the Anzen Credit Bank, however, Cosmo did not appear to have engaged in fraudulent lending activities. The bailout was accomplished with funds from the Sanwa Bank (Cosmo's largest creditor), several other banks, the National Federation of Credit Cooperatives, the Tokyo metropolitan government, and the DIC. Cosmo's operations were transferred to another institution (the Tokyo Kyodo Bank). The estimated cost of the bailout was ¥240 billion. The DIC contributed about ¥100 billion.

- Several weeks after the collapse of the Cosmo Credit Corporation, the Ministry of Finance decided to close down the Hyogo Bank (with about ¥3,400 billion in deposits) and Kizu Credit (with about ¥1,200 billion). Both institutions were experiencing deposit withdrawals as news spread of their financial position. The plan was to reorganize Hyogo into a new entity and to liquidate Kizu with its operations transferred to the Tokyo Kyodo Bank, the institution that absorbed Cosmo's operations. The total cost to the DIC of dealing with both institutions is estimated at ¥100 billion. This depleted the existing reserves of the DIC. As a technical matter, as of August 1995, the DIC had essentially zero net worth.

- Since the failures of the Hyogo Bank and the Kizu Credit Cooperative, in August 1995, there have been several more failures. Late in 1995 the Osaka, Sanyo, and Kenmin Daiwa Credit Cooperatives failed. The Taiheiyo Bank, a second-tier bank like Hyogo, failed in March 1996. In November 1996 the Ministry of Finance moved to liquidate the Hanwa Bank. The ministry's actions with regard to Hanwa were a departure from its previous actions in that there was no plan to arrange a merger and a bailout with shareholders at the time the decision to close the bank was made. Hanwa was simply ordered to cease operations except for meeting withdrawals of liquid deposits. The bank's assets are to be transferred to the RCB, and an explicit statement was made that the government would guarantee all of Hanwa's deposits. This statement reaffirmed a 1995 official announcement that all deposits at failed institutions would be guaranteed until the year 2000. Although it is too early to determine whether the Ministry of Finance has adopted a more aggressive attitude toward closing insolvent or nearly insolvent institutions, the closing of Hanwa without a merger or a shareholder bailout plan was a step in the right direction

The DIC has had a turbulent record in its short history. The first 20 years were uneventful, and few regarded the DIC as an important component of Japan's deposit-guarantee system (although a number of commentators mentioned that it was poorly funded—see, e.g., Cargill 1985 and Ito and Ueda 1993). Since 1991, however, the DIC has become a focal point of concern for two reasons: bailouts in late 1995 rendered the DIC insolvent,[11] and the DIC's approach to assisted mergers imposed few penalties on shareholders and none on depositors.

The Resolution of the Jusen *Problem and the Use of Public Money*

In December 1995, the government proposed a resolution plan for the seven insolvent *jusen* companies. This plan was passed by the Diet in the spring of 1996. Of the ¥13 trillion in assets of the seven *jusen* companies, ¥6.4 trillion was classified an immediate (primary) loss, ¥1.2 trillion was classified a "possible" (secondary) loss, ¥2.1 trillion was classified nonperforming but possibly recoverable, and ¥2.5 trillion was classified a normal performing asset. The primary loss of ¥6.4 trillion was to be borne by banks and life insurance companies, by agricultural cooperatives as a gift,[12] and by the government as public spending. The remaining assets were assumed by the Housing Loan Administration Corporation; special accounts will be used to deal with the secondary losses.

The plan has two shortcomings.

First, the sharing of the burden was not equitable; rather, it reflected the political strength of the agricultural sector. The plan is clearly lenient to the agricultural cooperatives. The strength of agriculture was revealed, for example, during the debate over sharing the costs of the financial crisis, when it became public that the Banking Bureau Director General of the Ministry of Finance had secretly signed a memorandum of understanding with his counterpart at the Ministry of Agriculture, Forestry, and Fisheries promising the Ministry of Finance's full backing of agricultural cooperatives' lending to *jusen* companies.[13] The heavier burden on banks also reflected the public perception that "founder banks" (banks that had set up *jusen* companies as subsidiaries) were providing personnel to manage operations and were referring potential borrowers (who turned out to be high-risk customers) to *jusen* companies.[14]

Second, the political opposition to using tax funds was strong. The resolution plan will spend only ¥685 billion of public funds in filling the gap between the primary loss and the private sector's burdens.[15] Many observers were puzzled by the extreme public opposition, since the amount of public funding was small in relation to the size of the nonperforming loans. In fact, the opposition was so strong that policymakers are likely to be very reluctant in the future to propose public funding as part of any solution in dealing with financial problems.

Unfortunately, the problem and its resolution were poorly presented by the Ministry of Finance. The plan was a reasonable starting point in tackling the financial debacle, but this purpose was lost in the debate over burden sharing and protection of the agriculture sector.

Capital-Adequacy Requirements

One issue that has complicated resolution of Japan's banking problems concerns stock-price fluctuations and the application of capital-adequacy requirements. Japan's banks commonly hold stocks of their

Table 6.5
Latent capital gains, in trillions of yen, among 21 leading banks in Japan. Source: Ito and Sasaki 1995.

Month	
1990:3	42.8
1990:9	24.0
1991:3	35.0
1991:9	30.1
1992:3	17.3
1992:9	14.6
1993:3	17.8
1993:9	23.6
1994:3	20.4
1994:9	19.3

large corporate customers with which they have long-term cross-shareholding relationships in the same enterprise groups.[16] Since these stocks have typically been held for some time, they contain unrealized capital gains that are not reported on balance sheets (in accordance with standard Japanese accounting practices). The latent capital gains (the difference between the current market value and the low book value), sometimes called *fukumi-eki* (hidden capital gains), have been a huge buffer in the capital position among the Japanese banks that had been relatively undercapitalized.

Bank regulators from major industrialized countries agreed in 1988 in Basle that standard capital requirements had to be set for banks that engaged in international businesses: 8 percent of total risky assets should be held in capital, and at least 4 percent of that in equities and the rest in near-capital such as subordinated debts. Risky assets, for example, include business lending but exclude cash and government bonds. The standard was to be phased in by the end of 1992 (or by March 1993, March being the end of accounting year for the Japanese banks).

In 1988, at the time of the adoption of the Basle capital-adequacy requirements, the Japanese monetary authority negotiated successfully for latent capital gains to be counted as a part of near-capital (tier II capital). This was expected to make it easier for Japanese banks to meet the Basle requirements. This seemed reasonable in 1988 and early 1989, before the bubble burst. As stock prices plummeted, banks suddenly faced a shortage of capital because latent capital gains fell significantly.

Table 6.5 shows the dramatic decline of *fukumi-eki* from 1990 to 1992. In September 1992, latent capital gains were one-third of the level in

March 1990. This made it difficult for Japanese banks to maintain the capital-adequacy ratio and to achieve the 8 percent by March 1993. The Japanese monetary authority was sufficiently concerned that the Ministry of Finance changed the guidelines to allow banks to issue subordinated debt, which grew substantially in 1992 and 1993 as banks responded to the loss of capital from stock-price declines (Ito and Sasaki 1995).

By the end of March 1993, all the major Japanese banks engaged in international business operations had satisfied the capital-adequacy requirement. However, stock-price declines such as those that occurred in the first half of 1995 reduce the hidden capital gains of Japanese banks and make the required capital-adequacy ratio more difficult to attain.

6.2 Deposit Guarantees

Deposit guarantees are an important part of Japanese financial regulation. As in other countries, they are intended to ensure public confidence in deposit money, to limit spillover (contagion) to the broader banking system from a problem with a single financial institution or a group of institutions, and in general to limit systemic risk. Before the start of liberalization in the mid 1970s, deposit guarantees in Japan were supported by an extensive set of constraints on portfolio decisions. From the 1950s to the early 1970s, Japan's financial system was one of the most regulated and administratively controlled in the world. These controls limited the ability of financial institutions to assume and manage risk; at the same time, they left the deposit-guarantee system untested.

Deposit-guarantee systems can be implemented in several ways. A number of countries, including the United States, have relied on deposit insurance. Deposit insurance is a passive system that comes into play whenever a local shock adversely affects one or a few banks. An explicit system of deposit insurance relies on codified regulations and on a willingness to accept bankruptcy as a normal part of business operations. Neither of these is characteristic of Japanese finance.

Japan has relied upon administrative guidance by the Bank of Japan and the Ministry of Finance to monitor institutions, impose regulatory discipline, intervene in financial markets, and force mergers. This is an activist approach, and the degree to which Japanese regulatory authorities are willing to regulate financial institutions is far greater than in most countries despite almost two decades of liberalization. Japanese financial regulation has historically been predicated on a "no-failure" policy (Tachibanaki 1991) and has not relied on a deposit-insurance framework that explicitly recognizes the possibility of failure. Conditions in Japan, however, have changed, forcing a reappraisal of the "no-failure" policy.

As a part of the "no-failure" policy, deposit guarantees are interpreted broadly. The Ministry of Finance in the past has made extraordinary efforts to ensure the health and protect the image of the financial system. This led to the rescue of a securities company in 1965; more recently, it has influenced the manner in which the ministry has handled public information on the nonperforming-loan problem and how it has arranged assisted mergers. It is illustrative that the Sumitomo Bank's announcement in January 1995 that it expected to become the first major Japanese bank to report an annual loss in the postwar period was regarded as a major attitudinal change on the part of the private banks and the Ministry of Finance (Choy 1995).

Until recently, Japan's deposit-guarantee system had not been tested. This is attributed to a variety of factors: Japan's macroeconomic environment has been conducive to a smooth and gradual evolution toward open and competitive markets; price stability generated only a small gap between regulated and unregulated interest rates and thus provided few incentives to innovate; the absence of open money markets limited the means to innovate; and regulation and administrative guidance have been quite binding.

Japan's system of deposit guarantees consists of three components: the Ministry of Finance's administrative guidance and the Bank of Japan's discount window (which provide the main support for deposit guarantees, especially for the large banks), two explicit deposit-insurance funds (one for large depository institutions and one for specialized depository institutions), and an explicit deposit-guarantee commitment to the Postal Savings System.

The Deposit Insurance Corporation and the much smaller Savings Insurance Corporation[17] have counterparts in many countries (Congressional Budget Office 1990). However, the Postal Savings System is a less well understood financial intermediary. The Postal Savings System, established in 1874, has come to play a major role in Japan's public-sector activities, especially in the postwar period.[18] It is regulated by the Ministry of Posts and Telecommunications, placing that Ministry among the major three financial agencies in Japan (after the Ministry of Finance and the Bank of Japan).

In addition to functioning as a typical postal service, Japan's more than 18,000 post offices accept transactions, savings, and time deposits, offer credit card services, and sell life insurance; however, the Postal Savings System is not permitted to make loans to postal customers, though it has repeatedly petitioned the Ministry of Finance for such authority. The Postal Savings System is the largest financial institution in the world in terms of deposits accounting for slightly more than 30 percent of total household deposits. These funds are an important component of the government's fiscal program, since the Postal Savings System contributes about 20 percent of the funding of the Fiscal Investment and Loan Program (FILP). The FILP, in turn, provides funds to support the general and special accounts of the government.

Regulation provides a number of comparative advantages to the Postal Savings System in attracting deposits, including complete government deposit guarantees. Past and current regulatory advantages provided by the Postal Savings System include more flexibility to permit multiple deposits by the same household to secure tax advantages prior to the Tax Reform Law of 1986, higher deposit rates relative to banks, and more attractive time-deposit instruments than banks.[19]

Late in 1992 the Ministry of Posts and Telecommunications and the Ministry of Finance agreed to reduce the competitive advantage of savings, time, and *teigaku*[20] accounts; however, the final agreement leaves considerable room for the Postal Savings System to retain its competitive advantage over private banks for household deposits. The Postal Savings System has not been a passive actor in this regard; it has shown considerable resistance to policies that would erode its regulatory advantages, despite the transition of finance toward more open and competitive structures. In 1992 the Postal Savings System even began to publicize the fact that postal deposits were more secure than bank deposits. In an effort to attract funds, it referred to the nonperforming-loan problem of private banks. The practice was officially criticized by top Ministry of Posts and Telecommunications officials.

The Bimodal Structure of Deposit Guarantees

The regulatory advantages provided to the Postal Savings System and the importance of postal receipts in the FILP explain why the Postal Savings System remains such a prominent part of Japan's financial system despite official efforts to liberalize the flow of funds. The Postal Savings System, however, has been a focal point of discussion during the past two decades. Two issues seem particularly important in the context of the deterioration of the financial system in the 1990s.[21]

First, a significant part of the flow of funds is likely to be allocated on the basis of strong political connections rather than on the basis of economic criteria. Postal savings funds are easily accessible to the Ministry of Finance to bail out troubled financial institutions, especially the housing-loan companies. To highlight the potential for inefficient use of Postal Savings System, the Ministry of Finance in 1992 directed the Ministry of Posts and Telecommunications to use funds from postal life insurance to support equity prices in the Tokyo stock market.

Second, the existence of the Postal Savings System in essence allows a dual system of complete deposit guarantees in Japan and ensures that Japan will not easily be able to solve the conflict between liberalization on the one hand and deposit guarantees that encourage risk taking and/or provide a foundation for destabilizing disintermediation from private banks to government-guaranteed deposits. Government deposit guarantees in Japan are evolving toward a bimodal structure as the financial system becomes more liberalized. In the past the Ministry of Finance took the position that no financial institution would fail, but as liberalization continues many specialized depositories will be under increasing competitive pressure as, at the same time, their status in the deposit-guarantee system becomes less certain. There are two components of the financial system, however, that continue to receive full deposit guarantees.

At one end of the spectrum are the large city and regional banks that for all practical purposes are regarded as too big to fail. It is not likely that the Ministry of Finance or the Bank of Japan would allow these institutions to fail, and close monitoring of these institutions means that actions would be taken as soon as insolvency appeared possible. Deposits in these institutions are, for all practical purposes, fully guaranteed despite the DIC limit. The policy of "too big to fail" creates problems, as it has in the United States, and the conflict is likely to increase as the liberalization process continues.[22] Japan has a smaller number of large banks, and that fact puts more pressure on regulators to ensure no large bank became insolvent. The Postal Savings System stands at the other end of the spectrum: postal deposits are guaranteed by the full faith and credit of the Japanese government.

A Politically Difficult Solution

Policymakers have several choices with respect to the role of the Postal Savings System. The alternatives include permitting the bimodal structure to become a permanent feature, extending deposit guarantees explicitly to all private depositories, eliminating the complete deposit guarantee on postal deposits through privatization of postal deposits while reducing deposit guarantees for all private depositories, and retaining the guarantee on postal deposits while eliminating deposit guarantees for private depositories.

The first policy is probably not viable over the long term, since problems in the "in-between" sector will continue to induce disintermediation of funds to the large banks and the Postal Savings System. The second policy may not be feasible, since it will merely worsen the moral hazard of deposit guarantees. The third policy may be consistent with a transition toward open and competitive markets; however, it has little chance of implementation in the near future, in view of the current economic and political status of the Postal Savings System. The fourth policy would limit government deposit guarantees to a narrow type of institution that accepts deposits and invests only in government securities. This radical approach to deposit guarantees is not likely to be feasible with the existing financial structure.

At some point Japan will need to deal explicitly with the Postal Savings System, because of its size and its potentially destabilizing role in the deposit-guarantee system. Privatization may appear the most efficient longer-term solution for a variety of reasons; however, privatization would run into stiff political opposition.

6.3 Lessons of the Nonperforming-Loan and *Jusen* Problems

There are several lessons to be learned from the regulatory response to the nonperforming-loan problem and the *jusen*-resolution problem against the backdrop of widespread deposit guarantees.

Delay in Regulatory Response

Delay in regulatory reaction raised the cost of the bailout and made it difficult to gain public support for any solution involving taxpayer funds. The regulatory response has been slow by any reasonable standard, and once regulatory action was initiated it often increased the magnitude of the problem. This outcome resulted from improper administration of the deposit-guarantee system and failure to appreciate the "moral hazard" of protecting depositors and assisting troubled institutions. This failure is even more striking in that the lessons from the

United States' experience with savings-and-loan and bank regulation starting in the 1980s were widely recognized by this time (see e.g. Barth 1991; Barth et al. 1992; Kane 1989; White 1991).

By 1995 Japan had come under intense international pressure to take decisive action to solve the problem of nonperforming loans. An International Monetary Fund report, highly publicized in Japan upon its release in the summer of 1995, criticized Japanese authorities for their delayed response. The market's judgment was also critical: the credit ratings of Japanese banks, previously at the top of the industry internationally, were downgraded sharply. The Daiwa Bank scandal and the Ministry of Finance's failure to properly inform US regulatory authorities of the problem in a timely manner further weakened confidence in Japanese financial institutions and Japanese regulatory authorities.

In the context of the growing public awareness of the nonperforming-loan and *jusen* problems, as well as intense international pressure, the government in December 1995 initiated a series of reforms to cope with future financial problems. Six legislative bills were introduced and passed by the Diet. One bill deals with *jusen* resolution. Another strengthens deposit insurance. The staff of the deposit-insurance system was enlarged, deposit reserves were strengthened by increasing deposit-insurance premiums sevenfold,[23] and a special deposit-insurance reserve was set up for credit cooperatives during the consolidation process. Another bill states that early corrective actions will be introduced to warn and limit operations of "weak" financial institutions (measured by capital ratio, nonperforming loans ratio, and other criteria), to minimize moral hazard and reduce the potential burden on taxpayers. It is also presumed that financial institutions will be closed before insolvency, to avoid losses.

Unfortunately, reform of the supervisory framework was omitted from this round of reform. In light of the poor performance of the Ministry of Finance in dealing with the financial problems, some observers questioned the effectiveness of any reform as long as the Ministry of Finance remained the primary financial regulatory authority. Some even proposed separating banking supervision from the ministry and creating an independent agency. Others suggested enhancing the regulatory authority of the Bank of Japan. Instead of focusing on the changes needed in the regulatory structure and on how banks and other depository institutions are regulated and supervised, the Ministry of Finance was able to shift the discussion to reforming the 1942 Bank of Japan Law and increasing the Bank of Japan's formal independence. While such a change in the Bank of Japan's legal charter is desirable for a variety of reasons, it is not very relevant to the structural problems of financial regulation in Japan. Shifting the focal point of the discussion to the Bank of Japan Law was partly a tactic by the Ministry of Finance to head off more widespread reform.[24]

Delay in shutting down an insolvent financial institution increases losses. This is a classical case of the moral hazard of deposit guarantees and the administration of those guarantees. Permitting an insolvent or nearly insolvent institution to operate provides incentives for the institution to gamble on a high-risk, high-return projects or to engage in fraudulent behavior (e.g., lending to top managers of related companies). There are numerous cases in the *jusen* industry of excessive risk taking and fraudulent behavior.

Indecision by the Ministry of Finance is primarily responsible for the delayed response—especially during 1992 and 1993, by which time the *jusen* problem had been evident to the ministry and to market insiders for several years. Documents submitted to the Diet in February 1996 show that the Ministry of Finance made the first on-site examinations of *jusen* companies in 1991–92. Those examinations revealed that 67 percent of loans made to the largest 50 borrowers were already nonperforming. *Jusen* companies, however, were allowed to operate, because it was assumed that land prices would rise in the near future. When land prices continued to decline, the *jusen* problem increased in magnitude. Nonperforming loans held by the *jusen* companies increased by 75 percent in the next four years.

A number of factors can be identified as contributing to the delay in regulatory response: lack of political leadership, problems in administering deposit guarantees, the political power of the agricultural sector, the existence of three separate and in some cases competing regulatory authorities (the Ministry of Finance, the Ministry of Agriculture, Forestry, and Fisheries, and the Ministry of Posts and Telecommunications), and a general unwillingness to recognize that Japan and Japanese financial institutions are susceptible to moral hazard associated with government deposit guarantees.

Moral Hazard

Moral hazard—incentives to assume more risk because deposit guarantees remove depositor discipline as a constraint on risk taking by depository institutions—is a serious problem despite a general unwillingness by Japanese regulatory authorities to recognize that fact. The moral-hazard problem facing Japan's financial institutions is similar in magnitude to that facing their counterparts abroad. The failure in December 1994 of two credit cooperatives, Tokyo Kyowa and Anzen Credit Cooperative, offers some insights. The Tokyo metropolitan government, the direct supervisor in the case, reportedly was aware of the insolvency of the two credit cooperatives as early as the spring of 1993, when a special joint examination with the Ministry of Finance was conducted. The delay in closing the two institutions substantially increased the ultimate cost of the bailout in early 1995.

The two credit cooperatives suffered from a classic case of moral hazard in their last two years of operation.[25] Deposits at both institutions increased from ¥139 billion in March 1992 to ¥244 billion in November 1994 (an annual rate of 32 percent), while lending increased from ¥137 billion to ¥225 billion (an annual rate of 22 percent). The majority of the new loans made during this period were ultimately classified as nonperforming. The total nonperforming loans of the two credit cooperatives increased from ¥250 billion (out of total loans of ¥1,371 billion) in March 1992 to ¥1,769 billion (out of total loans of ¥1,990 billion) in March 1994; moreover, unrecoverable losses increased from ¥65 billion in March 1992 to ¥1,118 billion in March 1994. Not only did the two credit unions aggressively expand deposits to make new, higher-risk, loans during their decline into insolvency; total nonperforming loans increased sevenfold and unrecoverable losses increased sixteenfold between March 1992 and March 1994. In addition, rapid increases in deposits were made possible by offering above-market deposit rates.

The portfolio behavior of the two credit cooperatives illustrates the incentives that face private depository institutions in the presence of government deposit guarantees when they are confronted with actual or impending insolvency. Insolvent or nearly insolvent institutions have an incentive to take on very risky investments, hoping to earn large returns and to become profitable again. But depositors have little incentive to monitor the portfolio shift, since they are protected by deposit guarantees.[26] The monitoring role must be taken by the supervisory agencies. In this respect, the Ministry of Finance did not respond sufficiently. The failure of deposit insurance in the United States in the late 1980s and the early 1990s and the current difficulty in Japan illustrate the universality of the problem.[27]

Public Funding and Involvement in the Solution

Public assistance is an important component of any plan to deal with widespread loan problems. However, the Japanese people were not initially informed of the need for substantial public funds expenditure to support failed institutions. Revelations of delays and special treatment of near-insolvent and solvent institutions by the Ministry of Finance also brought intense public criticism and great reluctance to commit public funds for financial restructuring. Public funding may be the least costly solution to the problem, however, since an efficient and equitable burden-sharing scheme was required and delay only increased the ultimate costs. Moreover, the justification for burden sharing in this case rests on the "public good" characteristic of the financial system. This was not readily accepted by the Japanese general public. The perception was that fiscal spending to make up the difference between the market values of assets and liabilities was little more than an effort to subsidize bankers and borrowers who had made bad business decisions.[28]

Concluding Comment

The problems experienced by Japan's financial system since 1985 raise a number of perplexing issues for Bank of Japan policy. These issues center on a series of conflicts faced by the Bank of Japan.

The conflict between price stability and external policy targets has been a recurring theme for the Bank of Japan in the postwar period. The postwar period offers two clear examples of the willingness of the Bank of Japan to pursue external policy targets at the expense of the domestic economy. The inflation of the early 1970s was the direct result of monetary expansion, and, although expansionary monetary policy may not have generated the asset-price inflation of the second half of the 1980s, it clearly played an accommodative role. The special structure of the financial system, liberalization, and deposit guarantees combined with the accommodative monetary policy to create the condition that allowed asset-price inflation and the bubble economy. The aftermath of asset inflation has revealed problems in Japan's financial system and structure of regulation. In many ways, Japan's regulatory authorities appear to be committing the same policy errors that US policymakers had committed several years earlier.

Japan's deposit-guarantee system remains bimodal, makes little effort to impose discipline on depositors or shareholders, and relies on a passive regulatory attitude. Whereas in the past the main monetary-policy conflict emanated from attempts to influence the value of the yen, the current deterioration of the financial system may force the Bank of Japan to give increasing consideration to prudential objectives when formulating policy—and those objectives may conflict with domestic price stability.

Concerns with prudential policy are always present; however, the willingness to directly subsidize the banking sector on the basis of vague arguments of "contagion" impose serious costs on the economy at large.[29] Recent events and concerns[30] expressed by the Bank of Japan suggest that greater involvement by central banks in prudential issues may be anticipated.[31]

Bank of Japan policy has been and will continue to be influenced by Japan's financial problems. It is important that the structural problems revealed in the first half of the 1990s be addressed, not only to provide a better operating environment for central-bank policy but also to ensure an efficient and stable financial system. In this regard, Prime Minister Hashimoto's announcement in late 1996 of a major reform and deregulation effort is a step in the right direction. Hopefully, the issues discussed in this chapter will be seriously considered.

7 Elections, Monetary Policy, and Political Business Cycles

The economy exhibits two types of time-varying behavior: short-run fluctuations in output, productivity, and inflation (referred to as *business cycles*) and longer-term secular trends. Although business cycles and secular trends are related, they present distinctly identifiable time-series behaviors. Although central banks cannot focus on one to the exclusion of the other, business cycles and secular trends present policymakers with distinctly different problems.

A central bank's policy generally has little influence on the long-run real path of the economy, but it is the primary determinant of the long-run inflation rate. There is substantial ambiguity, however, as to the role of monetary policy in business cycles. Some economists view monetary policy as capable of smoothing out fluctuations in economic activity; others argue that an activist stabilization policy may actually increase instability as well as deter the central bank from focusing on its long-run objective of price stability.

A review of the macroeconomic performance of various industrialized economies since World War II shows the regularity of business cycles despite the appearance of dampened fluctuations, longer expansions, and shorter recessions than in earlier decades.[1] Japan appeared to be an exception to this experience through the mid 1980s, as "growth recessions" seemed the Japanese norm for a business cycle downturn; however, recent swings in economic conditions highlight Japan's vulnerability to business cycles. A review of the long-run performance of most industrialized economies also shows that secular inflation continues to be a problem. Japan has achieved an excellent inflation record during the past 20 years, but over the entire postwar period there have been several bouts of high inflation.

The relationship among a central bank's policy, business cycles, and long-run inflation may be considered from either a technical or a political-economy perspective. The two perspectives are not independent; however, the political-economy approach explicitly considers the impact of a set of forces on the formulation and execution of monetary policy that are assumed exogenous in the technical approach. The focus of the political-economy perspective is on how political institutions, elections, regulatory structure, and policymakers' preferences influence policy. This approach, which has gained increasing attention in the past few decades, offers an interesting perspective on policy successes and failures. Political-economy analysis is particularly useful in understanding the persistence of business cycles and difficulty central banks have in achieving long-term price stability.

This chapter discusses the relationship between the Bank of Japan and business cycles from the perspective of political economy. We focus on short-term macroeconomic developments and on the political institutions (particularly the election system) that influence business cycles.

To date, the literature on political business cycles has devoted relatively little attention to the Japanese case. This reflects, in part, Japan's mild business-cycle fluctuations in the postwar period. It has also been suggested that Japan's economic and political structure are inconsistent with the basic assumptions of the political-business-cycle model. We show in this chapter that meaningful political-macroeconomic interactions that involve both monetary and fiscal policy can be identified in Japan, and that recent changes in Japan's political structure are likely to make this influence on the economy even greater in the future.

7.1 The Political-Business-Cycle Hypothesis: A Brief Review of the Literature

The literature on political business cycles has a long tradition in theories of economic fluctuations (see, e.g., Kalecki 1937 and Schumpeter 1939) and is evident in the writings of Karl Marx. However, not until 1975 was there a formal model showing how fluctuations in economic activity may be systematically attributed to political institutions in the form of election cycles.

The Nordhaus model[2] is relatively simple in terms of its underlying assumptions, but it stimulated the development of more complex models. Its basic assumptions include the following:

(i) Politicians are office-motivated: they are willing to generate economic fluctuations to remain in power.

(ii) Politicians have the ability to influence either monetary or fiscal policy.

(iii) There exists a short-run-exploitable Phillips curve in which shifts in aggregate demand generate short-run changes in output and employment.

(iv) There exists a voting function that is positively related to current and recent output and negatively related to current and recent inflation.

(v) Voters are irrational: they consider only the current and recent past performance of the economy in making political choices.

(vi) Politicians and voters possess the same utility function with respect to inflation and output.

(vii) Election cycles are fixed in terms of timing (as in the case of presidential and congressional elections in the United States).

(viii) Politicians perceive that their chance of remaining in power is tied more to the performance of the national economy than to regional conditions.

Figure 7.1 illustrates the basic Nordhaus model. Incumbent politicians starting from position A before an election pressure the monetary and/or fiscal authority to stimulate the economy. The stimulus moves the economy along a short-run-exploitable Phillips curve from position A to B (with anticipated inflation, $P_a = 5\%$), thereby generating a more favorable tradeoff between inflation and unemployment by placing the economy on a lower social disutility function (D_2). After the election, the economy shifts from position B to position C—that is, the economy returns to its natural growth path (with natural unemployment at 6%), but at a higher inflation rate as inflationary expectations catch up with recent experience ($P_a = 7\%$). The voters, having been fooled into thinking that the higher level of output was permanent, now find themselves at position C—that is, on a higher disutility frontier. The newly elected government now has two choices: it can leave the economy at position C, or it can disinflate and shift the economy from C to D (with a temporarily higher level of social disutility, D_3) and ultimately back to A. In either case, the incumbent politicians can repeat the stimulus before the next election and thereby increase the probability of their remaining in power. This behavior is referred to as *manipulative,* because the incumbent government manipulates monetary and/or fiscal policy to increase the probability of its remaining in power.

The Nordhaus model evolved to incorporate partisan considerations (Hibbs 1977) and endogenous election cycles (Chappell and Peel 1979;

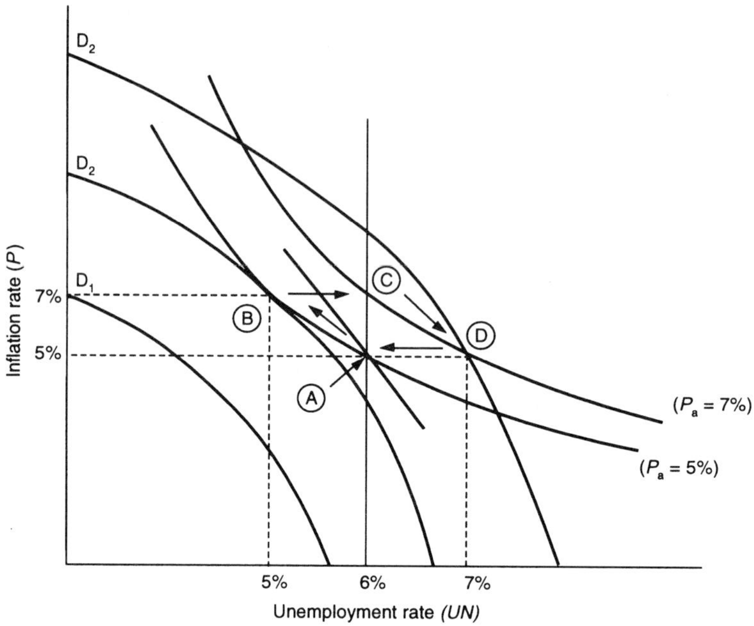

Figure 7.1
The Nordhaus model of political business cycles.

Lachler 1982). Partisan considerations permit at least two utility functions for politicians and voters: the utility function of one political party places higher importance on price stability than on output growth, while the utility function of another party places higher importance on output growth than on price stability. Each party imposes its political agenda on the economy when it assumes power. In a political system with endogenous election cycles, politicians select the election timing in response to favorable economic performance. This behavior is referred to as *opportunistic,* since the incumbent government takes advantage of non-policy-induced changes in the performance of the economy to increase the probability of its remaining in power.

Interest in models of political business cycles waned in the early 1980s as the economics profession began working out the implications of the rational-expectations approach to macroeconomic modeling. Many economists pointed out that Nordhaus-type models were inconsistent with rational voters and hence offered little insight into potential macroeconomic-political interrelationships (McCallum 1978). The rational-expectations premise is that politicians are not capable of systematically fooling surprising voters. Indeed, Nordhaus recognized that voters in his framework were not "rational," in the sense that voters failed to understand the incentives facing policymakers and their attempts to manipulate the economy to enhance the likelihood of electoral success.

A number of recent models, including those of Alesina (1987, 1988), have incorporated rational expectations into the basic political-business-cycle framework,[3] thus renewing interest in this general approach. By the early 1990s, a variety of models consistent with both rational and irrational voters predicted a relationship between macroeconomic performance and political institutions.[4]

7.2 Political Institutions in Japan

Determining the applicability of the political-business-cycle model to Japan first requires a brief review of Japan's political institutions, which, although rooted in Japan's history, were heavily influenced after World War II by the occupation and by the revised constitution.[5]

Japan's Diet (parliament) is divided into two houses: the House of Representatives (Lower House) and the House of Councillors (Upper House). An individual cannot serve in both houses at the same time. The head of the government, the prime minister, is elected by members of the Lower House; traditionally, a majority of the cabinet members are selected from the Lower House, as is the prime minister. The cabinet consists of the ministers of Justice; Foreign Affairs; Finance; Education; Health and Welfare; Agriculture, Forestry, and Fisheries; International Trade and Industry; Transport; Posts and Telecommunications; Labor; Construction; and Home Affairs.

The Lower House, the center of Japan's political system, clearly dominates the Upper House in appointing the prime minister and cabinet members and administering the country's economic and political programs. Members of the Upper House serve six-year terms with an election for half of the members taking place every three years. The Upper House cannot be dissolved. Members of the Lower House serve four-year terms unless that house is dissolved by the prime minister and a new election called. The Lower House has always been dissolved before the four-year limit except in 1976 and 1993, and there has been considerable variation in amount of time elapsed between the dissolution and the past election. When the Lower House is dissolved, an election must occur with 40 days of the dissolution and the Diet must be reconvened within 30 days of the election. The fact that the Lower House has been dissolved in varying times from the past election and the speed with which new elections can take place render the opportunistic channel of the political-business-cycle model potentially important in Japan.

Table 7.1 presents the Liberal Democratic Party (LDP) composition of the Diet from shortly after the end of World War II through late 1996. The LDP, formed on November 15, 1955, through a merger of the Japan Democratic Part and the Liberal Party, held the majority of the Lower House from that date until July 1993. At that time, the majority shifted to the New Japan Party, a coalition of LDP, Socialists, and other minor parties. The new coalition heralded the end to LDP dominance of the Lower House. Although the LDP returned to power in October 1996, a new and more unstable era in Japanese politics has begun.

7.3 Is Japan a Candidate for the Political-Business-Cycle Model?

Except for work done by the authors of this book and one other study, the literature on political business cycles includes few case studies of Japan. In multicountry studies,[6] where "one model fits all," little attention is paid to the special circumstances surrounding particular elections or other country-specific factors.

The lack of attention to Japan can be attributed to the belief that Japan does not satisfy a number of important preconditions for political business cycles. Japan's seemingly nonexistent short-run inflation-output tradeoff leaves no maneuvering room for a Nordhaus-type model. Furthermore, Japanese politics was dominated by a single party from 1955 to August 1993 (when the Liberal Democratic Party lost its majority in the Lower House), whereas researchers have stressed the importance of competing political regimes in creating political business cycles.

It is often argued that dominance by one party provides little incentive for manipulative behavior before elections, since officeholders know with a high degree of confidence that they will remain in power. This characterization is not correct for Japan, however. During most of the postwar period the LDP may have expected to retain power with a high degree of confidence, but, at the same time, that party had strong incentives to maximize its percentage of seats in the Diet in order to ensure smoother implementation of its programs. The number of chairpersons for committees is by tradition decided in proportion to the number of party members, and as table 7.1 shows there has been considerable variation in the percentage of seats held by the LDP in the Diet. In addition, the inter-party fighting in the Diet is legendary.

Researchers have found that in Japan neither the inflation-output tradeoff nor the short-run Phillips curve offers much potential for politi-

Table 7.1
Composition of Diet.

Quarter	Election date	LDP	Other	Total seats	Percent of LDP
House of Representatives					
46:2	4/10	234[a]	230	464	50.4
47:2	4/25	252[a]	214	466	54.1
49:1	1/23	333[a]	133	466	71.5
52:2	10/1	325[a]	141	466	69.7
53:2	4/19	310[a]	156	466	66.5
55:1	2/27	279[a]	188	467	59.7
58:2	5/22	287	180	467	61.5
60:4	11/20	296	171	467	63.4
63:4	11/21	283	184	467	60.6
67:1	1/1	277	209	486	57.0
69:4	12/27	288	198	486	59.3
72:4	12/10	271	220	491	55.2
76:4	12/5	249	262	511	48.7
79:4	10/7	248	263	511	48.5
80:2	6/22	284	227	511	55.6
83:4	12/18	250	261	511	48.9
86:3	7/6	300	212	512	58.6
90:1	2/18	275	237	512	53.7
93:3	7/18	233	278	511	45.6
96:4	10/20	239	261	500	47.8
House of Councillors					
47:2	4/20	75	175	250	30.0
50:2	6/4	61	69	130	46.9
53:2	4/24	54	74	128	42.2
56:3	7/8	61	66	127	48.0
59:2	6/2	71	56	127	55.9
62:3	7/1	69	67	136	50.7
65:3	7/4	71	56	127	55.9
68:3	7/7	69	57	126	54.8
71:2	6/27	63	63	126	50.0
74:3	7/7	62	68	130	47.7
77:3	7/10	63	63	126	50.0
80:2	6/22	69	57	126	54.8
83:2	6/26	68	58	126	54.0
86:3	7/6	72	54	126	57.1
89:3	7/23	36	90	126	28.6
92:3	7/23	68	59	127	53.5
95:3	7/23	65	61	126	51.6

a. Combined seats of Japan Democratic Party and Liberal Party, which formed LDP in November 1955.

cal exploitation (Gordon 1982; Grubb 1986; Hamada and Hayashi 1985). A combination of the nature of wage bargaining, lifetime employment, and flexible hours and pay renders Japan's short-run Phillips curve steeper than those for other industrial countries. In principle, a steeper Phillips curve reduces the political gain from political business cycles, since a small output gain would come at the cost of a large rise in inflation. Nonetheless, although Japan's Phillips curve appears to be relatively steep, there is still an exploitable tradeoff between inflation and growth in the short run. Manipulative behavior may still have its reward.

The traditional literature on political business cycles emphasizes that fluctuations in macroeconomic activity are likely to be centered around elections. However, the reverse causation may also be evident. That is, in a system with endogenous elections, macroeconomic performance can cause elections, as politicians choose, with a reasonable degree of flexibility, when to call an election. In fact, Japan's dominant-party system may reinforce the opportunistic channel of macroeconomic-political interactions relative to other countries where shifts in political regimes have been more likely. Thus, the dominance of the LDP increases the importance of the opportunistic channel while not rejecting the potential for the manipulative channel. Obviously, the difficulty lies in analytically separating manipulative behavior (designed to influence an election's outcome) from countercyclical policy actions of the Keynesian type (designed to stabilize the economy).

At least through the late 1980s, Japan surpassed other industrial countries in macroeconomic performance, and to some this suggests another reason why political business cycles were improbable. Moreover, the relatively stable Japanese economy suggests that political-macroeconomic interactions may be subtle and difficult to isolate empirically.

The Bank of Japan's contribution to price stability since the early 1970s is well documented and would also appear inconsistent with political business cycles. But while a well-functioning central bank may reduce the number of opportunities to engage in opportunistic behavior, there are sufficient economic shocks impacting Japan to leave latitude for politicians to at least exploit the opportunistic channel in an effort to remain in power.

Japanese politics changed dramatically in August 1993, when the LDP lost its majority in the Lower House. It is difficult to predict with any confidence how the system will evolve in the future, but it appears that a two-party system may emerge, making partisan considerations even more important.[7] In October 1996 the LDP regained some of its strength but did not achieve a clear majority in the Lower House. Of the 500 seats in that house, the LDP captured 239—up from 233 of 511 seats in the previous election. Combined with a less stable economic environment, these political developments may create greater opportunity to exploit both the manipulative and opportunistic channels in the future.

A Political-Business-Cycle Model for Japan

A political-business-cycle model for Japan must consider popularity functions, rational versus irrational voters, tradeoffs between output and inflation, incentives to politicians in a single-party structure to incorporate macroeconomic performance into their "office-motivated" behavior, and manipulative versus opportunistic behavior.

Popularity functions

Popularity (voter-preference) functions express the relationship between outcomes of elections or popularity of the incumbent government and a small set of economic variables, usually including the growth of real GDP, the unemployment rate, and the inflation rate. Because unemployment rates vary much less in Japan than in other industrial countries and reflect special features of Japanese labor markets, they are not suitable for establishing a relationship between election outcomes and macroeconomic performance.

A significant relationship between election outcomes or political popularity and economic variables is a necessary condition for political business cycles. Otherwise, politicians would have little incentive to engage in manipulative or opportunistic behavior. There exists a voluminous literature for the United States and several European countries linking economic variables to voting behavior and election results. In fact the association seems almost too high in view of the variety of economic and noneconomic influences government has on individuals (Nordhaus 1989, p. 30).

Inoguchi (1979, 1981) found only weak support for a statistically meaningful popularity function in Japan. Using annual data from surveys over the period 1960–1980, he found that the government's popularity was significantly related to inflation and a measure of nominal income, with the correct signs; however, he was unable to establish a significant relationship between election results (measured by the percentage of seats held by the LDP) and economic variables. Inoguchi concluded that economic variables appeared to be important in determining the popularity of the government, but less important in determining election outcomes. These results seemed at variance with those found for other countries; however, the use of annual data and a nominal rather than real measure of income may not have provided the most favorable basis for estimating popularity and voting functions in Japan.

Cargill and Hutchison (1988b) found stronger evidence for the existence of a popularity function. The percentage of total seats in each house held by the LDP at each election was regressed against the growth of real GNP and the rate of inflation measured by the GNP deflator. The regression was estimated with quarterly data over the period 1955–1986, with the two economic variables represented as four-quarter moving averages based on the contemporaneous value of the variable at the time of the election and in the preceding three quarters. The Lower and Upper House results were pooled into one regression, which included a time trend and a dummy variable equal to 0 for Lower House elections and 1 for Upper House elections. The results are presented in table 7.2 for both economic variables (column 1), inflation only (column 2), and real output only (column 3). LDP success at the polls, measured by percentage of seats achieved in each house, was found to be positively correlated with real output growth and negatively correlated with inflation, though the inflation variable was only significant at the 10 percent confidence level.

Ito (1990) estimated a voting function with a different specification and found even stronger evidence that economic conditions influenced voting outcomes. The dependent variable was the percentage of seats won by the LDP in the Lower House elections. In addition to real-GNP growth and inflation, a time trend and a dummy variable were included as explanatory factors. The dummy variable represented the occurrence of a double (*Dojitsu*) election in which the election for the Lower House occurred on the same day as the Upper House (dummy variable: 1). Ito argued that a Dojitsu election is advantageous to the LDP, since "passive" supporters of the status quo are more likely to show up at the polls when elections are taking place for both houses. In an effort to determine how far back the memory of the Japanese voter extended, Ito measured the output and inflation variables as changes from quarter to quarter (quarter-long memory), changes over the past four quarters (year-long memory), changes over the past eight quarters (two-year-long memory), and changes over the past twelve quarters (three-year memory).

Ito found that the Dojitsu variable was significant and positive, supporting the view that double elections help the LDP. LDP success at the

Table 7.2
Liberal Democratic Party election results related to economic variables. Independent variables: given in leftmost column. Dependent variable: percent of total representatives at each election who are members of LDP. Dummy: 0 if election is for House of Representatives, 1 if for House of Councillors. Q and P: average values over contemporaneous and previous three quarters or real-GNP growth and inflation (GNP deflator). Trend is a linear time trend. t statistics shown in parentheses. Source: Cargill and Hutchison 1988, p. 11.

	(1)		(2)		(3)	
Constant	52.87	(12.73)	60.43	(27.81)	51.21	(11.90)
Q	0.64	(2.08)			0.67	(2.04)
P	−0.35	(−1.79)	−0.36	(−1.74)		
Dummy	−0.67	(−0.39)	−1.70	(−0.94)	−0.97	(−0.53)
Trend	−0.04	(−0.19)	−0.33	(−2.05)	−0.03	(−0.14)
$\bar{R}^2$	0.35		0.23		0.27	
See	3.70		4.04		3.94	
DW	2.09		2.38		1.47	
OBS	21		21		21	

Table 7.3
Voter preference as indicated by $v_t = a_1 + a_2T + a_3D_t + b_1gt + b_2pt$, with v representing percentage of seats won by LDP, T representing trend in t, D the Dojitsu dummy (1 if election coincided with election of House of Councillors, 0 otherwise), g representing growth rate, and p representing inflation rate. Sample: t = election quarters only, including 1980 election. Period: 1955:1–1986:4. Number of observations: 12. Case 1: quarter-long memory, with g and p quarter-to-quarter rates. Case 2: year-long memory, with g and p changes over past four quarters (annualized rates). Case 3: two-year memory, with g and p changes over past eight quarters (annualized rates). Case 4: three-year memory, with g and p changes over past twelve quarters (annualized rates). Source: Ito 1990, p. 147.

	Constant	Trend	Dojitsu	Growth	Inflation	$\bar{R}^2$	DW
Case 1							
coefficient	63.39	−0.11	9.28	0.26	−0.40	0.94	2.01
t statistic	(26.18)	(−6.96)	(6.72)	(2.19)	(−3.47)		
Case 2							
coefficient	64.00	−0.11	7.42	0.42	−0.70	0.86	2.16
t statistic	(31.88)	(−5.12)	(3.70)	(2.78)	(−3.26)		
Case 3							
coefficient	63.55	−0.11	6.99	0.54	−0.74	0.84	1.64
t statistic	(18.83)	(−4.81)	(3.28)	(2.14)	(−2.58)		
Case 4							
coefficient	69.85	−0.14	5.82	−0.06	−0.48	0.72	1.30
t statistic	(18.47)	(−4.37)	(1.96)	(−0.53)	(−1.67)		

polls also was positively related to economic growth and negatively related to inflation, and both coefficients were highly significant. Finally, real output fluctuations seemed to be forgotten after about two years, but voters continued to penalize the LDP for inflation over the past three years.

Inoguchi's result should be discounted because he used annual data and a nominal rather than a real measure of income. The more correctly specified voting functions estimated by Cargill, Hutchison, and Ito support the existence of a voting function that depends positively on real output growth and negatively on the inflation rate, as assumed by the political-business-cycle model.

Rational versus irrational voters

A major debate in the literature on political business cycles concerns whether voters can be systematically fooled by politicians in subsequent elections or whether voters take all current and past information into account and adjust economic contracts to offset any attempt to manipulate the economy.

Several features of the Japanese economy may lead voters to be less than fully rational in the sense of Alesina et al. Until recently, economic fluctuations in Japan have been relatively mild and thus not likely to stand out in voters' memories. Ito's voting function results suggest that, at least for output, a voter's memory lasts only 2 years. Even in the case of inflation, he found that voters' memories dropped markedly after 2 years.

Nordhaus (1989) reviewed several empirical findings with respect to the United States and found no support for rational expectations in voting behavior. For example, the tendency of voters to repeatedly overvalue a new incumbent was "a clear violation of ultrarationality" (ibid., p. 32). The tendency to repeatedly overvalue a new government and prime minister, a common feature of postwar Japan, also leads us to question the assumption of voter rationality.

Tradeoffs between inflation and output

Short-run tradeoffs between output and inflation are generally assumed in political-business-cycle models. To the extent that output gains are the benefit and inflation is the cost of aggregate demand stimulus in appealing to the popularity or voting function, the short-term tradeoff is a major factor in the manipulative channel.

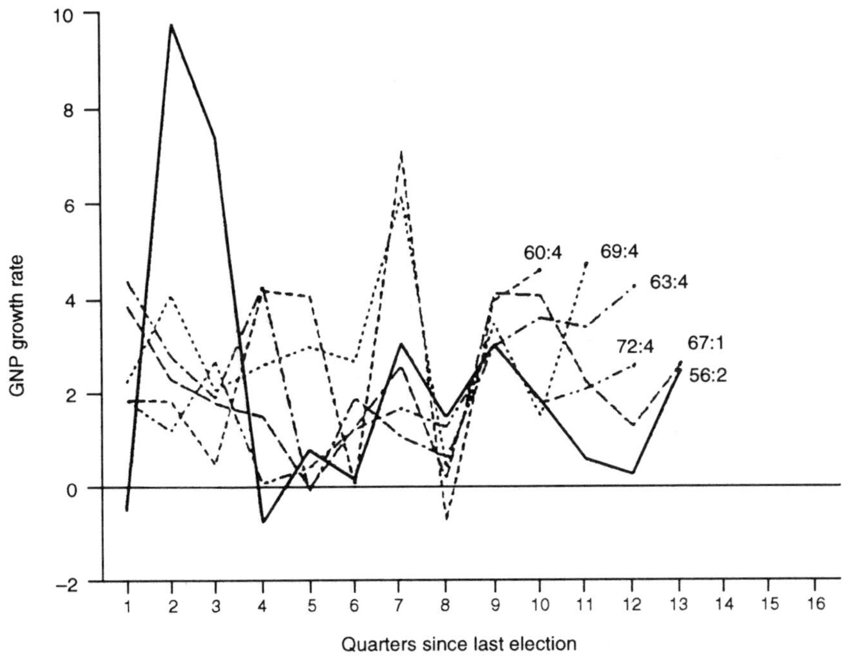

Figure 7.2
Election cycle before first oil crisis. Source: Ito 1990, p. 139.

8 months after the last election. This short cycle resulted from an "accidental" no-confidence vote on the Ohira cabinet, which was not related to economic performance.[9]

7.4 The Japanese Political-Business-Cycle Model: Empirical Evidence

This section reviews studies that have devoted considerable attention to special features of the Japanese political and economic environment in testing the political-business-cycle model. These studies are more detailed than the multicountry studies and, as a result, provide the most meaningful evidence on political business cycles in Japan.

Two sets of studies will be discussed. Those in the first set (Inoguchi 1979, 1981, 1983) present a conceptual framework and some basic statistical features.[10] Those in the second set (Cargill and Hutchison 1988b, 1991a, 1991b; Ito and Park 1988; Ito 1990; Kohno and Nishizawa 1990) are deeper empirical investigations.

Inoguchi explores the endogeneity of election timing and provides a number of important insights into the political business cycle in Japan.

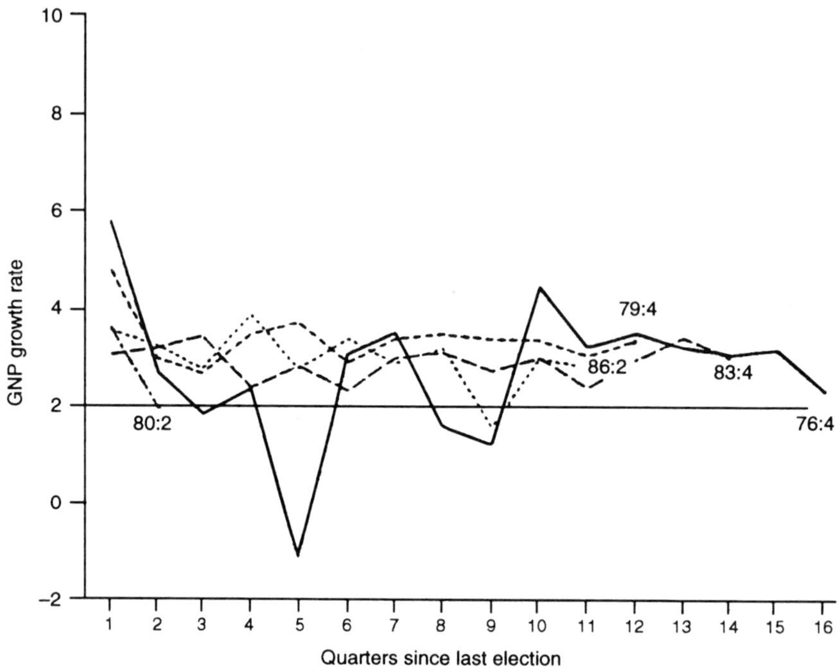

Figure 7.3
Election cycle after first oil crisis. Source: Ito 1990, p. 139.

Though others had recognized the importance of endogeneity of election cycles in parliamentary systems (e.g. Tuft 1978), Inoguchi's work is the first application to Japan. He concludes that the Japanese government seizes the opportunity of good economic performance to call a general election but does not systematically engage in manipulative behavior. He argues that the independence of the bureaucracy from politicians reduced the ability to manipulate the economy in advance of calling an election. Inoguchi also explores the relationship between popularity and voting functions and economic performance, but overall finds only weak evidence of a political business cycle.

More extensive and rigorous tests of the political business cycle in Japan, following this line of research, will now be summarized.

Ito 1990; Ito and Park 1988

Ito 1990 extends Ito and Park 1988 and is the focus of discussion here.[11] Ito carefully distinguished between the manipulative and opportunistic

Table 7.4
Policy manipulation. *T:* trend. D*i:* *i*th-quarter dummy ($i = 2,3,4$). REGIME: Bank of Japan policy-regime change (= 1 after 1975:1). *m:* quarter-to-quarter growth rate of M2 + CDs outstanding at end of quarter. *g:* quarter-to-quarter growth rate of real GNP. *p:* quarter-to-quarter growth rate of CPI. GC: government consumption/GNP (available after 1957:1). OIL: oil-crisis dummy (= 1 after 1974:1). EL: election variable (coefficients on the constant, trend, dummies, and monetary-regime dummy not reported). Source: Ito 1990, pp. 148–149.

Monetary-policy manipulation:

$m_t = a_1 + a_2T + a_3\text{D2} + a_4\text{D3} + a_5\text{D4} + a_6\text{REGIME} + b_2m_{t-1} + b_2p_{t-1} + b_3g_{t-1} + b_4\text{EL}_t$

	m_{t-1}	p_{t-1}	g_{t-1}	EL_t	R^2	DW
coefficient	0.24	−0.04	0.01	−0.16	0.84	1.95
t statistic	2.57	−0.50	0.38	−0.39		

Fiscal-policy manipulation:

$GC_t = a_1 + a_2T + a_3\text{D2} + a_4\text{D4} + a_6\text{OIL} + b_1 GC_{t-1} + b_2g_{t-1} + b_3E_t$

	GC_{t-1}	g_{t-1}	EL_t	R^2	DW
coefficient	0.91	$-0.82\times(E-3)$	$-0.18\times(E-2)$	0.89	1.95
t statistic	23.62	−1.68	−0.75		

channels of political-macroeconomic interaction in Japan, investigating the two channels separately and also jointly.

Manipulative behavior was investigated by determining whether monetary and fiscal policy instruments were sensitive to election periods, after accounting for factors that may influence monetary and fiscal policy. Table 7.4 presents selected[12] empirical results for monetary and fiscal policy, respectively, estimated with quarterly data over the period 1956:2–1986:4.

The monetary-policy-manipulation regression expresses the growth rate of M2 + CDs against a time trend; seasonal dummies; a dummy variable representing the Bank of Japan's change of policy regimes in 1975:1; past growth rates of money supply, real GNP, and CPI; and an election variable. The fiscal-policy-manipulation regression expresses the growth rate of government consumption against a time trend; seasonal dummies; an oil-crisis dummy; past growth rates of the fiscal-policy instrument and real GNP; and an election variable.

The estimated regressions explain much of the variation in the monetary-policy and fiscal-policy instruments over time (e.g., high R^2 values) without generating serially correlated errors. The coefficients, with the exception of the election variable, have the anticipated signs and are statistically significant in most cases. The election variable, however, is not statistically significant in any of the equations, and this leads Ito to reject the manipulative channel.

Ito also investigates the opportunistic channel by regressing election occurrences on economic growth, inflation, and time elapsed since the last election. The results (not reported here) show a statistically significant relationship between the probability of an election and economic variables. The probability of an election increases with higher real economic growth, decreases with higher inflation, and increases with the amount of time elapsed since the last election.

Separate tests of the manipulative and opportunistic channels, however, may pose a simultaneous-equations bias in estimation. A model incorporating both manipulative and opportunistic channels predicts a two-way relationship between elections and macroeconomic activity. The manipulative channel emphasizes causation from elections to macroeconomic performance, while the opportunistic channel emphasizes causation from macroeconomic performance to elections. Simultaneously estimating the influence of the two channels while taking into account the two-way feedback between macroeconomic performance and elections is the preferred methodology.

Ito presented LOGIT and PROBIT estimates that took the simultaneity problem into account by separating changes in real-GNP growth and inflation into policy-induced and non-policy-induced changes. The model then combines these two components into one regression, which tests the degree to which the probability of an election is related to policy-induced and non-policy-induced real-GNP growth and inflation. The results are presented in table 7.5. The coefficients for the policy-induced components (E_g and E_p) are not statistically significant; however, those for the non-policy-induced components (RES_g and RES_p) are statistically significant, as is the coefficient for the time-elapsed variable.

Thus, it appears from Ito's results that the probability of an election is increased when an unexpected increase in real-GNP growth or an unexpected decrease in inflation occurs with time elapsed since the last election held constant. The probability of an election appears unrelated to policy-induced changes in economic growth and inflation. On the basis of these results, Ito rejects the manipulative channel for Japan and, supporting Inoguchi's finding, argues that the opportunistic channel is the primarily conduit between elections and macroeconomic performance.

Table 7.5
Tests of manipulative- and opportunistic-government hypothesis. E_g = fitted values of GNP growth regressed on policy variables; RES_g = residuals of GNP growth regressed on policy variables; E_p = fitted values of inflation regressed on policy variables; RES_p = residuals of inflation regressed on policy variables; TSLE = quarters since last election. Source: Ito 1990, p. 152.

	Const.	E_g	E_p	RES_g	RES_p	TSLE
PROBIT						
coefficient	−12.24	0.00	−0.22	0.27	−0.16	1.02
t statistic	−3.00	−0.19	−1.51	2.83	−1.50	3.14
LL = −10.72						
Avr L = 0.91						
LOGIT						
coefficient	−21.32	0.00	−0.40	0.47	−0.29	1.79
t statistic	−2.85	−0.01	−1.54	2.68	−1.54	2.93
LL = −10.89						
Avr L = 0.91						

Kohno and Nishizawa 1990

Kohno and Nishizawa (1990) question Inoguchi's view that opportunistic rather than manipulative behavior is most prominent in Japan.[13] Although recognizing that the bureaucracy in Japan is relatively independent, they argue that politicians follow self-interest and often attempt to influence economic policy. In addition, they point out that many noneconomic factors have influenced election timing (p. 155).

Kohno and Nishizawa directly test the manipulative channel by estimating a time-series or Box-Jenkins model for various economic policies. They also include an election variable in their regressions. They consider three economic policies that could be subject to manipulation: industrial policy, monetary policy, and government spending. Government spending appears to be the most accessible to politicians. Time-series models are estimated for monthly data on government expenditures on public works in the budget (planned spending) and on public construction started by public corporations and agencies (actual spending). The latter is regarded as the more reliable, since the government expenditures in the budget represent attempts at government intervention, while the actual expenditures started in each month represent the outcomes of attempted intervention.

The election variable is positive and statistically significant in the time-series model for the public construction starts. This supports the view—commonly held in Japan—that during an election the government spends more on public-works projects in order to influence the election's outcome. The election variable in the time-series model for government expenditures on public works in the budget was not statistically significant, however,.

Cargill and Hutchison 1991a,b

Cargill and Hutchison investigate political business cycles in Japan from two perspectives. First, they directly examine the relationship between monetary-policy instruments (money supply and the interbank interest rate) and elections. Second, they formulate and estimate a simultaneous-equations model that incorporates both opportunistic and manipulative components.

The first set of results are based on a reaction-function approach to Bank of Japan policy. That is, a Bank of Japan policy instrument (interbank rate or money supply) is regressed against a time trend, a dummy variable representing the shift from fixed to flexible exchange rates, lagged values of the instrument, lagged values of other economic variables (real GNP, inflation, exchange rates, and trade balance), and three political-event variables. The three political-event variables are dummies representing post-election periods and pre-election periods and the percentage of seats held by the LDP in the Lower House. The advantage of the reaction-function approach is that it permits identification of political influence on monetary-policy instruments that may not show up in overall macroeconomic performance; in this respect, Cargill and Hutchison's reaction-function results are similar in concept to the framework adopted by Kohno and Nishizawa.

Table 7.6 presents selected results where reaction functions are estimated over two time periods, with the interbank rate used as the policy instrument. The break between the two time periods is 1975, at which time the Bank of Japan adopted a more "money-focused" approach to policy and, in addition, was freed from the constraints of the fixed-exchange-rate system (see chapter 3). The results provide only weak support for political-business-cycle behavior. Only changes in the interbank interest rate during the later period are consistent with political-business-cycle predictions. In particular, the interbank rate is decreas-

Table 7.6
Tests of the effects of election timing on Bank of Japan changes in the interbank interest rate, *I*. No trend included in this model, *Y* is growth of real GNP, *P* is GNP inflation rate, *M* is the M2 + CDs money supply, *E* is the exchange rate, *TB* is the trade balance, *D*PRE is a pre-election dummy, *D*POST is a post-election dummy, and *S*LDP is the strength of the LDP. I, E, and TB are in first differences. t statistics shown in parentheses. Source: Cargill and Hutchinson 1991a, p. 130.

	1958:2–1974:4	1975:1–1986:4
Constant	−0.433	−1.361
	(−0.650)	(−1.798)
DUM	1.500	—
	(3.150)	
ΣY_j	0.474	0.263
	(1.616)	(1.995)
ΣI_j	−0.110	0.486
	(−0.424)	(1.621)
ΣM_j	−0.007	0.044
	(−0.203)	(0.356)
ΣP_j	−0.020	−0.105
	(−0.394)	(−1.171)
ΣE_j	—	1.679
		(0.466)
ΣTB_j	−18.552	—
	(−1.735)	
*D*PRE	0.831	−8.317
	(0.236)	(2.400)
*D*POST	0.256	−0.043
	(1.130)	(−0.137)
*S*LDP	−0.014	0.168
	(−0.195)	(2.502)
R^2	0.537	0.44
OBS	67	48
F value[a]	0.473	2.560
Significance level of *F* value	0.703	0.079

a. For hypothesis that coefficient of political-event variables are jointly zero.

ing before an election, and the amount by which the interbank rate is decreasing is negatively related to the strength of the LDP (that is, the stronger the LDP's majority position, the smaller is the reduction in the interbank rate). The reaction functions with the money supply used as the policy instrument rejected political-business-cycle behavior, however.

The reaction-function results are extended by using a framework that permits coefficients of the basic relationships to evolve over time. This is accomplished by estimating a VAR model of the Japanese economy without political-event variables and using this model to calculate forecast errors for the money supply and the interbank interest rate. In principle, this approach is similar to Ito's decomposition of output and inflation into policy-induced and non-policy-induced changes. Deriving the VAR-model estimates from a time-varying procedure allows the coefficients to evolve over time. Specifically, estimates of the VAR model from time t to $t + n$ are used to estimate the forecast errors of the money supply and the interbank rate at time $t + n + 1$, estimates of the VAR model from $t + 1$ to $t + n + 1$ are used to estimate the forecast errors of the money supply and the interbank rate at time $t + n + 2$, and so on. The forecast errors of the money supply and interbank rate are then regressed on the three political event variables.

These results confirm the previous finding that only the interbank rate in the latter sample period (1975:1–1986:4) appears to respond to political events (Cargill and Hutchison 1990, p. 133). The downward shift in the interbank rate before an election is consistent with the political-business-cycle hypothesis. It is noteworthy that the magnitude of the decline is tempered by the electoral position (strength) of the LDP at the time. That is, the larger the majority of the LDP in the Diet, the smaller is the decline in the interbank rate before an election. Nonetheless, Cargill and Hutchison emphasize the tentative nature of the results, because the political-event variables were significant in only one of several empirical formulations of the model.

In a subsequent study, Cargill and Hutchison (1991b) directly address the issue of simultaneity between elections and economic activity. This is the most general test of the political-business-cycle model to date, and it is the only test of the model in the Japanese context applying a fully simultaneous estimation procedure.

The model encompasses two simultaneous equations, with real-GNP growth as an endogenous continuous variable and the timing of elections as an endogenous dichotomous choice variable. Consider the following simultaneous equations:

$$y_1 = \delta_1 y_2 + B_1 X_1 + u_1, \tag{7.1}$$

$$y_2 = \delta_2 y_1 + B_2 X_2 + u_2, \tag{7.2}$$

where y_1 is the observed continuous variable (growth of real GNP) and y_2 is a dummy variable indicating whether a House of Representatives election is held ($y_2 = 1$) or not ($y_2 = 0$) in that particular quarter. X_1 represents a vector of predetermined variables influencing real-GNP growth (including real oil prices, *ROIL;* a dummy variable for the post-1973 growth slowdown, D_{73}; lagged real-GNP growth, $RGNP_{t-1}$; and the number of quarters since the last election in the House of Representatives, *HRDIST*). X_2 represents a vector of predetermined variables influencing the decision of the government to call an election (including *HRDIST;* a dummy variable for Upper House elections, D_{HC}; a dummy variable for the "accidental" no-confidence vote and early 1980 election, D_{80}; a variable testing for the influence of elections in the United States on Japan, *US Election;* and a variable measuring the electoral strength of the LDP, *Strength*).

The manipulative component is indicated by $\delta_1 > 0$, the opportunistic component by $\delta_2 > 0$. Thus joint estimation of the two-equation system permits a simultaneous test of the two channels. A variety of estimation techniques and specifications are reported by Cargill and Hutchison, and tables 7.7 and 7.8 here present selected results. The results indicate that neither the manipulative nor the opportunistic component can be rejected for postwar Japan. That is, the growth rate of real GNP appears to be positively and significantly related to an election variable once a number of economic and noneconomic influences on real-GNP growth are taken into account (table 7.7). The probability of an election also appears to be positively and significantly related to the growth rate of real GNP (table 7.8). The manipulative channel is statistically more robust because the election coefficient is positive and significant in all the specifications of the model; the opportunistic channel is less robust since the real-GNP growth coefficient is positive and significant only in the single-equation estimation procedure.[14]

Table 7.7
Effects of election timing on growth of Japan's real GNP (two-stage model). Source: Cargill and Hutchison 1991b, p. 737.

Constant	7.01
	(1.99)
Election	6.23
	(2.63)
D_{73}	−5.00
	(−3.52)
$ROIL_t$	−0.03
	(−1.76)
R^2	0.29
SSE	5.22
DW	2.31
DF	115

Implications of the Empirical Results

The studies by Inoguchi, Cargill and Hutchison, Kohno and Nishizawa, Ito and Park, and Ito provide a fairly extensive investigation of the political business cycle in Japan. These studies, taken together, provide a far more important basis on which to judge the existence of political business cycles in Japan than multicountry studies where Japan is included. There are some differences among the studies, but overall the results suggest that Japan's macroeconomic performance has been influenced by political events despite the dominance of the LDP and, in turn, that politicians take advantage of favorable economic performance in calling elections.

There appears to be little debate over the opportunistic channel. Ito and Park, Ito, and Cargill and Hutchison find evidence to support Inoguchi's "political surfing" view. The manipulative component is debatable, however. Cargill and Hutchison and Kohno and Nishizawa do not reject the manipulative channel. They report evidence that some policy instruments are sensitive to elections and that macroeconomic performance is sensitive to elections. In contrast, Ito and Park, and Ito, reject the manipulative channel. The differences in results appear to be due to differences in estimation methods and model specifications. An important task for future research is to resolve this question, better identifying the links among policy instruments, macroeconomic performance, and political influence.

Table 7.8
PROBIT model for timing of Japanese elections. Source: Cargill and Hutchison 1991b, p. 738.

	Single equation		Two-stage	
	(1)	(2)	(3)	(4)
Constant	−1.43	0.13	−1.03	−0.37
	(−4.46)	(0.09)	(−1.74)	(−6.52)
$RGNP_t$	0.05	0.045	0.001	0.020
	(2.27)	(1.95)	(0.02)	(0.01)
HRDIST	0.06	0.05	0.05	0.05
	(1.93)	(1.72)	(1.62)	(1.50)
D_{HC}	8.83		8.14	
	(0.00)		(0.00)	
D_{80}	0.65		0.47	
	(0.00)		(0.00)	
$US\ Election_t$		0.33		0.42
		(1.01)		(1.11)
$Strength_{t-1}$		−0.03		−0.01
		(−0.95)		(−0.40)
Observations	119	119	119	119
Cases correct	90	88	89	89
Log likelihood	−62.56	−64.70	−65.18	−66.60
Average likelihood	0.59	0.58	0.58	0.57

7.5 The Future of the Japanese Political Business Cycle

The evidence suggests that Japan is not unique with respect to interactions between political events and macroeconomic performance. Despite a number of special features of Japan's politics and economy, several predictions of the political-business-cycle model are confirmed by empirical analysis.

The loss of the LDP's majority in the Lower House in August 1993 and the failure of any group to achieve the type of consensus common during the period of the LDP's dominance mark a new era in Japanese politics. This era will likely see even greater partisan pressure on the formulation of macroeconomic policy. At least three changes in the Japanese economy also point to increased partisan pressure on policy.

First, by the late 1980s Japan had achieved all reasonable expectations in its push to reindustrialize and catch up economically with the United

States. At this point, a major unifying element of Japanese politics—rapid economic growth—ended. As higher economic welfare had been achieved, more diverse political demands were to be expected. Japan will respond to these challenges, and the economy will be affected. For example, Japanese households have demanded more leisure time and more participation in the financial system, and demographic changes in the workforce have seen women assume more responsibility. As a result, it will be more difficult for one party to achieve the type of majority enjoyed by the LDP in the 1960s and the 1970s. Different political coalitions will likely arise to address these more diverse interests.

Second, despite efforts by regulatory authorities to insulate Japan's economy, world financial and trade pressures are forcing important structural changes. This has challenged the traditional power relationships among the business sector, bureaucrats, and politicians. Again, this creates an environment for new factions to arise and assume power.

Third, the Japanese economy has exhibited increased instability since 1989. The continuing problem of nonperforming loans, the fears about the financial system, and the long and deep 1991–mid 1995 recession suggest that politicians may now have more to gain by exploiting voters' concerns over the economy. The benefits from manipulative behavior may be higher in a more unstable environment.

In sum, Japan exhibits political-business-cycle behavior, and there is a large body of evidence linking economic performance to political events (especially the timing and outcome of elections). It appears that the Liberal Democratic Party acted opportunistically by calling elections early when economic conditions were particularly favorable. There is less support for the view that monetary and fiscal policies were systematically manipulated to generate booms in the hopes of improving electoral positions. However, changes in Japan's economic and political environment suggest that political interference with the conduct of macroeconomic policy is likely to become increasingly evident.

8 Inflation, Time Inconsistency, and Central-Bank Independence

Substantial long-lasting inflation is almost always associated with excessive money growth.[1] In this context, an explanation of a central bank's behavior and of the process of making decisions about monetary policy is necessary if we are to understand and explain ongoing (secular) inflation. Our focus in this chapter is on the political economy of secular inflation. Extending chapter 7's discussion of the political business cycle, we seek answers to three major questions about the Bank of Japan's behavior: Why did average inflation in Japan drop so sharply after the collapse of the Bretton Woods exchange-rate system? Why has average inflation in Japan been so low by international comparison since the mid 1970s? How has low inflation been achieved despite the legal dependence of the Bank of Japan on the Ministry of Finance?

The obvious answers to the first two questions are that Japanese monetary growth (figure 3.2) declined sharply after the mid 1970s and that since then it has been quite low by international comparison. The average annual growth rates of consumer prices and the broad money supply were 5.7 and 19 percent, respectively, during the period 1960–1972. After a period of turbulence associated with the collapse of Bretton Woods and the first oil shock, the average annual growth rates of prices and money declined sharply, averaging only 3.2 and 8.6 percent, respectively, during the period 1975–1994.

In this chapter we seek to explain the motivations and incentives behind the actions by the Bank of Japan that led to low monetary growth and low inflation. There is a large body of literature that seeks to explain persistent inflation as an "equilibrium" phenomenon: an outcome of political and economic interactions within the context of the institutional framework under which the central bank operates. This literature is primarily concerned with dynamic inconsistency as a source of inflation bias and with whether a politically independent central bank may be a solution. The problem is that central banks find it difficult to credibly commit to an announced policy consistent with low inflation. The private sector recognizes the incentives facing a central bank to inflate once wage and price contracts are set, and thus it anticipates more expansionary policies. The "equilibrium" rate of secular inflation in this case will be too high from a social-welfare point of view.

A number of proposals have been advanced to solve the problem of inflation bias. The traditional solution is to forgo discretionary policy and adopt a monetary rule (see, e.g., Friedman 1959). Kyland and Prescott's (1977) formulation of the dynamic-inconsistency problem was advanced as an argument for rules rather than discretion in macroeconomic policy.[2] A second solution is to delegate authority to a conservative and independent central banker Rogoff's (1985) conservative central banker dislikes inflation more, and places less value on output gains, than a government (i.e., the ruling political party or the administration in office) normally does.[3] In line with this argument, the Japanese government is at this writing considering a proposal to grant the Bank of Japan greater institutional independence from the Ministry of Finance. A third solution involves reputation. By acting consistently over a long period, a government builds up a reputation that causes the private sector to believe its announcements. Once a reputation has been built up, and expectations of inflation are in line with the announced low-inflation policy, there may be an incentive to inflate, but it will come at the cost of lost credibility and higher future expected (and realized) inflation rates.[4]

This chapter considers these alternative solutions to the problem of inflation bias to see if they are consistent with the facts and if they help explain observed Bank of Japan policy since the mid 1970s. Although a number of explanations have some support, our main conclusion is that reputational effects, magnified by a "long-lived" and highly autonomous government bureaucracy and supported by the Liberal Democratic Party's dominance between the mid 1950s and 1993 and by the memory of two inflationary episodes in the postwar period, best explain the low inflation bias in Japan. The shock of the high inflation that followed the collapse of the Bretton Woods system pushed the Bank of Japan to adopt a "money-focused" (i.e., price-stabilizing) policy, which gradually developed into a reputation as a conservative central bank credibly committed to low inflation. Japan provides the best counterexample to the view that formal central-bank independence is necessary if low-inflation (credible precommitment) equilibrium is to be achieved

(Cargill 1989 and 1995a). To some extent the Ministry of Finance, with its potentially strong influence over monetary policy, has cooperated to some extent with the Bank of Japan; they have jointly adopted the role of a politically independent and conservative maker of monetary policy. Reputational equilibria are by nature fragile, however, so a higher degree of institutional independence for the central bank may help sustain low inflation in the face of Japan's current economic problems and political uncertainty.

8.1 Rules Rather than Discretion in Monetary Policy

Figure 8.1 illustrates the basic problem of dynamic inconsistency and the argument for monetary-policy rules rather than discretion. The upper panel shows a series of short-run Phillips curves and policy indifference curves in the inflation space (π on the vertical axis) and in the unemployment space (μ on the horizontal axis). The Phillips curves are

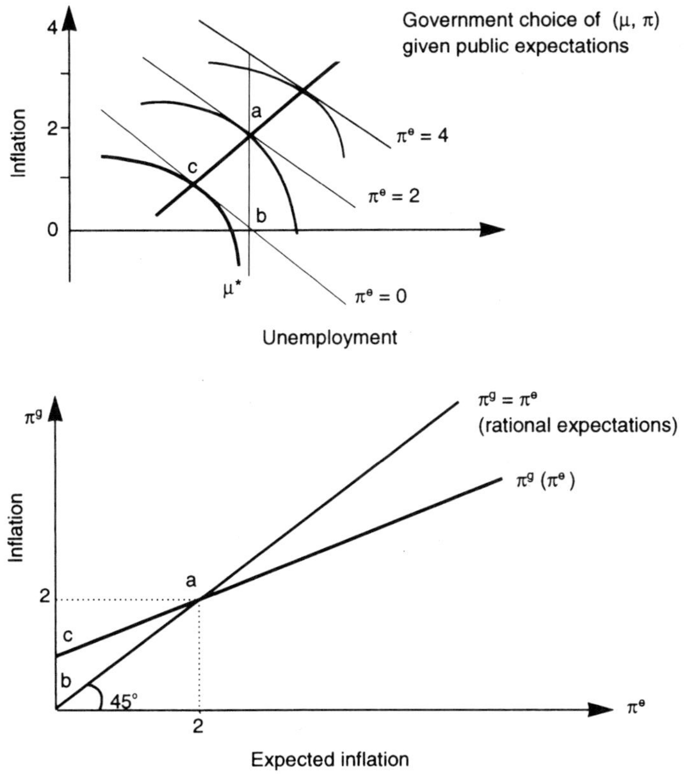

Figure 8.1
Time inconsistency and secular inflation.

represented by the downward-sloping lines, where the relevant curve at any point in time is set by the level of inflation expectations held by the private sector. Given expected inflation, the Phillips curve shows the combinations of inflation and unemployment that are possible in the short term and may be attained by varying the degree of monetary stimulus. The concave curves represent the preferences of the policymaker, showing points of indifference where slightly higher unemployment is traded off against slightly lower inflation. The curves closer to the origin are preferred by the policymaker, as they represent both lower inflation and lower unemployment.

The combination of inflation and unemployment at the point of tangency between a given Phillips curve (i.e., a given level of expected inflation) and the indifference curve is the optimal choice of the policymaker and reflects the monetary policy that would be followed under discretion. Varying the level of expected inflation gives the upward-sloping locus of (optimal) inflation-unemployment points that would be chosen by the policymaker. The inflation points chosen (π^g) by the policymaker for each level of expected inflation derived from the upper panel are also plotted in the lower panel.

The only long-run "expectations-consistent" or rational-expectations equilibrium is that where actual and expected inflation are equal and unemployment is at its "natural" or market-determined level (μ^*), indicated by **a** in each of the two panels of figure 8.1. In this constructed example, the equilibrium inflation rate is 2 percent. The problem with this discretionary equilibrium, where the policymaker simply chooses an optimal policy after expectations are given and wage contracts are set, is that no long-term gain in employment is able to make up for positive inflation. The policymaker would much prefer to be at point **b,** with the same rate of unemployment and no inflation, but without some means of credibly committing to this low inflation rate the private sector would anticipate a move from **b** to **c** (the short-run optimal choice) once expected inflation is set. That is, without some means of committing to the low-inflation policy, people would expect a "surprise" monetary stimulus moving the economy to point **c.** On the other hand, if the central bank were able to credibly commit to the low-inflation policy, convincing firms and workers that it would follow a policy consistent with point **b,** then everyone would be better off than at the discretionary equilibrium attained at point **a.**

To put the argument in more formal terms, consider an intertemporal policy loss function, a discounted sum (with discount δ) of the single-period losses which are quadratic in inflation (π) and deviations in real output from the desired level ($y - ky^*$):

$$L_t = \sum_{i=0}^{T} (1 + \delta)^{-i}[a\pi^2 + (y - ky^*)^2]_{t+i}, a > 0, k > 1 \quad (8.1)$$

where y is real output, y^* is full employment output, ky^* is the level of output desired, and a is the weight placed on inflation in the loss function. The desired output is above the full-employment level, either because distortions in the economy make the "natural" full employment level too low or because the policymaker has different preferences than the private sector.[5]

A short-run Phillips curve describes the movement of output around the natural rate in response to inflation surprises:

$$y = y^* + b(\pi - \pi^e), \quad (8.2)$$

where π^e is expected inflation.

The outcome of a one-period game ($T = 0$), where the private sector commits itself to π^e and then the policymaker sets monetary policy to hit a particular inflation rate, generally gives an equilibrium with an inflation bias. This is because once π^e is determined it is possible for the government to "surprise" the market and extract additional output at the expense of additional inflation, as the marginal benefits from output exceed the marginal costs of inflation in the mind of the policymaker at that moment. The rational-expectations equilibrium where expectations are correct (on average) gives, under discretionary policy, the inflation rate

$$\pi_d = a^{-1}b(k - 1)y^* \quad (8.3)$$

and the loss function

$$L_d = (k - 1)^2 y^{*2} (1 + a^{-1}b^2). \quad (8.4)$$

This equilibrium is worse than if the government were able to credibly commit to a zero inflation policy, giving $\pi_p = \pi_p^e = 0$, and a loss function (with unchanged equilibrium output at y^*) of

$$L_p = (k - 1)^2 y^{*2}. \quad (8.5)$$

The discretionary outcome is worse for the policymaker; however, without the ability to precommit credibly, the discretionary outcome is the equilibrium that will be obtained.

The practical implication of this theory is that moderate or even high ongoing inflation may be explained by the inability of the central bank to convince firms and wage earners that it will not take advantage of a situation where it could temporarily create an economic boom. After nominal wage and price contracts have been signed, firms and workers are "vulnerable" to an unanticipated monetary expansion and to an associated jump in inflation. They know that the government will have difficulty resisting this temptation, at least when the inflation rate is below a certain threshold, since it wants to increase output and lower unemployment. Without commitment by the central bank to a particular low-inflation policy stance, the private sector will expect an inflation rate just high enough so that the government has no incentive to increase it further—that is, a rate at which the costs of more inflation are balanced by the perceived benefits of the output gain. One way the central bank signals commitment is by its independence from the government.

A Monetary Rule as a Solution to Dynamic Inconsistency?

One proposed solution to the dynamic-inconsistency problem is to impose a monetary rule on the central bank. Kydland and Prescott argued for a rule in the broad sense, preempting discretionary actions on the part of the central bank to generate surprise inflations. Friedman's (1959) constant-monetary-growth rule is a much stricter version of this general principle.

The Bank of Japan followed a rule of sorts and had limited discretion over the stance of monetary policy during the Bretton Woods period (see chapter 4). The value of the yen against the US dollar remained at ¥360 from 1949 until the summer of 1971. With limited foreign-exchange reserves and capital controls, the current account was the primary binding constraint on monetary policy. Discretionary control over monetary policy did not really become an issue until after the collapse of the Bretton Woods system, when the external constraint was formally relaxed.[6] Nonetheless, the Bretton Woods rule wasn't designed to provide credibility for a low-inflation policy or to "import" credibility from abroad by having trend inflation determined by Japan's major trading partner countries, especially the United States.

The Bank of Japan moved toward a "money-focused" monetary policy in the mid 1970s, after the bout of high inflation. The monetary-growth trend, shown by the dashed line in figure 3.2, fell between 1975 and 1985, and the deviations from the announced M2 (later M2 + CDs) forecasts were seemingly small. Nonetheless, as we discussed in detail in chapter 3, the Bank of Japan never followed a constant-monetary-growth rule or targeted monetary growth.[7]

Economic Structure and Dynamic Inconsistency

Dynamic inconsistency is less of a problem, at least in principle, when there is relatively little output gain associated with inflation surprises (small b in equation 8.2) or, equivalently, when the short-run Phillips curve is steep. It should also be less of a problem when the policymaker's desired output level is close to the natural rate (k close to unity). Can either of these factors help explain Japan's relatively low inflation rate?

The short-run Phillips curve in Japan appears to be relatively steep by international comparison, indicating that there is relatively little to be gained in terms of output from a surprise inflation. This is consistent with a low ongoing inflation bias in Japan (Cargill and Hutchison 1990); it also suggests that there is little incentive for incumbent politicians to pressure the central bank to inflate before an election (see chapter 7). Table 8.1 presents Walsh's (1994) estimates of the short-run output gain from a nominal demand shock and Ball's (1994) calculations of the average "sacrifice ratio" during deflationary periods. Both sets of estimates suggest that output moves relatively little in response to changes in nominal demand or price in Japan compared to most other industrial countries. Walsh's estimate indicates that a 1 percent rise in aggregate demand increases output only 0.3 percent, ranking Japan 14th among the 21 countries he studied; Ball's (1994) calculations give Japan the lowest ranking among the 19 countries he studied. Other studies also indicate that the output gain (loss) associated with an inflation (disinflation) surprise is relatively low in Japan compared with most industrial countries.

Now let us turn to the desired or target output in Japan (ky^*). It may be the case that k is relatively close to unity because the policymakers' preferences are closer to the private sector's or because fewer distortions operate on the Japanese economy. Average unemployment in Japan during the period 1960–1994 was around 2 percent, the lowest among the industrial countries with the exception of Switzerland. The Japanese economy has grown quickly during most of the postwar period, consistently having lower unemployment and higher capacity-utilization rates than almost all other industrial countries. This may have led Japanese policymakers to more readily accept the "natural" output level (y^*) the economy was generating, placing little pressure on them to target even higher rates of growth. Indeed, Walsh (1996) finds that in a panel

Table 8.1
Tradeoff and sacrifice ratios of output to inflation.

	Estimated output gain after nominal demand shock[a]	Calculated sacrifice ratio[b]
Denmark	1.2	0.6
Germany	0.9	2.5
United States	0.8	2.3
Austria	0.7	0.5
Switzerland	0.7	0.9
Finland	0.6	0.7
Netherlands	0.6	0.3
Canada	0.5	1.2
Italy	0.5	1.5
Luxembourg	0.5	0.5
Australia	0.5	0.3
France	0.4	0.2
Belgium	0.3	1.0
Japan	**0.3**	**−0.2**
Sweden	0.3	0.5
Spain	0.3	0.9
New Zealand	0.2	0.5
Iceland	0.1	n.a.
Norway	0.1	n.a.
Ireland	0.1	0.7
United Kingdom	0.0	0.7

a. Estimated coefficients from regressions of (log) real GNP on change in (log) nominal GNP using annual data for 1972–1990 for each industrial country noted. A constant, a time trend, and a lagged (log) real GNP were also included in the regressions. Source: Walsh 1994.
b. Sacrifice ratios calculated as percentage real GNP (or GDP) decline divided by decline in CPI inflation. Average ratios for period of disinflation 1960–1991 are reported. Annual data are employed. Source: Ball 1994.

regression of 18 industrial countries low unemployment helps explain Japan's low average inflation rate. At the same time, Japan's recent memory includes near hyperinflation after the end of World War II and the "wild inflation" of the early 1970s. This may have convinced the public of the need for a low-inflation policy across a wide range of natural growth rates.

8.2 The Bank of Japan's Formal Decision-Making Structure

One of the main policy implications drawn from the literature on dynamic inconsistency is that an independent central bank, by being able to formulate and execute monetary policy without major interference from other government agencies or political authorities, may avoid inflation bias.[8] Consider the advantages of appointing a conservative central banker who gives a higher personal weight to inflation (a_b) than would the government (a)—again in the context of a single-period loss function (Rogoff 1985). And assume that this conservative central banker is given the opportunity to pursue these aims within an independent central-banking institution. Under these circumstances,

$$L_b = [1 + (b^2 / a_b)]L_p, \tag{8.6}$$

and the higher is the conservative central banker's inflation aversion (a_b), the lower is inflation and the closer is the equilibrium (and the policy loss) to the credible precommitment solution.[9]

Institutions

To what extent has low inflation in Japan been associated with an independent and conservative institutional structure for central banking? The Bank of Japan Law stipulates that the Policy Board is the highest authority on domestic monetary policy in Japan.[10] This board usually meets twice a week. There are seven members:

the Governor of the Bank of Japan (five-year term with voting rights)

four voting members (four-year terms), each with expertise or experience from city banking, regional banking, commerce and industry, or agriculture but not directly representing any of these interests

two nonvoting representatives, one from the Ministry of Finance and one from the Economic Planning Agency.

The governor is appointed by the cabinet and, by law, serves as the chairman of the Policy Board. Since 1969, governors have been picked alternately from within the Bank of Japan and from among former Ministry of Finance officials (table 8.2). The other four voting members of the Policy Board also are appointed by the cabinet subject to approval by both houses of the Diet. The representatives of the Ministry of Finance and the Economic Planning Agency, though not voting members of the board, facilitate "communication and consultation between the government and the Bank" (Nakao and Horii 1991, p. 27). Board members may not be dismissed except for such an obvious reason as physical or mental incapacity. No minutes of Policy Board meetings are disclosed.

Table 8.2
Governors of Bank of Japan.

Tenure	Name	Background
10/45–6/46	Eikichi Araki (first term)	Bank of Japan
6/46–12/54	Naoto Ichimada	Bank of Japan
12/54–11/56	Eikichi Araki (second term)	Bank of Japan
11/56–12/64	Masamichi Yamagiwa	Ministry of Finance
12/64–12/69	Makoto Usami	Mitsubishi Bank
12/69–12/74	Tadashi Sasaki	Bank of Japan
12/74–12/79	Teiichiro Morinaga	Ministry of Finance
12/79–12/84	Haruo Mayekawa	Bank of Japan
12/84–12/89	Satoshi Sumita	Ministry of Finance
12/89–12/94	Yasushi Mieno	Bank of Japan
12/94–present	Yasuo Matsushita	Ministry of Finance

Most important issues for the implementation of monetary policy are discussed and decided by an Executive Committee in a *marutaku* (round-table) meeting, in "accordance with the orientation of the Policy Board" (Nakao and Horii 1991, p. 27). The Executive Committee, made up of senior executives of the Bank of Japan, generally meets every business day except Wednesday. The governor plays the key role, serving both as the chief executive officer of the Bank and as a member of the Policy Board. Other members of the Executive Committee are the Senior Deputy Governor (five-year term), the Deputy Governor for International Relations (four-year term), and the Executive Directors of the Bank (at least three, serving four-year terms). The Senior Deputy Governor is appointed by the cabinet, while the Deputy Governor for International Relations and the Executive Directors (and other senior executives of the Bank) are appointed by the Finance Minister from persons recommended by the Governor. Traditionally, one Executive Director is a former Ministry of Finance official and the remainder are from inside the Bank of Japan.

An Executive Director may be dismissed for violating the law or if, in the view of the cabinet or Finance Minister, dismissal is necessary to achieve the goals of the Bank of Japan.

Division of Responsibilities

The Bank of Japan Law empowers the Bank to determine the official discount rate and the reserve requirements and to conduct open-market operations. The Policy Board of the Bank is given this formal responsibility, and, more generally, it sets the orientation of monetary policy and the framework for its implementation. Reserve-requirement changes decided by the Policy Board, however, require approval by the Finance Minister. The Finance Minister also is consulted on important policy matters such as changes in the discount rate.

Since 1947 the Finance Law has prohibited the Bank from underwriting government bonds or extending loans to the government. But the law allows the Bank to underwrite bills for short-term government finance (the balance remaining after public auction), which it routinely does, as well as to underwrite government bonds issued to refinance maturing debt (up to an amount authorized by the Diet). The latter occurred during the period of high government deficits between fiscal 1973 and fiscal 1988.

Formal Objectives

The Bank of Japan Law, enacted in 1882, is the original legal basis for a central bank in Japan. The law was revised in 1942 to reflect wartime conditions. The only significant change to the law since that time was the 1949 amendment establishing the Policy Board and giving it power over interest-rate policy.[11] In terms of formal objectives, Article 1 of the Bank of Japan Law provides the following:

> The Bank of Japan has, for its objective, the regulation of the currency, the control and facilitation of credit and finance, and the maintenance and fostering of the credit system, pursuant to the national policy, in order that the general economic activities of the nation might adequately be enhanced.

The fact that no mention is made of price stability reflects the fact that the law was revised in 1942, when institutional support of the war effort was given highest priority. According to the law, the Bank of Japan is clearly subordinate to the government; its mission is set "solely for achievement of national aims."

8.3 How Independent Is the Bank of Japan?

There are a number of possible ways to measure a central bank's independence. Perhaps the most important distinction, however, is between political independence and economic or functional independence.

Broadly, political independence is the ability of the central bank to select its policy objectives without excessive influence from the government. The criteria for political independence include the following:

whether the bank's governor and the board of directors are appointed by the government

whether government representatives sit on the bank's board

the length of the appointments of the bank's directors

whether government approval of monetary-policy decisions is required

whether the objective of "price stability" is explicitly or prominently part of the central-bank statute.

Economic independence, on the other hand, is the ability of the central bank to use the instruments of monetary policy without restrictions—for example,

the extent to which the central bank is required to finance government deficits

the extent to which interest-rate controls are imposed on the economy by the Ministry of Finance, the Treasury, or some other government agency

whether changes in the discount rate or in the reserve ratio must be approved by the government.

By these political and economic criteria, the Bank of Japan appears to be a formally *dependent* central bank. The governor of the Bank generally is chosen alternately from among former Ministry of Finance officials and from among individuals with Bank of Japan backgrounds. The Policy Board's members are appointed by the cabinet or directly by the Ministry of Finance. A Ministry of Finance representative is a nonvoting member of the Policy Board. The most senior Bank of Japan officials on the Executive Committee are also appointed either by the cabinet or directly by the Ministry of Finance, and one of the Executive Directors is usually a former Ministry of Finance official.

On major policy changes, the Bank of Japan generally seeks agreement from the Ministry of Finance. This is a formal obligation for changes in the reserve requirement, but the Bank of Japan also closely "consults" with the Ministry over changes in the discount rate.[12] Rarely have public disputes over policy arisen, but such disputes appear to have been more frequent in recent years. For example, in February 1990 contradictory statements by the Governor of the Bank of Japan and the Deputy Minister of Finance led to a public controversy over interest-rate policy between the two authorities (Eijffinger and van Rixtel 1992).

The Bank of Japan's mandate is consistent with virtually any set of formal objectives, depending on the national priorities of the moment as formulated by the government. These may include fostering high growth, directing credit to targeted sectors, achieving stability, or other objectives. Suzuki (1987, p. 305) interprets the last part of Article 1 quite broadly as a mandate to "foster the stable development of the Japanese economy."

In any case, no formal restrictions preclude the government, and the Ministry of Finance in particular, from pressuring the Bank of Japan to follow certain objectives.[13] Indeed, the main policy objectives of the Bank have changed significantly over time. In the 1950s, and to a lesser extent in the 1960s, an important aim was to channel credit to high-priority sectors identified by the government. This aim was imbedded in an overall governmental strategy of rapid reindustrialization and economic growth. Since the mid 1970s, however, the Bank has focused on price and financial stability as its primary objectives. For example, a recent Bank of Japan report (1993, p. 1) states: "The Bank of Japan has two missions: stabilizing the value of money and fostering a sound and safe financial system—both of which contribute to the stability of the Japanese economy." But at times other factors—particularly attempts to stabilize exchange rates—have played important roles in the formulation of policy. The latter objective clearly came into conflict with price stability after the Plaza Agreement. (See chapter 4.)

International Rankings of Central-Bank Independence

International rankings of central banks by their relative degrees of independence generally give the Bank of Japan a low rating. Cargill (1994) compares the rankings given by four recent studies. Bade and Parkin (1982), Burdekin et al. (1991), and Grilli et al. (1991) use an average of political and economic indicators of central-bank independence in their indices, while the index of Cukierman, Webb, and Neyapti (1993) is based entirely on legal institutional structure. Three of the indices are consistent, with relatively low rankings for the Bank of Japan.[14]

Cukierman, Webb, and Neyapti 1993, in the most ambitious effort to date, give the Bank of Japan a rank of 0.18 on a 0–1 scale, with 1

Table 8.3
Measurements of central-bank independence, 1980–1989, with 0 representing minimal independence and 1 representing maximum independence. Source: Cukierman 1992.

	Japan	US	Germany	Switzerland
Chief executive officer				
Term of office?	0.50	0.25	1.00	0.75
Who appoints?	0.25	0.50	0.75	0.25
Provisions for dismissal?	0.83	0.00	1.00	n.a.
Allowed to hold another office?	0.50	1.00	0.00	1.00
Policy formulation				
Who formulates monetary policy?	0.67	n.a.	0.67	n.a.
Government directives and resolution of conflict?	0.00	0.20	1.00	1.00
CB role in formulation of govt. budget?	0.00	0.00	0.00	0.00
Price stability given high priority?	0.00	0.40	1.00	0.00
Limitations on lending				
Limitations on advances to govt.?	0.00	1.00	0.67	1.00
Limitations on securitized lending?	0.00	0.33	0.67	n.a.
Restrictions on interest rates?	0.25	0.25	0.25	0.25
Ranking from summary measures of central-bank independence				
Overall legal independence[a]	64	6	2	1
Overall legal independence[b]	20	4	2	1
CB governor turnover rate[c]	18	10	9	13

a. Sample: 68 countries.
b. Sample: 21 industrial countries.
c. Sample: 19 industrial countries.

representing maximum independence. The details of the study as it applies to the Bank of Japan are given in table 8.3, where we compare the results for Japan, the United States, Germany, and Switzerland. In terms of "legal independence," using an average of the indicators shown in the table and other indicators not shown in the table, the Bank of Japan ranks 64th out of a group of 68 central banks in the study and 20th out of a group of 21 central banks in the industrial countries. Using a measure of the turnover rate of central-bank governors, the Bank of Japan ranks 18th out of 19 central banks in the industrial countries.

Although the negative association between inflation and central-bank independence is not as strong as is generally claimed, there is still a significant link between the two for the industrial countries.[15] The simple

Table 8.4
Central-bank independence and predicted inflation in 17 industrial countries: values predicted from a regression of inflation on a constant and an index of legal independence for 17 industrial countries (Switzerland, Germany, Austria, United States, Canada, Netherlands, Ireland, Luxembourg, United Kingdom, France, Sweden, Finland, Italy, Spain, Belgium, Japan, Norway).

	1960–1973	1975–1994	1960–1994
Japan			
Actual	5.7	3.2	5.0
Predicted	4.8	7.3	6.8
Error	0.9	−4.1	−1.8
United States			
Actual	2.9	5.3	4.7
Predicted	3.7	4.8	4.7
Error	−0.8	0.5	−0.0
Germany			
Actual	3.1	3.2	3.4
Predicted	3.3	3.8	3.8
Error	−0.2	−0.6	−0.4
Regression statistics			
R^2	0.28	0.28	0.37
SEE	0.86	1.99	1.99
Inflation average	4.2	5.9	5.6

relationship between average inflation rates for 17 industrial countries and the Cukierman-Webb-Neyapti (1993) ranking of independence is captured by simple regressions run separately over the periods 1960–1973, 1975–1994, and 1960–1994. The summary statistics and predicted values (for Japan, the United States, and Germany) are given in table 8.4. The model is reasonably accurate for Japan in the Bretton Woods period (1960–1973), predicting 4.8 percent inflation against an actual value of 5.7 percent. However, the model performs poorly for Japan in the latter period, predicting 7.3 percent inflation against the 3.2 percent realized. Japan is the largest outlier (prediction error: −4.1 percent) in the 1973–1994 regression. This is evident from figure 8.2, where the squares represent actual values of inflation, the diamonds represent predicted value of inflation, and the symbol in the lower left corner represents Japan. Germany and Switzerland, represented by the two symbols in the lower right corner of the figure, have low prediction errors.[16]

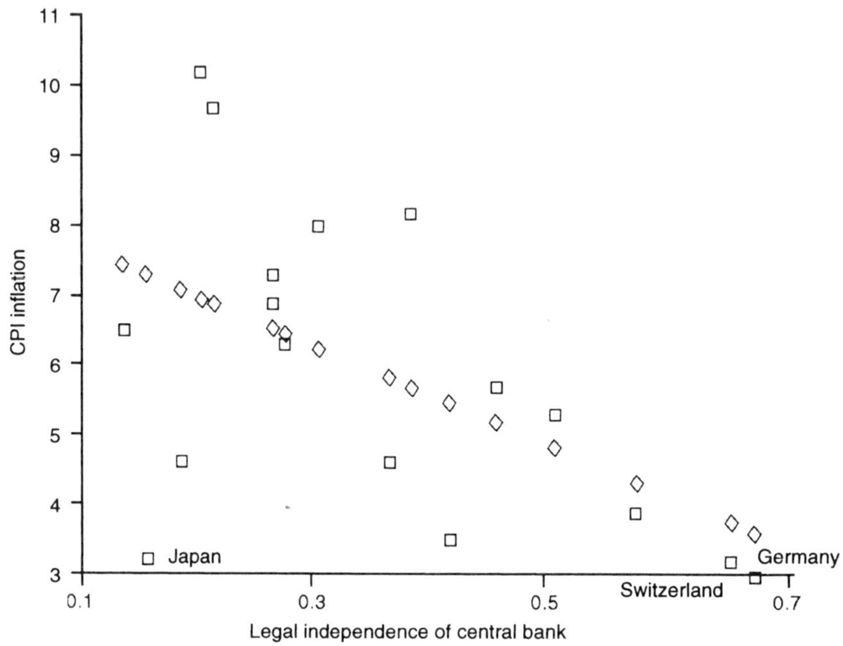

Figure 8.2
Central-bank independence and inflation, 1975–1994. Actual (squares) and predicted (diamonds) inflation.

Formal Dependence and Price Stabilization

Japan's good inflation record since 1975 suggests that price stability can be achieved within an institutional setting in which the central bank lacks formal independence. This experience also raises questions about whether formal independence is either necessary or sufficient for good price performance.[17]

Although we have emphasized the Bank of Japan's formal dependence on the Ministry of Finance and the cooperation between these institutions in setting policy, in a number of instances conflicts over interest-rate and regulatory policies have emerged. For example, the Bank of Japan has been in conflict with the Ministry of Finance over the pace and the extent of interest-rate liberalization, the subsidizing of the Postal Savings System, the development of secondary markets in government securities, and deposit insurance (Cargill 1989). There have also been public disputes over the timing and extent of discount-rate changes.[18]

In all these circumstances, the Bank of Japan has asserted a degree of policy independence beyond its legislated charter. Its policy stance is given force by its technical expertise, by the memory of the wild inflation, by its considerable prestige in the financial and political communities, and in several instances by the strength of personality of the central bank's governor.

8.4 Would an Anti-Inflation Ministry of Finance Be Functionally Equivalent to an Independent Central Bank?

The Bank of Japan is not formally independent of the Ministry of Finance. However, inflation bias might be avoided if the ministry itself were an independent agent of the government, delegated authority over monetary policy and was able to credibly commit to long-term price stability. If the Ministry of Finance were conservative in the sense of having a stronger aversion to inflation than politicians or other ministries of the government have, that would help explain low inflation.

The Ministry of Finance is indeed conservative in the sense of being very reluctant to use fiscal policy to manage aggregate demand. This reluctance to use discretionary policy, known in Japan as the "Ministry of Finance view," may be characterized as anti-Keynesian. It is rooted in the early postwar experience with near-hyperinflation and in the wild inflation. Moreover, the Ministry of Finance demonstrated the ability to commit to a long-term policy of budget deficit reduction in the late 1970s and in the 1980s, despite strong domestic and international pressure for fiscal expansion at several points (Cargill and Hutchison, forthcoming). The program included a spending freeze and repeated proposals (which eventually succeeded after a decade of attempts) to introduce a consumption tax.[19] The serious mistake of expansionary fiscal and monetary policy in the early 1970s, pushed through by Prime Minister Tanaka, was resented and resisted by most high-level Ministry of Finance officials (Henning 1994).

The conservative views of the Ministry of Finance on monetary policy are reflected by the performance of former officials of this ministry during their terms as governors of the Bank of Japan. Some have argued that governors chosen from former Ministry of Finance officials are less "independent minded" and give in more readily to political pressure.[20] However, there is no clear statistical evidence supporting this argument, and the casual evidence may be misleading.[21] It has been pointed out, for example, that when Haruo Mayekawa (a career Bank of Japan official) was appointed governor, in December 1979, he immediately petitioned the government to raise interest rates, taking a more aggressive anti-inflationary stance than his predecessor, Teiichiro Morinaga, a former Ministry of Finance official. But it was under Governor Morinaga's leadership that the "money-focused" policy, which led to a drop in inflation, was introduced.

More generally, the power and the comparative autonomy of the Japanese bureaucracy are well known. A high percentage of the top officials of Japanese ministries are career bureaucrats rather than political appointees, and many have spent an entire career within one ministry. This fosters institutional loyalty and independence from the political process. Moreover, the stability of control at the top echelons of decision making in the ministries, despite numerous changes in LDP leadership, gives the bureaucracy considerable control over economic policy. The ministers of finance change frequently (generally with each change in prime minister), but most of the top officials stay, and the operation of the ministry is little affected.[22,23]

Burdekin and Willet (1991) also observe that Japanese monetary policy appears less politicized than the formal dependence of the Bank of Japan on the government would suggest. They attribute this to the centrality of the finance ministry's role and to "an unusually autonomous position for that Ministry within the government bureaucracy."

Indeed, in numerous cases the Bank of Japan was shielded by the Ministry of Finance from political pressures to run more expansionary policies. The cost of such protection is high: by tradition the Ministry of Finance appoints an official from its own ranks for the governorship of the Bank of Japan for alternating terms. Nonetheless, as Henning (1994) points out, the objectives of the Ministry of Finance are broader than those of the Bank of Japan, and although ministerial autonomy shields the Bank from politicians it does not shield the Bank from pressures from the Ministry to use monetary policy to achieve those objectives.

An autonomous Ministry of Finance is not functionally equivalent to a conservative central banker focusing primarily on price stability. For example, in the second half of the 1980s the Ministry of Finance, preoccupied with fiscal austerity, reportedly pushed for a more stimulative monetary policy to pursue exchange-rate objectives—a policy stance that contributed to the bubble economy.

8.5 Reputation and Long-Lived Agents

A highly autonomous and independent finance ministry may not be the functional equivalent of an independent central bank, in that it may have identical preferences to other parts of the government. But relative autonomy and independence may increase the ability of the Ministry of Finance to credibly commit to a longer-term policy of low inflation. Fratianni and Huang (1992) show that independent central banks are better able to commit, leading to lower inflation even if the central bank and the government have identical preferences. The same logic applies to the Ministry of Finance.

The stability and the longevity of the Ministry of Finance bureaucracy means that reputation may be more important in Japan than it is in most other industrial countries. One result derived from the Kreps-Wilson (1982) reputation framework is that, as the horizon (T) of the policymaker goes into the indefinite future, provided discount rates (δ) are sufficiently low, the likelihood of obtaining the reputational equilibrium with zero inflation increases.

Suppose that the horizon is infinite ($T = \infty$) and that policymakers have the loss function specified in equation 8.1. Fischer (1990) considers the nonstochastic case where the government starts by consistently following a non-inflationary policy ($\pi = 0$) but then is tempted to deviate and generate an inflation surprise. If an inflation surprise is generated (i.e., if "fooling" occurs), then the net gain is equal to the one-period gain (equal to the precommitment loss less the "fooling" loss function) less the present discounted value (PDV) of the loss that starts one period later (discretionary loss less the precommitment loss) and continues indefinitely:

$$\text{PDV net gain} = \lambda L_p[\delta - (1 + \lambda)][\delta(1 + \lambda)]^{-1},$$

where $\lambda = b^2/a$ and where δ is the discount rate of the government. (A lower value of δ implies that a high value is placed on future outcomes.) The lower the discount rate (i.e., the more forward looking the government), the lower is the PDV net gain from an inflationary surprise (opportunistic behavior) and the more likely it is that the government will continue with the precommitment policy. The role of λ is indeterminate, since both the gains and the losses are increasing in λ. Moreover, in stochastic models (Tabellini 1985; Backus and Driffill 1985) one general result is that, as the horizon goes to infinity (i.e., when a policymaker, a government, or a political party has been power for along time), the reputational equilibrium with zero inflation is obtained (Fischer 1990). The reason for this is that, once credibility as a low-inflation central bank is lost, there is a long period during which the private sector expects higher inflation, and that makes for a higher loss function.

The notion that the public "punishes" policymakers for inflation may be unrealistic and is subject to a coordination problem.[24] Another interpretation, emphasized by Cukierman (1992), is that punishment is a by product of the public's attempt to rationally learn about the changing objectives of policymakers. The private sector, trying to ascertain the private information held by the central bank, tries to discern the central bank's preferences from the realized inflation rate and thereby sets its own expectations about future inflation. The public may interpret an inflation surprise as indicating the central bank's preferences (i.e., little aversion to inflation) and set inflation expectations higher accordingly. This, in turn, raises the future costs to the central bank of inflating. In this sense, an inflation surprise causes the central bank to lose its reputation as an inflation fighter.

Single-Party Control and Reputation

In most respects, however, it would be difficult to differentiate empirically the "reputation" explanation for low inflation in Japan and the explanation of a conservative and independent Ministry of Finance—Bank of Japan coalition. Cargill and Hutchison (1990) and Henning (1994) argue that there is little shifting of responsibility for the control of economic policy and its consequences among the government, the ministries, and the central bank. The Bank of Japan is legally subordinate to the Ministry of Finance, and no claims of formal independence are suggested. The Ministry of Finance and the LDP (until 1993, at least) had generally assumed responsibility for monetary policy and its inflationary consequences. The government agencies, viewed in their entirety, took responsibility for economic policy, and the government agencies were closely identified with the LDP.[25]

The LDP had a very long-term view of economic policy, and this may have translated into the precommitment low-inflation situation associated with a reputational equilibrium. A very strong dominant political party may generate discipline on politicians for other reasons. Harrington (1992), for example, argues that, because political parties are long-lived and politicians value the ideology reflected by the party, they will not "cheat" on promises. It is clear that the LDP is long-lived, but whether its politicians value a particular ideology is questionable.[26]

The Japanese experience is also consistent with a body of literature suggesting that political stability (i.e., few shifts in government) is associated with low inflation (Cukierman, Edwards, and Tabellini 1993).

8.6 Is Reputation Enough?

The autonomy of the Japanese Ministry of Finance and its ability to shield the Bank of Japan from outside political pressures have limits, however. These limits have been tested, and there have been some concessions, such as the monetary expansion after the 1987 Louvre Accord. Without a formally independent central bank—or, perhaps preferably, an explicit contract (see Walsh 1995c) specifying the objectives of the central bank (goal dependence) but allowing instruments to be chosen freely (instrument independence)—how these conflicts are resolved will depend on a number of political and economic factors. Resolution is also likely to vary over time, depending on particular circumstances and personalities.[27] In this context, the personalities of the Prime Minister, the Minister of Finance, and the Governor of the Bank of Japan are especially important. In Japan, personality factors have usually played only a small role in determining the overall stance of policy, but several notable exceptions stand out.

In 1972, Prime Minister Kekuei Tanaka, the most colorful and powerful Japanese politician of the postwar era, insisted on lowering interest rates despite Bank of Japan officials' recommendations to do precisely the opposite (Ito 1992). Tanaka wanted a strong economy and sought support of his regional development policy under the slogan "Transforming the Japanese Archipelago." The result was disastrous, contributing to the infamous wild inflation. In 1974, the inflation rate peaked at over 30 percent. This was caused by a combination of easy monetary policy in the early 1970s (due in part to Tanaka's insistence on discount-rate cuts) and the 1973 oil shock.[28] The immediate effect of this experience was to give the Bank of Japan and the Ministry of Finance more power to follow policies with less political pressure. Politicians' confidence in the monetary field was undermined, a social consensus on keeping politicians out of the monetary field was emerging, and Bank of Japan and Ministry of Finance officials increased their resolve to resist political pressures in formulating policy (Henning 1994, p. 78). In particular, the

Bank of Japan introduced a "money-focused" policy orientation in the mid 1970s and began to act decisively at other critical junctures when inflation threats were evident. At the time of the second oil shock, the Bank of Japan moved (with little resistance from the Ministry of Finance) quickly and decisively against inflation, increasing the discount rate from 3.5 to 9.0 percent between mid 1979 and early 1980. Similarly, a decade later, former governor Yasushi Mieno, widely viewed as the strongest and most independent-minded governor ever, raised interest rates from 2.5 to 6.0 percent between early 1989 and the end of 1990 in a (perhaps too) successful effort to stop the "bubble economy" and asset-price inflation.[29]

The Bank of Japan, working with the Ministry of Finance, has built up a high reputation as a price-stabilizing central bank over the past 20 years. With the Bank of Japan's reputation as a "strong" central bank increasing, however, the benefits from a bout of inflation also rise. Will this create a problem in Japan? The policy uncertainty that followed the defeat of the LDP in 1993, combined with the greater short-term benefits associated with an inflation surprise, may provide stronger incentives for politicians to override Ministry of Finance's traditional power over monetary policy. The comparative autonomy of the Ministry-Bank coalition has not yet been seriously challenged, and the reputations of these two institutions remains intact, though the reputation of the Ministry has fallen in response to the banking problems discussed in chapter 6. But with the long period of LDP dominance over, and with new political coalitions forming, it is unclear whether the autonomy afforded Japanese ministries generally, and the Ministry of Finance in particular, will continue.

A general characteristic of reputational models is that multiple equilibria exist. Large shocks, both economic (e.g., a large recession) and political (e.g., a weak central-bank governor) may destabilize the system, moving the economy to the high-inflation discretionary situation. Furthermore, as memories of the wild inflation wane, the anti-inflationary fervor of the Bank-Ministry coalition may diminish.

Conclusion

The literature linking central-bank independence to good inflation performance has devoted relatively little attention to the Bank of Japan. Debelle and Fischer (1994), for example, state that one of the foundations for the "new orthodoxy" as to the desirability of central-bank independence is based on the success of the Bundesbank and the German economy. Clearly, Germany has both a very independent central bank and a good inflation record and is an interesting case study. However, Japan's average inflation since the mid 1970s has been about the same as Germany's, and its economic performance has been far better despite the Bank of Japan's ranking as one of the least independent central banks. Whereas most international comparisons linking central-bank independence and economic performance simply treat the Bank of Japan as an exceptional case, we emphasize the independence of the Bank-Ministry coalition from the agendas of politicians.

The central banks of Chile, France, Mexico, New Zealand, and Venezuela all have had their independence enhanced, and the Bank of France and the Bank of England are debating the merits of more independence. Walsh (1995b) provides a survey of recent movements toward independence, and Posen (1995) and Fischer (1995) offer related discussions. The Maastricht Treaty also requires national central banks participating in the European System of Central Banks (a precursor to monetary union) to meet a prescribed standard of independence. Similarly, the Bank of Japan has pushed for legislative changes giving it more independence. In November 1996 the Central Bank Study Group, a working group set up by the government, issued a report[30] recommending reforms that would enhance the central bank's institutional independence. The Central Bank Study Group recommended a number of reforms, including abolishing the Bank of Japan's Executive Committee, giving more prominence to the Policy Board, giving the Policy Board authority to make final judgments on monetary policy (provided its relationship with the government is clarified), forbidding the government to dismiss the Bank's executives or members of the Policy Board for reasons of differences of opinion over policy, and abolishing the government's broad power to give orders to the Bank. The report also calls for the Policy Board to publicize summaries and minutes of its meetings.

Prime Minister Ryutaro Hashimoto accepted the report and stated that reform of the central bank is the most important policy item on his cabinet's agenda.[31] The Financial System Research Council, an advisory body to the Minister of Finance, is charged with making specific suggestions for changes in the Bank of Japan Law taking the recommendations of the Central Bank Study Group into account. It appears likely that the Bank of Japan will be given more independence, not because of economic arguments over the desirability of this institutional change, but rather as an attempt by the Ministry of Finance to avoid deeper and more widespread reforms that may be inspired by public criticism of its handling of the financial crisis.

The experience of Japan, however, demonstrates that avoiding inflation bias does not require central-bank independence. Japan's relatively autonomous government bureaucracy generally, and the position of the Ministry of Finance in particular, has contributed to a credible commitment to low inflation. But the objectives of the Ministry of Finance are much broader than price stability alone, so an independent Ministry of Finance—Bank of Japan coalition is not functionally equivalent to an independent central bank. Rather, we argue, discipline on monetary policy is derived from the long-lived nature of the bureaucracy and from the long dominance of the Liberal Democratic Party. Because of the long tenure of Japanese policymakers, reputation is more important in Japan than most other industrial countries.

However, this state of affairs may not be stable, particularly in light of the changing nature of Japan's politics (due to the LDP's loss of power) and of the country's weaker economic performance. An equilibrium based on reputation may be destabilized by large shocks. The wild inflation gave the Bank of Japan—Ministry of Finance coalition greater insulation from politicians, pushed it to adopt a "money-focused" policy, and set the stage for 20 years of low inflation. Another large shock could push inflation higher. The susceptibility of the present system to large political and economic shocks provides an argument for institutional independence. Independence serves as a buffer against large shocks even when a central bank has an established reputation as an inflation fighter. With this uncertainty in mind, granting the Bank of Japan greater political independence could prove worthwhile.

9 Concluding Comments

Various aspects of central banking in Japan, ranging from its historical roots to the present crisis, have been explored in this book. Particular attention has been devoted to the relationship among central banking, politics, and institutional structure in Japan. The issues of most interest have changed over time, in line with the fundamental transformations in Japan's real and financial sectors, fluctuations in economic performance, and domestic and foreign political pressures. Most of these issues, however, may be viewed as problems of political economy, which analyzes the traditional problems of central banking within a political and institutional context.

A number of our themes have broader implications for our understanding of the workings of central banks, monetary policy, and financial structure. We conclude by highlighting some of the main themes of our work and drawing out some of the broader implications.

9.1 The Bank of Japan and the Japanese Economy

The High-Growth Period

The Japanese economy underwent fundamental changes in the postwar period, and Bank of Japan policy both reacted to and played an important role in this process. Japan's rapid reindustrialization, with double-digit output growth in the 1950s and the 1960s, is impressive by any standard, and it became the model for the East Asian economic "miracle." Monetary policy in Japan during this period operated under constraints and with objectives similar to those facing many newly industrialized economies today. The primary economic objective was rapid economic growth, and monetary policy and financial policy were expected to play important roles in this process by providing adequate liquidity and ensuring that funds flowed smoothly from the large surplus household sector to the large-deficit corporate sector. Price stability was also a desired objective, but it was secondary to rapid economic growth.

During this time, the Bank of Japan was constrained by the requirement under the Bretton Woods system that the exchange rate remain fixed at 360 yen per dollar, and it was operating in a financial environment with extensive interest-rate regulations and administrative guidance over an internationally isolated financial structure. Despite these constraints, the Bank of Japan achieved the majority of its objectives. While Japan's average inflation rate (4–5 percent) was higher than those of other industrialized economies, the Bank of Japan's policy can be regarded as successful in view of the special needs of the Japanese economy and the priority placed on growth and reindustrialization.

"Wild Inflation" and Transition

Fundamental changes in the economic environment and political pressures (including a slowdown in growth potential, the oil shock, and the increasing misalignment of exchange rates under the Bretton Woods system) led to the first major failure of Bank of Japan policy. In the late 1960s and the early 1970s, the Bank of Japan was pressured into an overly expansionary monetary policy in a futile effort to maintain double-digit GDP growth. The attempt to maintain the exchange rate fixed at 360 yen per dollar, despite mounting evidence that this rate was substantially undervalued, also contributed to expansionary policy. The result was severe inflation pressure. In 1973, when the central bank moved to restrain monetary growth, the first oil-price shock occurred. The result was the infamous "wild inflation."

This first major mistake by the Bank of Japan since the move to floating rates is attributable to a combination of economic and political causes. The economic environment was highly volatile; however, it was not clear at the time that the decline in output growth reflected a drop in the economy's full-employment growth path. The inflationary consequences of the oil shock and of the attempt to keep the exchange rate fixed also were not obvious. Opposition to expansionary monetary policy would probably have been stronger if the true risks had been clearer. This experience points not only to the difficulties of assessing the correct monetary stance in a rapidly changing and uncertain economic environment, but also to the risks of allowing policy to be determined by political expediency.

Economic Stability and the "Money-Focused" Policy

By 1975, the recognition of the policy mistake and a new operating environment allowed the Bank of Japan to focus attention on gradually slowing the rate of monetary growth and achieving greater price stability. The real sector quickly adjusted to the oil-price shock, and by this time it was clear that a slower economic growth path was inevitable. But although economic growth slowed in the 1970s and 1980s, it was still impressive on an absolute standard. Japan experienced sustained growth in the 3–5 percent range and low rates of inflation over this period, despite a very large real appreciation of the yen exchange rate after the collapse of the Bretton Woods system, despite significant structural changes, and despite a second oil-price shock in 1979–80.

The financial system evolved to a more competitive and internationally open structure as the result of a series of market and regulatory innovations that removed interest-rate controls, relaxed constraints on the inflow and outflow of capital, and permitted an enhanced role for competitive forces in the allocation of credit. By the mid 1980s, sustained economic growth had also elevated Japan's economic position: with an aggregate GNP second only to that of the United States, Japan was the largest creditor nation in the world. Japan's international financial ties also rapidly expanded during the late 1980s as many Japanese corporations and financial institutions went abroad with direct and portfolio investments.

Our work has depicted the mid 1970s as a watershed in the evolution of Bank of Japan policy. The transformation from a fixed exchange rate and a rather closed economy to a large open economy and a floating exchange rate changed the Bank of Japan's operating environment. The Bank now had more flexibility to pursue various objectives of policy, since it was free of the fixed-exchange-rate constraint and since financial liberalization enhanced the channels through which monetary policy impacted the economy. In addition, the policy errors made during the late 1960s and the early 1970s, which inflated the economy, provided the Bank of Japan with enhanced political independence with which to pursue the objective of price stability.

Public consensus called for greater price stability, and the Bank of Japan introduced a new "money-focused" monetary policy to achieve this objective. The policy called for greater attention to monetary growth, more flexibility in interest rates, and quarterly announcements of monetary-growth projections. The new monetary procedures were not traditional "monetarist." That is, short-term monetary targets were not followed strictly, base drift was allowed (indeed, deviations from publicly announced projections were typically followed by further deviations), and policy was formulated both in response to the state of the business cycle and in response to other considerations (such as the level of the exchange rate). These procedures proved sufficient, however, to establish a high degree of credibility with the public and to stabilize inflationary expectations. This became particularly evident when the Bank of Japan reacted to the second oil-price shock by quickly and substantially raising interest rates to hold inflation in check, which resulted in a short-lived and (by international standards) modest rise in inflation and in the best economic performance among the major industrial countries—GNP growth in Japan never fell below 3 percent during the worldwide 1980–1982 recession. We characterized this episode as the high-water mark of the new "money-focused" policy.

The Bubble Economy and the Bank Crisis

The desire to manage exchange rates more actively and to coordinate economic policies internationally after the Plaza and Louvre G7 meetings overshadowed policy in the second half of the 1980s, when Japan's monetary policy was set on a more expansionary course. This was not fully apparent at the time, both because financial deregulation had made growth in the monetary aggregates difficult to interpret and because Japan was experiencing (at least initially) virtual price stability. However, the period was characterized by a surge in economic activity and a rapid rise in asset prices (land, equities, etc.). Monetary policy accommodated this "bubble," which had its roots as well in the far-reaching changes in financial structure and regulation over the previous decade, in the extensive government deposit guarantees, and in the general optimism over the continued growth prospects and rapid accumulation of wealth of the Japanese economy.

The collapse of asset prices was initiated by the decision of the Bank of Japan to raise the discount rate in May 1989 despite opposition from the Ministry of Finance. But though the timing may have varied, there appears little doubt that asset prices would eventually have fallen to bring them more in line with economic fundamentals. As it happened, the collapse of asset prices and the deep recession that followed revealed significant weaknesses in Japan's financial and regulatory structure.

9.2 Exchange Rates and International Policy Cooperation

Japanese monetary policy is quite sensitive to exchange-rate developments, despite the move to a floating exchange rate in the early 1970s. The Bank of Japan's intervention in the foreign-exchange market has been designed primarily to moderate exchange-rate movements, following a "leaning against the wind" operating strategy. The Japanese experience clearly demonstrates the conflict between exchange-rate stability and the achievement of domestic objectives—a central theme of chapter 4. This conflict has been exacerbated by the intense pressure on the real value of the yen exchange rate to appreciate in line with high productivity growth over most of the past 25 years (Marston 1987). Rather than contribute to domestic stability (as often argued in the European context, where emphasis is placed on importing "credibility" from the center country), attempts to limit exchange-rate fluctuations have greatly increased economic volatility in Japan. A number of East Asian countries, also with strong fundamentals leading to pressure for real appreciation, have recently experienced a similar conflict (Glick et al. 1995).

Exchange-rate stability is often viewed as desirable in its own right, and the specific objective of moderating yen appreciation has strong political support from those concerned with export competitiveness. Despite efforts by the Bank of Japan to sterilize intervention operations, Japan's monetary policy has tended to be expansionary when the yen appreciates. Of the four episodes of sharp yen appreciation, two clearly resulted in expansionary monetary policies and one led to an expansionary fiscal policy.

The three episodes that led to expansionary policy responses, in turn, had adverse effects. Pressures on the yen to appreciate in the last stage of the Bretton Woods system and the consequent stimulative monetary policy in 1971–72 were partly responsible for the wild inflation of 1973–74. The Bonn summit coincided with the 1978 yen appreciation (or dollar depreciation), at which time Japan agreed to implement public-spending measures if growth fell short of an ambitious 7 percent target. These measures were subsequently implemented, and the already-large budget deficits and the government debt burden grew worse. The sharp appreciation of 1985–86 coincided with the Plaza Agreement and was followed by the Louvre Accord, both of which sanctioned more activist attempts to manage exchange rates. In the Plaza communiqué, dollar depreciation was welcomed, and Japan alone committed to the "flexible management of monetary policy with due attention to the exchange rate." Continued sharp yen appreciation was eventually viewed with alarm, however, and after the spring of 1986 the Bank of Japan undertook massive intervention operations and switched to an expansionary monetary stance, thus contributing to the asset-price inflation of the late 1980s and the dramatic boom-and-bust cycle of 1986–1995.

9.3 Money, Financial Regulation, and the Bubble Economy

Several causes of the bubble economy beyond expansionary monetary policy were identified in chapter 5: financial liberalization, rapid wealth accumulation, expectations of continued strong economic growth, and a great deal of speculative activity in property and equity markets. Lax monetary policy was initiated in an attempt to limit yen appreciation and fulfill promises made in the Louvre Accord. But fears of a financial collapse after the October 1987 stock market collapse, and technical difficulties in interpreting monetary growth during a period of significant financial transformation, also led to an overly expansionary monetary stance, which was maintained too long.

In view of the rise in asset prices so far above fundamental values, a collapse at some point was inevitable. When it occurred in the first half of the 1990s, many financial institutions were faced with a nonperforming-loan problem of major dimensions. This was the focus of chapter 6. With benefit of hindsight, it is clear that bank supervision was too lenient during the asset-inflation years—especially in the context of a pervasive system of deposit guarantees, which provided additional incentives to assume risk. Financial liberalization, which started in the mid 1970s and picked up pace in the 1980s, should have been accompanied by stricter supervision of bank balance sheets and lending practices and by a more explicit consideration of the risk incentives embedded in deposit guarantees.

In view of the number of bank failures and insolvencies of *jusen* (housing-loan) companies, it is also clear that the problem of nonperforming loans should have been dealt with more aggressively and much earlier, probably in 1991 or 1992. Forbearance policy, or wait-and-see attitudes, with the faint hope of quick asset-price recovery, proved to be very costly. Nonperforming loans and insolvent financial institutions will plague Japanese financial regulators for some time and will necessitate a substantial infusion of public funds at some point. The upturn in the economy that started in mid 1996 will ease the nonperforming loan problem, but at some point the Bank of Japan may face a difficult choice between providing sufficient liquidity to support a weak financial system and limiting monetary growth to control inflation. This was not a conflict during the lengthy recession, but it may arise once the recovery is in full swing.

The nonperforming-loan problem and related issues have been a subject of intense discussion and debate in Japan. The need for reform is clear. Prime Minister Ryutaro Hashimoto announced in November 1996 that his government would undertake an extensive deregulation of Japan's financial system by 2001—a proposal likened by senior officials to the "Big Bang" financial deregulation in the United Kingdom more than a decade ago. The exact nature of these reforms, the timetable for implementation, and indeed whether the reforms will be as sweeping as promised, is still uncertain at this time.

9.4 Political Business Cycles and Central-Bank Independence

The Bank of Japan must be given credit for achieving one of the lowest average inflation rates in the world, on a par with Germany and Switzerland, since the mid 1970s. In part this reflects the move to a money-focused monetary policy, which was allowed by the dissolution of the Bretton Woods system of fixed exchange rates (under which monetary policy was in large part set by balance-of-payments conditions). The new operating procedure and the relaxation of external constraints gave the Bank of Japan the freedom to initially pursue a disinflationary policy and then maintain a consistently low rate of inflation. But what motivated the Bank of Japan, given this opportunity, to pursue such a low-inflation policy? Presumably there were forces pushing for more expansionary policies than were in fact pursued.

We have seen that low inflation on average does not imply that the Bank of Japan focused solely on an inflation target, and that the Bank was not immune from political pressures. The state of the business cycle, exchange considerations, and political agreements to coordinate policies internationally all figured in the formulation of policy.

In chapter 7 we also saw that there is a discernible "political business cycle" in Japan, though it is not of the form usually postulated for the

United States. The Japanese political system has been characterized by the dominance of the Liberal Democratic Party for most of the period since World War II, and Japan's parliamentary system allows for irregular intervals between elections. In this context, the LDP has often taken the state of business cycle into account when deciding the timing of elections, in the hope of strengthening its position in the Diet. Economic conditions are a factor in electoral outcomes in Japan, justifying "opportunistic" behavior of this form. There is also some evidence, albeit not conclusive, that fiscal and monetary policies tend to be more expansionary before elections ("manipulative" behavior). Moreover, in view of recent political and economic developments in Japan, political-economic interactions of this sort are likely to increase.

Despite these pressures, the Bank of Japan has achieved a remarkable inflation performance on average over a 20-year period. We explored this in chapter 8, seeking to explain the motivations and incentives behind Bank of Japan actions (as opposed to changes in technical operating procedures) that led to low monetary growth and low inflation. The Japanese solution to "inflation bias" is relevant to the broad issue of central-bank institutional reform, which is either on the agenda or already in place in many countries (including New Zealand, Canada, and France) and in some regions (as in the case of the European Central Bank).

Two frequently suggested solutions to the problem of inflation bias—setting a mechanical monetary growth rule and granting the central bank legal independence—were not adopted in Japan during the period covered by this book. The "money-focused" policy did not encompass a monetary-growth rule, and the Bank of Japan is formally, legally, and institutionally dependent on the Ministry of Finance. By conventional measures Japan is one of the most dependent central banks among the industrial countries, and this calls into question the received wisdom that granting central banks independence is a necessary condition for low inflation. However, we argue that in practice the Bank of Japan is more independent than its legal status would suggest. We also conclude that reputation effects, magnified by a "long-lived" and highly autonomous government bureaucracy and supported by the LDP's dominance between the mid 1950s and 1993, explain much of Japan's good inflation performance. In particular, there is less incentive to be tempted by the short-term benefits (on output) of surprise inflation if the same bureaucrats and politicians are still in office when the costs of sustained high inflation are inflicted on the economy.

The shock of the wild inflation also effectively gave the Bank of Japan more independence from political pressure and, together with the relaxation of the external constraint, allowed it to pursue a disinflationary policy with broad public support. To some extent, the Ministry of Finance (itself a powerful and in many respects autonomous bureaucracy) has shielded the Bank of Japan from political pressures. But attributing low inflation to a coalition (jointly independent and conservative) between the Bank of Japan and the Ministry of Finance may be pushed only so far. In numerous instances the Ministry of Finance has desired a more expansionary policy stance than the Bank of Japan has pursued, and there have been occasional public disputes over other policy issues.

9.5 Institutional Reform

New roles will be defined for the Bank of Japan in the coming years. The political and economic environment is changing rapidly, and the institutional framework of central-bank policy must adapt to the new environment. As the political scenery changes from LDP domination to some other form with greater competition among political views, the temptation for political parties to influence monetary policy may increase. One may also expect that the high degree of autonomy currently enjoyed by Japan's powerful ministries will be curbed by these political changes. Under these conditions, pressure to direct economic policy toward short-term political ends would likely rise.

The low-inflation "equilibrium" in Japan, based on reputation and on autonomous and long-lived bureaucracies, may be fragile. Twenty years of price stability were initiated by the bad experience with the wild inflation, which gave the Bank of Japan the independence to purse a new policy course with broad public support. Another large shock to the economy—perhaps a second lengthy and deep recession—could turn the balance in the other direction, toward more inflationary policies. Against the background of recent political and economic developments, this provides an argument for greater legal and institutional independence for the Bank of Japan. More independence would allow the buffer between the political process and the Bank of Japan now in place to continue despite far-reaching changes in the political landscape.

In fact, at the time of this writing it appears the Bank of Japan will obtain a greater degree of institutional independence than it has ever experienced since its establishment in 1882. In November 1996 an official working group appointed by Prime Minister Hashimoto issued a report proposing legislation that would give the Bank of Japan far greater institutional independence from the government. However, the motivation for the Ministry of Finance's willingness to support a revision of the 1942 Bank of Japan Law has little to do with either dissatisfaction with the Bank's past performance or the expectation that greater independence is needed to deal with the concerns of the future. Rather, it represents an effort to divert attention away from reforming the Ministry of Finance and to shift the discussion away from the Ministry's performance in handling the nonperforming loans of banks and *jusen* companies in the early 1990s.

Banking regulations (most of which are supervised jointly under the Bank of Japan and the Ministry of Finance) and regulation of the Postal Savings System by the Ministry of Posts and Telecommunications also need to adapt to a deregulated financial environment. Most of the regulations on interest rates, number of bank branches, and types of financial products have been removed. With deregulation, the deposit-insurance system, capital standards, and oversight of the payment system are much more important. Increased prudential regulation of banks to ensure sound management is necessary in order to maintain a stable financial system. Whether the Japanese financial system continues to perform well depends on its ability to adapt to changing circumstances in future years. We have pointed out several desirable directions, but institutional design in practice involves many difficult choices and must be able to evolve in step with these other developments. This is a challenge facing Japan in the years to come. The events of 1996 and the effort to shift attention away from reforming the Ministry of Finance (for all practical purposes the primary financial regulator) leave one with concern about Japan's willingness to effectively regulate the financial system as liberalization continues.

The Ministry has come under unprecedented attack in the past few years and is targeted for some type of reform as part of the "Big Bang" announced by Prime Minister Hashimoto, who also announced, to the surprise of many, that some of the regulatory responsibilities of the Ministry would be transferred to a new independent agency called the Financial Inspection and Supervisory Agency. The new agency would report directly to the prime minister's office. As with other aspects of the new reform effort, it is far too early to determine to what extent, if any, these changes will occur.

Notes

Chapter 2

1. Even Milton Friedman (1959), despite his criticism of government involvement in the economy, argued that government has the right and responsibility to establish central banking institutions to limit contagion and limit the equivalent of "economic counterfeiting."

2. It is possible to establish a private-sector agency to take up the supervision role. A nonprofit agency such as a central bank can separate the supervisory role from the role of issuing notes.

3. Goodhart's (1991, pp. 122–128) historical account calls into question whether the honor of the first central bank should be given to the Riksbank. Although it was the only bank in existence, and thus the only note-issuing agency, it was operated more like a commercial bank in the beginning. Not until 1726, when its notes were declared legal tender, did the Riksbank take on some of the characteristics of a central bank. "Despite its long history as the main, publicly owned bank of the country, the Riksbank had not developed many of the chief features of a true Central Bank by the beginning of the twentieth century." (ibid., p. 128)

4. The July 1996 issue of *Monetary and Economic Studies*, published by the Bank of Japan's Institute for Monetary and Economic Studies, provides illustrations and a brief description of these coins.

5. For a brief description of the rice market see pp. 29–30 of Ito 1992. For a more detailed discussion see Schaede 1989.

6. The first Westerners appeared on Japanese soil in 1543. The Tokugawa shoguns, the first having started in 1603, increasingly took steps to prohibit foreign contact with Japan. English ships were banned from Japan in 1623, Spanish ships in 1624, and Portuguese ships in 1639. Christianity was banned in 1630, and in 1633 it was decided that any Japanese who had lived abroad and returned to Japan would be executed. The only port open for contacts with foreign traders was Dejima, an island off Nagasaki which Dutch and Chinese ships were permitted to visit. Japan also permitted a limited number of Dutch merchants to remain on Dejima. Japanese ships, however, did visit neighboring countries.

7. Japan's postwar growth is often portrayed as a unique experience, and some even argue that the structural changes established during the occupation provided the base for rapid reindustrialization. No doubt the economic and political structural changes played some

role; however, in historical perspective, Japan's postwar experience appears to be more correctly regarded as an accelerated growth rate that reestablished prewar trends by the early 1970s. For more on this see chapter 3 of Ito 1992.

8. The national bank known as Dai-ichi (Number 1), established in Tokyo, survived until the postwar period and then merged with Kangyo Bank to become Dai-ichi Kangyo Bank ("Ikkan"), one of Japan's major banks. Dai-shi (Number 4) Bank, a national bank established in Niigata, is still operating as a regional bank; it is now the oldest bank, predating even the Bank of Japan.

9. Bank notes were ordered from the Continental Banknote Company in New York.

10. One of the objectives in the revision was to absorb special government bonds issued to former imperial relatives (*kazoku*) to compensate for the loss for cash compensation. In the revised national banking law, these special bonds were deemed qualified to be part of capital.

11. Michelacci (1993) provides an interesting comparative analysis of the regulatory responsibilities of central banks in nine industrialized countries. The Bank of Japan appears to be one of the central banks least involved in regulation and supervision.

12. Earthquake bills were concentrated in only a few banks, with about half of the outstanding bills held by the Taiwan Bank. Another problem was that the Taiwan Bank concentrated 70 percent of its lending to Suzuki Shoten (a trading company). The core of the bad-loan problem was thus concentrated in the Taiwan Bank and its relationship to the Suzuki Shoten. The government's policy error was the failure to prevent one problem bank from contaminating other banks. In the absence of a deposit guarantee, and with a lack of political will to rescue the Taiwan Bank and the Suzuki Shoten, widespread runs on other weaker banks ensued.

13. The Finance Minister's mistaken claim derived from an conversation between the bank's president and a ministry official on the possibility of a cash shortfall for settlement. In fact, the bank met its settlement liability by borrowing funds from other banks; however, that fact was not conveyed in time to the minister, who was sitting in the legislative chamber. Whether the Tokyo Watanabe Bank would have survived and a wave of bank runs would have been prevented if the Finance Minister had not relayed incorrect information is an interesting counterfactual hypothesis.

14. Cited from p. 87 of Tsutsui 1988. Original source: Letter, Dodge to Marquat, June 16, 1950 (Dodge manuscripts, Japan 1950, box 7).

Chapter 3

1. Although monetary policy was passively responding to pressures on the exchange rate, the fundamental shocks to the exchange rate and balance of payments were primarily domestic in origin (Hutchison and Walsh 1992).

2. See Cargill 1985, Cargill and Royama 1988, Cargill and Royama 1992, and Suzuki 1986.

3. Suzuki (1980) gives a comprehensive analysis of the conduct and control of monetary policy during the period of fixed exchange rates and restricted financial markets. See also Cargill 1986b and Cargill and Hutchison 1988a.

4. For a review of the literature on Japan's economic growth and industrial transformation in the postwar period, see Ito 1992. Also, see Hamada and Horiuchi 1987.

Table N.1

Japanese term	Interpretation: Floor	Target	Ceiling	Translation
10.0 zengo	9.5	10.0	10.5	around 10.0
10.0 dai	10.0	10.5	11.0	the 10s
10.0 teido	9.75	10.0	10.25	near 10.0
10.0 jaku	9.5	9.75	10.0	less than 10.0
10.0 dai, jakkan no fure wa attemo 11.0 zengo	10.0	10.75	11.5	the 10s, but could be around 11.0

5. The 1969 OECD survey of Japan noted that "Japan may remain an important surplus country for some time to come [and that] the beginning of this trend could be traced as far back as 1964" (Organization for Economic Cooperation and Development 1969, pp. 39–42).

6. Figure 3.2 illustrates the following points: Between 1958 and 1974, monetary growth rates fluctuated greatly. Accordingly, both the real GDP growth rate and the inflation rate were quite volatile. From 1975 to 1987, the monetary growth rate was gradually reduced. The inflation rate (the difference between the middle and bottom lines) came down steadily without affecting the trend of the real GDP growth rate (bottom line). From 1987 to 1995, monetary growth rates deviated from the trend line, first positively and then negatively. This corresponds to the bubble years (1986–1990) and the burst-bubble years (1990–1995). The GDP growth rate came down substantially in the burst-bubble years.

7. Quarterly M2 + CDs is a three-month average of monthly average balances. To be precise, before May 1979 no CDs were issued. Thus, original statistics are M2 before 1979:3 and M2 + CDs on and after 1979:3.

8. An actual announcement of a "forecast" does not contain the range, but certain wording suggests some range. Table N.1 shows Ito's interpretation of the expression.

9. Periods of "large shocks" are defined as ones in which actual growth rates are either above the high or below the low of the forecasts. In the former, the difference between actual and high, in the latter, the difference between actual and low are recorded.

10. This is equivalent to permitting what has been called in the United States "full base drift" each quarter, and "forgiving" past misses of the level of the money target. See Hutchison and Judd 1992 for a comparison of the Japanese procedure with the one used in the US.

11. See note 8 above.

12. The calculations in table 3.3 are actual percentage growth rates rather than the log approximations in equation 3.1.

13. In contrast, Hutchison and Judd (1992) find that the Federal Reserve money forecasts, which are kept secret when they are in force, do significantly reduce the forecast error derived from a simple VAR model. It is paradoxical that the Bank of Japan's forecasts provide relatively little new information to the public, while the Federal Reserve's forecasts (which are not disclosed) potentially are valuable in reducing the public's money projection errors. Making public the Federal Reserve's internal monetary paths could reduce monetary uncertainty in the US.

14. For discussions of the transition see Cargill 1985, 1986a, 1990; Cargill and Royama 1988; Feldman 1986.

15. See Ito 1991b for more details.

16. The Basle requirements are standards on capital-to-asset ratios established by agreement among the major central banks.

17. Milton Friedman (1985), for example, has argued that "the Bank of Japan has been the least monetarist central bank in its rhetoric, the most monetarist in its policy." Friedman bases his observation on the fact that Japan's broad money growth declined fairly steadily from the mid 1970s until the mid 1980s, and this trend has coincided with the decline in price inflation. For contrasting views see Hutchison 1986, Hutchison 1988, Ito 1989a, and Ito 1992.

18. See Ito 1991b for further details. Ito also estimates money-demand equations with the WPI deflator that indicate larger forecast errors.

Chapter 4

1. The identification of these episodes draws on Glick and Hutchison 1994a.

2. Inflation began to accelerate toward the end of 1988; however; 2 years later it peaked at almost 4 percent.

3. The actual intervention operations are difficult to determine, as the cost of financing the 1991 Persian Gulf War caused foreign-exchange reserves to decline.

4. For an international comparison of macroeconomic developments and policy responses at the time of oil-price shocks in the 1970s and in 1990, see Hutchison 1991.

5. Broad money growth declined from over 25 percent in early 1973 to about 11 percent in the middle of 1974, and short-term interest rates increased from 6 percent to 13 percent.

6. Earlier studies of Japan's intervention policy testing a similar equation include Hutchison 1984, Quirk 1977, and Takagi 1991.

7. Glick and Hutchison (1994a) considered three different measures of intervention: the change in the yen-denominated value of (net) official holdings of foreign assets, the equivalent in dollar terms, and the change in holdings of foreign assets in dollars adjusted for interest-rate earnings.

8. The instruments for the current exchange-rate change were (three lags each of) the Japanese call money rate, the Federal Reserve funds rate, and logarithmic changes in the Japanese CPI index and the exchange rate.

9. The first variable is constructed by multiplying the change in the log exchange rate by a dummy variable which has a value of 1 when the change is positive and a value of 0 otherwise; the second variable is constructed analogously with a dummy variable which has a value of 1 when the change is negative.

10. An F test indicates that this difference is statistically significant.

11. The inconsistency of this finding with the finding reported in Hutchison 1984 may be due to the earlier and more limited sample period (March 1973–November 1981) employed in Hutchison's study.

12. Watanabe (1994) shows that shifts in policy responses and other factors have led to a substantial "unexpected" component of intervention, which in turn has provided a signal for future developments in monetary policy. In particular, Watanabe finds that dollar (sales) purchases against yen in the foreign-exchange market signal future monetary ease (tightening)—i.e., future declines (increases) in the discount rate.

13. This assumes that intervention operations *per se* have not changed the long-term trend in the yen-dollar exchange rate.

14. It is debatable whether sterilized intervention has an effect on the exchange rate, however. The bulk of the empirical literature finds that sterilized intervention does not offset the exchange rate through the "portfolio balance" channel (e.g. Rogoff 1984), but that it may work through the "signaling" channel (Dominguez and Frankel 1983). Watanabe (1994) argues that intervention has provided an effective signal of future monetary policy in Japan.

15. There is a tradeoff, of course, when the authorities decide to insulate the monetary base from intervention. That is, the likely effect on the exchange rate from the initial operation is likely to be less in the case of sterilized intervention than in the case of unsterilized intervention. For example, in the latter case a foreign-exchange purchase (sale) is followed by a domestic monetary expansion (contraction), thereby providing additional pressure on the domestic currency to depreciate (appreciate). See Glick and Hutchison 1994b.

16. Domestic credit changes are regressed on current and lagged changes in reserves as well as autoregressive lags. Whether or not foreign-exchange interventions are sterilized completely in the long run depends on the lagged pattern of intervention. Seasonally adjusted monthly data over the managed-floating-rate period is employed, and to correct for potential simultaneity bias the equation is estimated using both the ordinary least-squares (OLS) method and the instrumental-variables (INST) technique.

17. Here the number after the colon indicates the month rather than the quarter.

18. Takagi (1991), who also makes this point, emphasizes the role of declining interest rates in raising money demand during this period. See also Yoshida and Rasche 1990.

19. Announcement of ministers of finance and central-bank governors of France, Germany, Japan, the UK, and the US, September 22, 1985, paragraph 18. This announcement, and the other policy-coordination announcements cited, are reprinted in Funabashi 1988.

20. Ibid.

21. Ito (1987) investigates the determinants of yen appreciation for the year after the Plaza Agreement. Ito identifies five waves of appreciation, each lasting a few weeks, separated by periods of relative calm. He finds that major determinants included the United States' policy switch on intervention (first wave), the Bank of Japan's "high interest policy" (second wave), and various mixes of the sharp decline in oil prices and declines in US interest rates (third, fourth, and fifth waves). This evidence is consistent with the view that exchange rates mainly respond to news of fundamentals and that exchange rates are not manageable by coordinated intervention alone.

22. In the preparatory discussions before the Plaza meeting, Japanese officials entertained multilateral interest-rate cuts but toned down this suggestion when the Germans reportedly showed no interest (Funabashi 1988). Nonetheless, there was speculation in Japan that the Bank of Japan would lower the discount rate after the Plaza Agreement as part of its "flexible" approach to monetary policy—hardly the policy to spur yen appreciation in the absence of coordinated moves in the United States and elsewhere.

23. This was a meeting of the G7 less Italy. Italy, protesting its exclusion from earlier meetings, did not participate.

24. In contrast, monetary policy in the United Kingdom and in Canada was committed to reducing inflation. Monetary policy in Germany would be directed at "improving conditions for sustained economic growth while maintaining price stability," while US monetary policy would be "consistent with economic expansion at a sustainable non-inflationary pace." France made no commitment on monetary policy.

25. The Bank of Japan reportedly purchased $1.7 billion on March 24, $2 billion on March 27, and lesser amounts on other days (Ito 1992). Total dollar purchases in the first quarter of 1987 amounted to $16 billion. The United States also intervened, purchasing $3 billion between March 23 and April 6 (Funabashi 1988). The European central banks intervened to a lesser extent.

26. CPI inflation (capacity utilization) was essentially zero (94.0 percent) in 1986, 1 percent (99.6 percent) in 1987, 1 percent in 1988 (103.3 percent), 2.7 percent in 1989 (102.6 percent), and 3.7 percent (106.5 percent) in 1990. Inflation and economic activity declined sharply in the period 1991–1993.

27. The switch in policy illustrated in table 4.4 indicates that both the short-run and the long-run sterilization coefficients were much higher after 1978:7 than in the 1973:5–1978:6 period. The average coefficients did not change after the Plaza Agreement. This probably reflects the fact that the initial policy of greater accommodation immediately after Plaza was reversed only a few months later to one of greater sterilization.

28. The idea was pushed strongly by Malaysian Prime Minister Mahatir. The EAEG, as originally proposed, was to exclude the United States, Australia, and New Zealand. Japan has been reluctant to endorse the EAEG proposal, partly because of opposition from the United States.

Chapter 5

1. See Hamada 1994 for a comparison of the recent bubble and burst with earlier financial crises in Japan. See Konya 1994 for additional discussion of the recent bubble economy.

2. On dramatic speculative bubbles in a historical context, see Kindleberger 1995.

3. The land-price index is an average of land in six metropolitan cities (average of residential, industrial, commercial zoning) published by the Japan Real Estate Institute. The land prices are monitored at the end of March and at the end of September. These numbers are recorded as representing the first and the third quarter. The numbers for the second and the fourth quarter are interpolated from simple averages of the neighboring quarters. The quarterly stock price index is the Nikkei 225 stock index average of daily closing for the quarter. See Ito 1992 for particular characteristics of these indices.

4. The base year for GDP numbers (source: Economic Planning Agency) is 1990. The growth rates of both real and nominal GDP are annualized rates of the quarter-to-quarter changes.

5. French and Poterba (1991) and Ueda (1990) argued that stock prices were alarmingly high, whereas Konya and Wakasugi (1987) argued that the rise of the stock prices was consistent with fundamentals. Nishimura (1990) and Noguchi (1989) examined the issues related to land prices.

6. For general discussions of financial bubbles see Blanchard and Watson 1982.

7. For a more detailed discussion of stochastic bubbles see Ito and Iwaisako 1996.

8. For relevant statistics see chapter 14 of Ito 1992.

9. Implications using a real rate of interest instead of the nominal rate illustrated in table 5.2 would be similar since nominal and real rates moved together in the period under consideration (see figures 5.4 and 5.5).

10. Replicated in figure 14.6 of Ito 1992.

11. Identification of these disturbances is achieved with a structural vector autoregressive model, using the methodology of Blanchard and Quah (1989).

12. ". . . In those countries where the asset-price boom was most marked in the 1980s (Finland, Sweden, Norway, Japan, and the United Kingdom) or where the disruption caused by the downward correct in valuations has caused great concern (Australia and the United States) there is a relatively close correlation between the ratio of private credit to GDP and asset-price movements. . . . To a large extent, the major expansion of credit during the past decade reflected a relaxation of credit constraints in the financial industry in wake of both market-driven and policy-determined structural developments." (Borio et al. 1994, pp. 27–28)

13. For an interesting study of the effects of moral hazard on portfolio choice, see Iwamura 1993.

14. See, e.g., Grossman 1992; Kane 1985; Kane and Kaufman 1993; Kaufman 1994; Karaken 1983; Short and Gunther 1989; White 1991.

15. For details see Barthold and Ito 1992.

16. The increases in the margin requirements on Nikkei futures trading in the Osaka Securities Exchanges are commonly thought to have contributed to a decline in trading volumes in Osaka and an increase in trading volumes in Singapore, where the same product is traded.

17. See chapter 3 for a detailed discussion of these "forecasts."

18. As an aside, the Bank of Japan lowered the interbank market rate earlier than the discount rate during this period. The interbank market rate or call rate was cut on March 31, two weeks before the discount rate was cut. Similarly, the September discount-rate cut was preceded by a decline in the market rate. This reflected the changing operating environment of the Bank of Japan. Liberalization of interest rates after 1993 rendered the discount-rate changes more symbolic. The decision to lower interbank rates through market operations rather than through a formalistic relationship to the discount rate reflected the new environment. The market reaction was mixed. On March 31 when the interbank rate was lowered, the yen/dollar rate hardly moved and the stock market in fact declined. Lowering interbank market rates during the summer (before the September discount-rate cut) may have contributed to stopping yen appreciation and stock-price declines.

Chapter 6

1. Japan's most severe postwar recession itself can, in large part, be traced to the decline in asset prices. Consumption fell as households saw the real value of their equity and

real-estate holdings decline precipitously. The fall in consumption induced a fall in fixed investment, which was weakened further, in turn, by the overhang of excess capacity accumulated during the asset-inflation phase and the credit crunch induced by the decline in "hidden" bank capital. Japanese banks are permitted to hold equities in nonfinancial corporations. Bank equity holdings form an important part of the "customer relationship system" or main bank system. Regulation permits 45% of the latent capital gains (market value minus value at which equity was originally booked) to be counted toward tier II bank capital. The fact that the majority of equities were obtained in the past and are carried on the balance sheet at historical cost means that the bank's balance sheet understated capital during the bubble phase because equities appreciated in value.

2. International Monetary Fund 1995, p. 21.

3. See the *International Herald Tribune* of January 24, 1996.

4. The eighth *jusen* company (established by agricultural cooperatives and their national federation, Norin Chukin) was exempted from the plan and is not regarded as a problem institution in current estimates of the nonperforming-loan problem.

5. The losses were revealed by the press in late September 1995; however, it was later revealed that at the beginning of August the Daiwa Bank had notified the Ministry of Finance of a "problem" in the New York branch. The Daiwa Bank, however, did not file a detailed report until late September. Federal Reserve authorities were notified before the public announcement, but not until 6 weeks after the bank discovered the losses. During this period, the trader was permitted to continue trading. At the time of the public announcement, the losses were covered by realizing hidden reserves (difference between market and book values of long-term held securities) and written off in the biannual earnings report of September 1995. US regulatory authorities treated the delay in informing them of the problem most seriously. Later in the fall of 1995, US authorities banned the Daiwa Bank from conducting business in the US, citing delayed reporting to the US authorities and the cover-up of losses. Daiwa's operations in the US were sold to the Sumitomo Bank.

6. Until March 1993 the Ministry of Finance reported the sum of nonperforming loans only for the 21 major banks combined. The Ministry of Finance's definition of a nonperforming loan is narrow. Nonperforming loans are those loans for which the principal is not likely to be collected and those for which interest has not been collected in the past 6 months. This leaves considerable room to exclude loans that are clearly in serious default; for example, restructured loans in which the interest rate has been drastically reduced or even set to zero are not regarded as nonperforming. Loans that receive only a fraction of an interest payment also can be excluded from the nonperforming category. Moreover, there is evidence that banks make additional loans to enable borrowers to pay interest on previous loans so that the amount of nonperforming loans is understated. This type of activity on the part of private depositories was widespread in the S&L industry in the 1980s, and it had disastrous consequences. Judged by the loss ratios reported by the Cooperative Credit Purchasing Company and the experience with insolvent institutions, the Ministry of Finance's estimates of recoverable loans also appear conservative.

7. In comparison to the slow efforts of Japanese banks, US banks took drastic steps when faced with nonperforming loans in 1989 and 1990.

8. The Agricultural and Fisheries Cooperative Savings Insurance Corporation (AFCSIC) is the other deposit-insurance agency. It was established September 1973 and was based on principles similar to those of the DIC; however, it is administered by the Ministry of Agricultural, Forestry, and Fisheries and the Ministry of Finance. It insures the deposits

of about 5,500 agricultural and Fisheries cooperatives, and it has the authority to pay off depositors of a failed institution or assist the merger between an insolvent and a solvent institution. Membership is mandatory. Much like the DIC, the AFCSIC has made no actual payments to depositors of a failed institution. However, it did assist a merger between the insolvent Kagoshima City Cooperative with the Tagami Agricultural Cooperative in 1978. This was a relatively small assistance in comparison with the more public assistance offered by the DIC since 1991. The AFCSIC is much smaller than the DIC; as of March 1993, its reserves were ¥82 billion whereas those of the DIC were ¥696 billion.

9. Before 1989, regional banks of the second association were known as *sogo* banks.

10. This is not surprising, since the DIC was grossly underfunded in terms of ability to deal with even a few insolvencies of large institutions. To gain an appreciation of the degree of underfunding, we can compare the DIC to the Federal Deposit Insurance Corporation. Although close to 80% of deposits are insured in both countries, the reserve-to-deposit ratios are significantly lower in Japan. In 1994, for example, the ratio of insurance-fund reserves to insured deposits was 0.16 in Japan and 1.15 in the US (Deposit Insurance Corporation of Japan 1995; Federal Deposit Insurance Corporation 1994).

11. The AFCSIC, like the DIC, is grossly underfunded relative to deposits and the potential amount of nonperforming loans held by insured institutions. At the end of 1992, agricultural and Fisheries cooperatives held ¥66,025 billion in deposits (¥13.6 billion per institution). The ratio of March 1993 reserves to 1992 deposits was 0.0012, which was considerably less than the reserve ratio for the DIC was at that time. Agricultural cooperatives have extended significant funds to the *jusen*. In view of the small capital base of the cooperatives and the reserves of the AFCSIC, Japan's other system of deposit insurance can also be considered insolvent for all practical purposes.

12. The agricultural cooperatives insisted on having their lending repaid in full; thus, they recovered their loans to *jusen* in full. At the same time, agricultural cooperatives made a "gift" of ¥0.53 trillion to the *Jusen* Resolution Corporation.

13. The memorandum was signed in 1993, when a 10-year plan to rehabilitate *jusen* was established. The existence of the memorandum was revealed in the fall of 1995 during the debate over burden sharing. The language of the memorandum is vague, but the media and the public interpreted it as saying the Ministry of Finance, in principle, guaranteed the agricultural cooperatives' lending to *jusen*. Although the Ministry of Finance denied the legality of such a memorandum and asserted an abundance of empty promises during the budget process, public opinion shifted to blaming the Ministry of Finance for the *jusen* problem rather than questioning the lending practice of the agricultural cooperatives.

14. This seems an odd justification for imposing a greater-than-pro-rata burden sharing. To the extent that the close relationship was the basis for a greater burden, exposure of *jusen* lending should have been included in founder banks' risk measurement in the "consolidated basis." Additionally, if supervision had been extended to *jusen* as a part of banks' supervision, *jusen* would not have been permitted to expand through borrowing from agricultural cooperatives from 1990 to 1995.

15. The amount ¥685 billion came about in a curious manner. During the negotiations between the Ministry of Finance and the Ministry of Agriculture, Forestry, and Fisheries, the ministry originally proposed that agricultural cooperatives share the burden of ¥1.2 trillion. Political opposition from farmers' lobby was so strong that it was bargained down to ¥530 billion. The difference between the estimate by the Ministry of Finance and the accepted amount of the Ministry of Agriculture, Forestry, and Fisheries—¥685 billion—became the amount of fiscal spending proposed for resolving the *jusen* problem.

16. For a description and an analysis of the *keiretsu* relationship see chapter 7 of Ito 1992.

17. For a more detailed discussion of the two deposit-insurance agencies see Cargill, Hutchison, and Ito 1996.

18. For more detailed discussions of the Postal Savings System see Anderson 1990; Calder 1990; Ito 1992; Ogura and Yoshino 1988; Sakakibara 1991; Suzuki 1987; Yoshino 1992; Yoshino 1993.

19. The ability to hold multiple accounts was a major advantage before the Tax Reform Act of 1986, which eliminated the tax-free status of interest on small savings. Postal savings customers had greater opportunity to spread deposits over a large number of accounts so as not to exceed the ¥3 million maximum on tax-free interest. Some efforts, such as the "green card" effort (Feldman 1986), were made to reduce the ability to hold multiple accounts; however, evading taxes through postal savings deposits was widespread and officially tolerated. This advantage was eliminated with the Tax Reform Act of 1986, which extended income taxes to all interest income. The Postal Savings System has also timed interest-rate changes in response to changes in the Bank of Japan's discount rate to maximize the inflow of funds (Suzuki 1987, p. 150). Even when the official interest rates are the same, the Postal Savings System offers more flexible savings instruments that generate a higher effective yield. The most significant advantage currently enjoyed by the Postal Savings System is the *teigaku* time deposit. Sakakibara (1991, p. 66) refers to this as the "jewel" of the Postal Savings System because it is superior to any time deposit issued by private banks. The *teigaku* time deposit offers greater liquidity and yield than any private time deposit, especially in periods of fluctuating and uncertain interest rates. The *teigaku* deposit is a 10-year fixed-rate time deposit; however, the funds can be withdrawn after 6 months with no penalty. The *teigaku* deposit is essentially a long-term deposit with a short-term option to be exercised solely at the discretion of the depositor. It has been shown to provide the Postal Savings System with a significant competitive advantage over bank time deposits (Kamada 1993).

20. See note 19.

21. The Bank of Japan has also argued that the Postal Savings System interferes with monetary policy and exposes the banking system to liquidity risks during periods of tight monetary policy. For example, when the Bank of Japan shifts toward tight monetary policy and interest rates begin to increase, *teigaku* deposits offer an attractive feature to depositors. Funds can be placed in these accounts at the increasing rates and the flexibility to withdraw funds after 6 months without penalty provides depositors with an option to take advantage of further increase rate increases or to lock in higher interest rates if rates should decline. Yoshino (1994) provides some direct information on the potential disintermediation from banks to the Postal Savings System in response to shifts in monetary policy. Two distinct shifts toward tight monetary policy in 1973 and 1980 were associated with disintermediation from banks to the Postal Savings System; however, disintermediation did not take place in 1989 and 1990 when the Bank of Japan initiated tight monetary policy. The Postal Savings System in 1991, however, did experience a marked inflow relative to the banking system. This is most likely the result of increasing publicity given to the nonperforming-loan problem of Japanese banks and the aggressive efforts of individual postal offices to publicize the bank problems in the context of their complete government deposit guarantees. The Bank of Japan's overall performance in the postwar period, however, suggests that the Bank has not been seriously burdened by either actual or potential disintermediation of funds from banks to Postal Savings System. At the same time, the disproportional impact of monetary policy leaves much to be desired, and the potential

for disintermediation may in the future restrain Bank of Japan policy—especially if there is already concern with the financial condition of the banking system.

22. For a detailed discussion of the "too big to fail" policy in the context of the US financial system see Hetzel 1991.

23. The premium rate was increased from 0.012% of deposits to 0.084% of deposits, of which 0.048 percentage points of the increase represents a rise in regular rates and the remainder represents a temporary surcharge to cope with the coming consolidation of credit cooperatives

24. *Wall Street Journal*, August 2, 1996.

25. The numbers are based on the Tokyo Metropolitan Government documents, as reported in the daily newspaper *Asahi Shinbun* on February 16, 1995.

26. A deposit-insurance system has two relevant characteristics in this regard: the intended function of preventing a bank run and systemic risk and a side effect that causes moral hazard. Since deposits are protected, depositors do not put pressure on weak institutions by withdrawing funds.

27. Several authors had argued, before the series of credit-cooperative failures in late 1994 and 1995, that Japan was missing a chance to learn from the US deposit-insurance failure when the Financial System Reform Law (Cargill and Todd 1993 and Kane 1993) was being discussed prior to its passage in June 1992.

28. This impression was enhanced by a scheme that set up a new bank to assume business instead of outright liquidation, and also by the prolonged debate over burden sharing among the lenders to the *jusen*.

29. For a review of the literature on contagion with respect to the United States see Kaufman 1994.

30. Recent Bank of Japan conferences have focused on prudential concerns more than past ones. To judge by the 1993 conference (Sawamoto et al. 1995), the Bank of Japan anticipates that it will be more preoccupied with prudential issues in the future. Comments by Governor Mieno (1995) reflect the same view.

31. The widely accepted view that price stability contributes to a stable financial and monetary environment is a reason for concern whenever the central bank is diverted from goal of price stability. Cukierman (1996) offers a contrasting and interesting view that there is no tradeoff between price stability and financial stability in the long run.

Chapter 7

1. This view has been challenged by Romer (1986) and Watson (1994).

2. See Nordhaus 1975.

3. These models differ from the Nordhaus-type models because rational expectations make it more difficult to exploit a short-run Phillips curve, because voters cannot be consistently fooled by politicians, because well-defined cycles in macroeconomic activity are not necessarily predicted, and because much of the adjustment in macroeconomic activity in response to political institutions occurs after the election.

4. For an extensive review of the literature see Nordhaus 1989. Also see Willet 1988.

5. For a useful summary of political institutions in Japan see Kishimoto 1982.

6. Nordhaus 1975, Tufte 1978, Hee Soh 1986, and Alesina and Roubini 1992 are representative of the multicountry studies that include Japan. Overall, the multicountry studies suggest political-business-cycle behavior in postwar Japan, though the evidence is difficult to interpret. In an effort to have "one model fit all," the results fail to capture the specific institutional and historical environment of postwar Japan, which would influence the political business cycles. Although partisan considerations have not been important in Japan during most of the postwar period, none of the multicountry studies have incorporated into their frameworks the critical role played by changes in the percentage of seats held by the LDP as a measure of the willingness to engage in manipulative behavior. Nor do the multicountry studies incorporate the opportunistic channel, which turns out to be rather significant in the case of Japan.

7. Recent political reforms created an election system for the House of Representatives based on single-representative districts and proportional representation, which were employed in 1996.

8. Ito (1990) also presents a theoretical model consistent with the observations presented in figures 7.2 and 7.3.

9. This vote was accidental in the sense that some LDP members were absent from the House floor. However, some argue that their absence from the floor was deliberate, and that it stemmed from factional discontent with the prime minister. Even in the latter case, however, the motivation for passing the resolution was quite personal and factional rather than anything of a political-economy nature.

10. Cargill and Hutchison (1990) also provide a conceptual discussion of the political business cycle in Japan.

11. Ito (1991a) extends the framework to incorporate the influence of international variables on the timing of elections in Japan.

12. Only selected results from the various studies on Japan's political business cycles are reproduced here.

13. Kohno and Nishizawa did not cite Ito and Park 1988; however, they would also likely have been critical of this study's conclusion that only opportunistic political interaction could be found in Japan.

14. Each equation in the two-equation system (equations 7.1 and 7.2) can be estimated either by single-equation methods (OLS applied to the economic growth equation and PROBIt applied to the election equation) or by a simultaneous procedure that takes into account the two-way feedback between real GNP growth and elections. The simultaneous procedure needs to be modified to take into account the fact that one equation has a binary (0 or 1) dependent variable. The simultaneous-equations estimates are generally regarded as more reliable than single-equation estimates; however, the inherent problems of simultaneous-equations estimation procedures suggest that single-equation estimates cannot be discarded.

Chapter 8

1. There is some controversy over Milton Friedman's famous dictum that "inflation is always and everywhere a monetary phenomenon." However, most dispute concerns the ex-

tent to which monetary growth may be taken as exogenous. Even by 1975 there was general agreement that a steady and sustained rise in prices must be accommodated by a steady and sustained rise in monetary aggregates (Gordon 1975). For an overview of theoretical models of inflation and a discussion of the empirical evidence over the causes of inflation, see McCallum 1990.

2. Friedman's (1959) constant-monetary-growth proposal is one possible (and highly restrictive) rule that would help a central bank to credibly commit to a long-run policy of low inflation. Friedman argued for rules rather than discretion in monetary policy, using arguments similar to those formalized in the dynamic-inconsistency literature. Because of long and variable policy lags, Friedman also proposed simple rules, such as the rule of constant monetary growth, rather than complicated activist rules. It should also be pointed out that Friedman discussed the time-inconsistency problem in the 1960s.

3. Given independence from political and other pressures to deviate from its announced policy intentions, a conservative central banker can credibly commit to and deliver low inflation.

4. The reputation of the central bank (or, more generally, the government) will be damaged when it deviates from its announced policies and fails to honor its commitments. If the central bank fails to honor its commitments, the public will "punish" it by expecting high inflation for some periods in the future, creating an incentive to follow through with the announced policy.

5. For a good survey of the literature of dynamic inconsistency, on which this section draws, see Fischer 1990.

6. Henning (1994, p. 77) writes that in the early 1970s "domestic conflict over who within Japan would reap the discretionary benefit of this newfound policy latitude therefore reemerged."

7. After the 1985 Plaza Agreement, monetary growth began an upward trend that continued until 1990, when the asset-price bubble collapsed and the economy slowed down. No one suggests that a "monetary rule" has been in operation since 1985.

8. See Cargill 1989 and 1995a for an analysis of central-bank independence and for a comparison of the Bank of Japan and the Federal Reserve System. Cargill (1995b) finds that the statistical link between institutional measures of central-bank independence and inflation performance is not robust to small changes in model specification and in sample-period selection.

9. For useful discussions see Fischer 1990 and Blanchard and Fischer 1989.

10. The Bank of Japan Law was amended in 1949 as part of the Dodge Plan. This section draws on Nakao and Horii 1991 (a special paper issued by the Bank of Japan) for institutional details and facts about the decision-making structure of the Bank of Japan.

11. For a discussion of the Bank of Japan Law and of the efforts to have it changed see Cargill 1994.

12. Henning (1994) argues that the Bank of Japan does not act on discount-rate changes without explicit private approval by the Ministry of Finance; however, this formal requirement overstates the Ministry's influence over discount-rate changes in recent years (*International Herald Tribune* 1989).

13. Reflecting this concern, a former Governor of the Bank of Japan, Yasushi Mieno, recently called for public discussion of central-bank independence, stating that "a suitable

time for scrutiny [of the Bank of Japan Law] will come." In this speech Mieno emphasized that the existing law "reflects wartime features that pose a number of problems in terms of central-bank independence, including the government's broad authority over the Bank" and "authorizes the government to issue orders regarding the administration of the Bank" (Mieno 1995, p. 14). Moreover, he argues that this part of the law is inconsistent with the establishment of the Policy Board and with its authority over interest-rate policies.

14. However, Bade and Parkin (1982) give the Bank of Japan a higher ranking, putting it on a par with the Federal Reserve System. This ranking, which seems very odd on the basis of objective criteria (Cargill 1989), has been criticized by Eijffinger and Schaling (1993). For a detailed discussion of this issue see Cargill 1994.

15. Cargill (1995b) shows, however, that the statistical relationship between central-bank independence and relatively low inflation is not as robust as is generally claimed. He shows that only about 44% of inflation variance (16 industrial countries, 1973–1988) is explained by an index of central-bank independence once the correct index measure for Japan is included—disputing Alesina and Summers's (1993, p. 154) claim of "a near perfect negative correlation between inflation and central-bank' independence." Moreover, Cukierman, Webb, and Neyapti (1993) do not find a statistical correlation between legal independence of the central bank and inflation in the less-developed countries.

16. Walsh (1996) finds that a model including unemployment helps explain Japanese inflation. In a panel data set with 18 countries, the model continues to overpredict Japanese inflation (in view of the relative dependence of Japan's central bank). But the prediction error is reduced when unemployment is included in the prediction equation. Cargill and Hutchison (1990) also argue that Japan's low unemployment rate tended to reduce inflation bias ("demand" for inflation) by international comparison.

17. Cargill (1993a) characterizes the Bank of Japan as a "dependent but price stabilizing central bank" and argues that Japan runs counter to the conventional wisdom that formally independent central banks are better able to control inflation.

18. See, e.g., *International Herald Tribute* 1989.

19. This tax (actually a value-added tax) was first proposed in 1978, by the Ohira government; the Nakasone government proposed it again in 1987, and the Takeshita government in 1988. The tax was finally introduced into law in 1989. See Ito 1992.

20. *The Economist* (1992) makes this point, citing the example of 1972–1974, when the government, under the leadership of Prime Minister Tanaka, insisted on expansionary policies. The problem with this example is that Tadashi Sasaki, the governor from December 1969 to December 1974, was appointed from the ranks of the Bank of Japan, not the Ministry of Finance.

21. A simple test of the hypothesis that more expansionary monetary policies are generally followed during periods when former Ministry of Finance officials serve as governors of the Bank of Japan is rejected.

22. In this context, it would appear that an "implicit" contract between the principal (government) and the agent (Ministry of Finance—Bank of Japan coalition) is not evident in the sense that the Ministry officials are not removed if they fail to meet performance standards (i.e., stated objectives). It would be difficult to interpret the Japanese case as an "implicit" contract, drawing an analogy to the explicit contract employed in New Zealand, whereby the problem of inflation bias is explicitly addressed and, at the same time, enough flexibility to respond to some shocks is retained. On the design of optimal contracts in cen-

tral banking as a solution to the dynamic inconsistency problem, see Walsh 1995a; for an interpretation of the New Zealand Reserve Bank Act of 1989 as the design of an optimal contract, see Walsh 1995b.

23. There is a sign of changes in this respect. In 1993–1995, there were incidences in which the top executives in the Ministry of International Trade and Industry and in the Ministry of Finance resigned or took early retirement after heavy pressure from politicians (ministers and other politicians). Whether these incidences are aberrations or omens of a two-party system remains to be seen.

24. For details see sections 4 and 5 of chapter 11 of Cukierman 1992.

25. Supporting this view, Henning (1994) argues that single-party control limited the granting of greater independence to the Bank of Japan, perpetuating its subordinate position to the Ministry of Finance and the Liberal Democratic Party. LDP politicians were not motivated to create a more independent central bank, which might limit their successors' power over future monetary-policy decisions. Henning also notes that the LDP itself was accountable for (and, in the eyes of the public, identified with) economic policy in the post-war period.

26. Cargill and Hutchison (1990) present several political arguments for the small inflation bias, including these two: (1) The opposition parties in Japan generally have been weak, offering primarily radical positions on noneconomic issues that have overshadowed concerns over the conditions of the economy (Pempel 1987). The weak position of the opposition parties meant that the LDP was not effectively pressured to pursue more stimulative monetary policies. (2) The dominance of one party also decreased the incentive for expansionary policies before elections (e.g., political business cycles), which led to average inflation rates lower than would have been the case if elections had been hotly contested.

27. Debelle and Fischer (1994) present statistical evidence that inflation performance is likely to be better if the central bank has a mandate for monetary stability—i.e., a well defined long-term goal (no goal independence)—and if the central bank is allowed to pursue that objective in ways it deems most appropriate (instrument independence). They argue that the Federal Reserve needs a clearer mandate, and that the Bundesbank should be held more accountable for its actions (to keep it from being too conservative).

28. Other factors contributing to domestic monetary expansion included the undervalued exchange rate and the support for a policy of inflation in order to avoid a revaluation of the currency (the "inflation adjustment" argument). For a discussion, see Ito 1992.

29. Governor Mieno came under pressure from politicians to lower rates more aggressively when the economy started to slow in early 1992. Shin Kanemaru, vice-president of the LDP and leader of its largest faction at the time, warned Mieno that he might be dismissed by the prime minister if the discount rate wasn't cut (*Wall Street Journal*, February 28, 1992). The Ministry of Finance at times was also critical of the Bank of Japan's policy in the asset-deflation period.

30. This report is entitled Report of the Central Bank System—In Pursuit of "Open Independence."

31. *Japan Times*, November 13, 1996.

References

Agricultural and Fishery Cooperative Savings Insurance Corporation. 1993. Depositor Protection System in the Agricultural and Fishing Cooperative Sector.

Alesina, Alberto. 1987. Macroeconomic policy in a two-party system as a repeated game. *Quarterly Journal of Economics* 102, August: 651–678.

Alesina, Alberto. 1988. Macroeconomics and politics. In *NBER Macroeconomics Annual 1988*, ed. S. Fischer. MIT Press.

Alesina, Alberto, and Nouriel Roubini. 1992. Political cycles in OECD economies. *Review of Economic Studies Journal* 59: 663–688.

Alesina, Alberto, and Lawrence Summers. 1993. Central bank independence and macroeconomic performance: Some comparative evidence. *Journal of Money, Credit and Banking.* 25: 151–162.

Backus, David, and John Driffill. Inflation and reputation. 1985. *American Economic Review* 75, June: 530–538.

Bade, Robert, and Michael Parkin. 1982. Central Bank Laws and Monetary Policy. Unpublished manuscript.

Ball, Lawrence. 1984. What determines the sacrifice ratio? In *Monetary Policy,* ed. N. Mankiw University of Chicago Press.

Bank of Japan Bureau of Research. 1972. *Japanese Money.*

Bank of Japan Research and Statistics Bureau. 1975. On the importance of the money supply in Japan. [In Japanese] *Monthly Review,* July: 1–11.

Bank of Japan Institute for Monetary and Economic Studies. 1986. *Wagakuni no kin-yu seido.* [English version: *The Japanese Financial System,* ed. Y. Suzuki. Clarendon, 1987]

Bank of Japan. 1993. Treasury Business of the Bank of Japan. Special Paper No. 226.

Barth, James R. 1991. *The Great Savings and Loan Debacle.* American Enterprise Institute.

Barth, James R., R. Dan Brumbaugh Jr., and Robert E. Litan. 1992. *The Future of American Banking.* Sharpe.

Barthold, Thomas, and Takatoshi Ito. 1992. Bequest taxes and accumulation of household wealth: U.S.-Japan comparison. In *Political Economy of Tax Reform,* ed. T. Ito and A. Krueger. University of Chicago Press.

Black, Stanley W. 1991. Transactions costs and vehicle currencies. *Journal of International Money and Finance* 10: 512–526.

Blanchard, Olivier, and Stanley Fischer. 1989. *Lectures on Macroeconomics*. MIT Press.

Blanchard, Olivier, and Quah, Danny. 1989. The dynamic effects of aggregate demand and supply disturbances. *American Economic Review* 79, September: 655–673.

Blanchard, Olivier, and Mark W. Watson. 1982. Bubbles, rational expectations, and financial markets. In *Crisis in the Economic and Financial Structure*, ed. P. Wachtel. Lexington Books.

Borio, C. E. V, N. Kennedy, and S. D. Prowse. 1994. Exploring Aggregate Asset Price Fluctuations Across Countries. Economic Paper 40, Bank for International Settlements.

Bryant, Ralph. 1991. Model representations of Japanese money policy. *Monetary and Economic Studies* (Bank of Japan Institute for Monetary and Economic Studies) 9, September: 11–61.

Burdekin, Richard C. K., and Thomas D. Willet. 1991. Central bank reform: The Federal Reserve in international perspective. *Public Budgeting and Financial Management* 3: 619–649.

Calder, Kent E. 1990. Linking welfare and the developmental state: postal savings in Japan. *Journal of Japanese Studies* 16, winter: 31–60.

Cargill, Thomas F. 1985. A U.S. perspective on Japanese financial liberation. *Monetary and Economic Studies* (Bank of Japan Institute for Monetary and Economic Studies) 3, May: 115–161.

Cargill, Thomas F. 1986a. Financial reform in the United States and Japan: A comparative overview. In *Financial Policy and Reform in the Pacific Basin Countries*, ed. H. Cheng. Heath.

Cargill, Thomas F. 1986b. Japanese monetary policy, flow of funds and domestic financial liberalization. *Economic Review* (Federal Reserve Bank of San Francisco), summer: 21–32.

Cargill, Thomas F. 1989. *Central Bank Independence and Regulatory Responsibilities: The Bank of Japan and The Federal Reserve*. Salomon Brothers Center for the Study of Financial Institutions, New York University.

Cargill, Thomas F. 1990. Financial reform, inflation, and monetary policy in Japan: Lessons for U.S. policy. In *Japan's Economic Challenge*. U.S. Government Printing Office.

Cargill, Thomas F. 1993a. The Bank of Japan: A dependent but price stabilizing central bank. *Public Budgeting and Financial Management* 5: 131–139.

Cargill, Thomas F. 1993b. Deposit guarantees, nonperforming loans, and the postal savings system in Japan. In *FDICIA: An Appraisal*. Federal Reserve Bank of Chicago.

Cargill, Thomas F. 1994. The Bank of Japan and the Federal Reserve: financial liberalization, independence, and regulatory responsibility. In *Studies in the Contemporary Japanese Economy*, ed. M. Okabe. Macmillan.

Cargill, Thomas F. 1995a. An essay on central bank independence: The Bank of Japan and the Federal Reserve. In *Essays in Honor of Thomas Mayer*, ed. K. Hoover and S. Sheffrin. Elgar.

Cargill, Thomas F. 1995b. The statistical association between central bank independence and inflation. *Banca Nazionale Del Lavoro: Quarterly Review*, June: 159–172.

Cargill, Thomas F., and Michael M. Hutchison. 1988a. The Bank of Japan's response to macroeconomic and financial change. In *Monetary Policy in Pacific Basin Countries,* ed. H. Cheng. Kluwer.

Cargill, Thomas F., and Michael M. Hutchison. 1988b. Political Business Cycles in a Parliamentary Setting: The Case of Japan. Working Paper 88–08, Federal Reserve Bank of San Francisco.

Cargill, Thomas F., and Michael M. Hutchison. 1990. Monetary policy and political economy: the Federal Reserve and the Bank of Japan. In *The Political Economy of American Monetary Policy,* ed. T. Mayer. Cambridge University Press.

Cargill, Thomas F., and Michael M. Hutchison. 1991a. Political business cycles with endogenous election timing: Evidence from Japan. *Review of Economics and Statistics* 4, November: 733–739.

Cargill, Thomas F., and Michael M. Hutchison. 1991b. The Bank of Japan's response to elections. *Journal of Japanese and International Economics* 5: 120–139.

Cargill, Thomas F., and Michael M. Hutchison. Forthcoming. Macroeconomic policy in Japan: International and comparative perspectives. In *Handbook of Macroeconomic Policy in Open Economies,* ed. M. Fratianni et al. Greenwood/North-Holland.

Cargill, Thomas F., Michael M. Hutchison, and Takatoshi Ito. 1996. Deposit guarantees in Japan: Aftermath of the bubble and burst of the bubble economy. *Contemporary Economic Policy* 14, July: 41–52.

Cargill, Thomas F., and Shoichi Royama. 1988. *The Transition of Finance in Japan and the United States: A Comparative Perspective.* Hoover Institution Press.

Cargill, Thomas F., and Shoichi Royama. 1992. The evolution of Japanese banking and finance. In *Banking Structures in Major Countries,* ed. G. Kaufman. Kluwer.

Cargill, Thomas F., and Gregory F. W. Todd. 1993. Japan's Financial System Reform Law: Progress toward financial liberalization? *Brooklyn Journal of International Law* 19: 47–84.

Chappell, D., and D. Peel. 1979. On the political theory of the business cycle. *Economics Letters* 2: 327–332.

Chinn, Menzie, and Jeffrey Frankel. 1994. Financial links around the Pacific Rim: 1982–1992. In *Exchange Rate Policy and Interdependence: Perspectives from the Pacific Basin,* ed. R. Glick and M. Hutchison. Cambridge University Press.

Choy, Jon. 1992. Japanese banks' self-help questioned. *Japan Economic Institute Report,* November 6: 1–3.

Choy, Jon. 1994. Deregulation of Japan's financial markets: Update and impact. *Japan Economic Institute Report,* May 20: 1–17.

Choy, Jon. 1995. Japanese bank sees loss, market cheers. *Japan Economic Institute Report,* February 10: 1–4.

Cukierman, Alex. *Central Bank Strategy, Credibility and Independence.* MIT Press, 1991.

Cukierman, Alex. Forthcoming. The economics of central banking. In *Macroeconomic Policy and Financial Systems,* ed. W. Holger. Macmillan.

Cukierman, Alex, Sebastian Edwards, and Guido Tabellini. 1993. Seigniorage and political instability. *American Economic Review* 82: 537–555.

Cukierman, Alex, Steven B. Webb, and Bilin Neyapti. 1993. Measuring the independence of central banks and its effect on policy outcomes. *World Bank Economic Review* 6: 353–398.

Debelle, Guy, and Stanley Fischer. 1994. How Independent Should a Central Bank Be? Stanford University CEPR Publication 392.

Denison, E. F., and W. K. Chung. 1976. *How Japan's Economy Grew So Fast.* Brookings Institution.

Deposit Insurance Corporation of Japan. *1995 Annual Report.*

Dominguez, Kathryn, and Jeffrey Frankel. 1993. Does foreign exchange intervention matter? The portfolio effect. *American Economic Review.* 83, December: 1356–1369.

Dotsey, Michael. 1986. Japanese monetary policy: A comparative analysis. *Monetary and Economic Studies* 4: 105–127.

Economist. 1992. Central Banks: America v Japan, The rewards of independence. January 25: 19–21.

Eijffinger, Sylvester, and Adrian van Rixtel. 1992. The Japanese financial system and monetary policy: A descriptive analysis. *Japan and the World Economy* 4: 291–309.

Eijffinger, Sylvester, and Eric Schaling. 1993. Central bank independence in twelve industrial countries. *Banco Nazionale del Lavoro Quarterly Review,* March: 49–89.

Federal Deposit Insurance Corporation. *1994 Annual Report.*

Federal Reserve Bank of New York. 1985–86. *Quarterly Review* 10, winter.

Feldman, Robert Alan. 1986. *Japanese Financial Markets: Deficits, Dilemmas, and Deregulation.* MIT Press.

Fischer, Stanley. 1990. Rules versus discretion in monetary policy. *Handbook of Monetary Economics* 2: 1155–1184.

Fischer, Stanley. 1995. The unending search for monetary salvation. *National Bureau of Economic Research Macroeconomics Annual 1995:* 275–286.

Frankel, Jeffrey A. 1993. Is Japan Creating a Yen Bloc in East Asia and the Pacific? In *Regionalism and Rivalry: Japan and the United States in Pacific Asia,* ed. J. Frankel and M. Kahler. University of Chicago Press.

Frankel, Jeffrey A., and Shang-Jiu Wei. 1994. Yen bloc or dollar bloc? Exchange rate policies of the East Asian economies. In *Macroeconomic Linkage: Savings, Exchange Rates, and Capital Flows,* ed. T. Ito and A. Krueger. University of Chicago Press.

Fratianni, Michele, and Haizhou Huang. 1992. Central Bank Independence and Optimal Conservativeness. Working Paper in Economics 92–030, Indiana University.

French, Kenneth, and James Poterba. 1991. Were Japanese stock prices too high? *Journal of Financial Economics* 29: 23–50.

Fries, Steven, Robin Mason, and William Perraudin. 1993. Evaluating deposit insurance for Japanese banks. *Journal of the Japanese and International Economies* 7, December: 356–386.

Friedman, Milton. 1959. *A Program for Monetary Stability.* Fordham University Press.

Friedman, Milton. 1983. Monetary variability: United States and Japan. *Journal of Money, Credit and Banking* 15, August: 339–343.

Friedman, Milton. 1985. Monetarism in rhetoric and practice. In *Monetary Policy in Our Times*, ed. A. Ando et al. MIT Press.

Fukui, Toshiko. 1986. The recent development of the short-term money market in Japan and changes in the techniques and procedures of monetary control used by the Bank of Japan. In *Changes in Money Market Instruments and Procedures: Objectives and Implications*. Bank for International Settlements, Basel.

Funabashi, Yoichi. 1988. *Managing the Dollar: From the Plaza to the Lourve*. International Economics Institute.

Glick, Reuven, and Michael Hutchison. 1990. Financial liberalization in the Pacific Basin: Implications for real interest rate linkages. *Journal of the Japanese and International Economies* 4: 36–48.

Glick, Reuven, and Michael Hutchison. 1994a. Monetary policy, intervention and exchange rates in Japan. In *Exchange Rate Policy and Interdependence: Perspectives from the Pacific Basin*, ed. R. Glick and M. Hutchison. Cambridge University Press.

Glick, Reuven, and Michael Hutchison. 1994b. Foreign Reserve and Money Dynamics with Asset Portfolio Adjustment: International Evidence. Working Paper PB94–09, Federal Reserve Bank of San Francisco, Pacific Basin Working Paper Series.

Glick, Reuven, Michael Hutchison, and Ramon Moreno. 1995. Is Pegging the Exchange Rate a Cure for Inflation? East Asian Experiences. Working Paper PB95-08, Federal Reserve Bank of San Francisco Pacific Basin Working Paper Series.

Goodhart, Charles. 1991. *The Evolution of Central Banks*. MIT Press.

Gordon, Robert J. 1975. The demand for and supply of inflation. *Journal of Law and Economics* 18, December: 807–836.

Gordon, Robert J. 1982. Why U.S. wage and employment behavior differs from that in Britain and Japan. *Economic Journal* 92, March: 13–44.

Grilli, Vittorio, Donato Masciandaro, and Guido Tabellini. 1991. Political and monetary institutions and public finance policies in the industrial countries. *Economy Policy* 13, October: 341–392.

Grossman, Richard S. 1992. Deposit insurance, regulation, and moral hazard in the thrift industry: Evidence from the 1930s. *American Economic Review* 82, September: 800–821.

Grubb, David. 1986. Topics in the OECD Phillips curve. *Economic Journal* 96, March: 55–79.

Hamada, Koichi. 1994. Bubbles, bursts and bail-outs: A comparison of three episodes of financial crisis in Japan. In *The Structure of the Japanese Economy*, ed. M. Okabe. Macmillan.

Hamada, Koichi, and Fumio Hayashi. 1985. Monetary policy in postwar Japan. In *Monetary Policy in Our Times*, ed. A. Ando et al. MIT Press.

Hamada, Koichi, and Akiyoshi Horiuchi. 1987. The political economy of the financial market. In *The Political Economic of Japan*, volume I, ed. K. Yamamura and Y. Yasuba. Standford University Press.

Harrington, Joseph E. 1992. The role of party reputation in the formulation of policy. *Journal of Public Economics* 49, October: 107–121.

Hee Soh, Byung. 1986. Political business cycles in industrialized democratic countries. *Kyklos* 39: 31–46.

Henning, C. Randall. 1994. *Currencies and Politics in the United States, Germany, and Japan.* Institute for International Economics.

Hetzel, Robert L. 1991. Too big to fail: Origins, consequences, and outlook. *Economic Review* (Federal Reserve Bank of Richmond) 77, no. 6: 3–15.

Hibbs, Douglas A. 1977. Political parties and macroeconomic policy. *American Political Science Review* 71: 1467–1487.

Hutchison, Michael. 1984. Official Japanese intervention in the foreign exchange market: Leaning against the wind? *Economics Letters* 15: 115–120.

Hutchison, Michael M. 1986. Japan's 'money focused' monetary policy. *Economic Review* (Federal Reserve Bank of San Francisco) 3, summer: 33–46.

Hutchison, Michael M. 1988. Monetary control with an exchange rate objective: The Bank of Japan, 1973–86. *Journal of International Money and Finance* 7, September: 261–271.

Hutchison, Michael M. 1991. Aggregate demand, uncertainty, and oil prices: The 1990 oil shock in comparative perspective. Economic Paper 31, Bank for International Settlements.

Hutchison, Michael M. 1992. Budget Policy and the Decline of National Saving Revisited. Economic Paper 33, Bank for International Settlements.

Hutchison, Michael M. 1994. Asset price fluctuations in Japan: What role for monetary policy? *Monetary and Economic Studies* (Bank of Japan Institute for Monetary and Economic Studies) 12, December: 61–83.

Hutchison, Michael M., and John P. Judd. 1992. Central bank secrecy and money surprises: International evidence. *Review of Economics and Statistics* 74: 135–145.

Hutchison, Michael M., and Nirvikar Singh. 1993. Long-Term International Capital Mobility: New Evidence from Equilibrium Real Interest Rates Linkages. Working Paper PB93–06, Federal Reserve Bank of San Francisco (forthcoming in *Journal of the Japanese and International Economies*).

Hutchison, Michael, and Carl E. Walsh. 1992. Empirical evidence on the insulation properties of fixed and flexible exchange rates: The Japanese experience. *Journal of International Economics* 32, May: 241–263.

Inoguchi, Takashi. 1979. Political Surfing over Economic Waves: A Simple Model of the Japanese Political-Economic System in Comparative Perspective. Presented at Eleventh World Congress of International Political Science Association, Moscow.

Inoguchi, Takashi. 1981. Explaining and predicting Japanese general elections, 1960–1980. *Journal of Japanese Studies* 7: 285–318.

Inoguchi, Takashi. 1983. Gendai no Nihon Seiji Keizai no Kozu. Toyo Keizai Shinposha.

International Monetary Fund. 1995. *International Capital Markets: Developments, Prospects, and Policy Issues.*

Ito, Takatoshi. 1987. The intraday exchange rate dynamics and monetary policies after the Group of Five agreement. *Journal of Japanese and International Economies* 1: 275–298.

Ito, Takatoshi. 1989a. Is the Bank of Japan a Closet Monetarist? Monetary Targeting in Japan, 1978–1988.Working Paper 2874, National Bureau of Economic Research.

Ito, Takatoshi. 1989b. Was There a Target Zone? Japan Center for International Finance Policy Study Series 14.

Ito, Takatoshi. 1990. The timing of elections and political business cycles in Japan. *Journal of Asian Economics* 1: 135–156.

Ito, Takatoshi. 1991a. International impacts on domestic political economy: A case of Japanese general elections. *Journal of International Money and Finance* 10, March: S73—S89.

Ito, Takatoshi. 1991b. Monetary Policy in the Age of Financial Innovations: The Case of Japan, 1985–1990. Manuscript.

Ito, Takatoshi. 1992. *The Japanese Economy.* MIT Press.

Ito, Takatoshi. 1994. On the possibility of a yen bloc. In *Exchange Rate Policy and Interdependence: Perspectives from the Pacific Basin,* ed. R. Glick and M. Hutchison. Cambridge University Press.

Ito, Takatoshi, and Keiko Nosse Hirono. 1993. Efficiency of the Tokyo housing market. *Monetary and Economic Studies* (Bank of Japan Institute for Monetary and Economic Studies) 11, July: 1–32.

Ito, Takatoshi, and Tokuo Iwaisako. 1996. Explaining asset bubbles in Japan. *Monetary and Economic Studies* (Bank of Japan Institute for Monetary and Economic Studies) 14, July: 143–193.

Ito, Takatoshi, and Jin Hyuk Park. 1988. Political business cycles in the parliamentary system. *Economics Letters* 27: 233–238.

Ito, Takatoshi, and Yuri Nagataki Sasaki. 1995. Impacts of the Basle Capital Standard on Japanese Banks' Behavior. Memorandum.

Ito, Takatoshi, and Kazuo Ueda. 1981. Tests of the equilibrium hypothesis in disequilibrium econometrics: An international comparison of credit rationing in business loans. *International Economic Review* 22: 691–708.

Ito, Takatoshi, and Kazuo Ueda. 1993. Editors' introduction. *Journal of the Japanese and International Economies* 7, December: 323–328.

Iwamura, Mitsuru. 1993. Deposit insurance and moral hazard. *Monetary and Economic Studies* (Bank of Japan Institute for Monetary and Economic Studies) 11, July: 63–85.

Kalecki, Michael. 1937. A theory of the business cycle. *Review of Economic Studies* 4, February: 77–97.

Kamada, Koichiro. 1993. The real value of postal savings certificates. *Monetary and Economic Studies* (Bank of Japan Institute for Monetary and Economic Studies) 11, November: 59–96.

Kane, Edward J. 1985. *The Gathering Crisis in Federal Deposit Insurance.* MIT Press.

Kane, Edward J. 1993. What lessons should Japan Learn from the U.S. deposit-insurance mess? *Journal of the Japanese and International Economies* 7, December: 329–355.

Kane, Edward J., and George G. Kaufman. 1993. Incentive conflict in deposit-institution regulation: Evidence from Australia. *Pacific Basin Finance Journal* 1, March: 13–29.

Karaken, John H. 1983. Deposit insurance reform or deregulation is the cart not the horse. *Quarterly Review* (Federal Reserve Bank of Minneapolis) 7, spring: 1–9.

Kaufman, George G. 1994. Bank contagion: A review of the theory and evidence. *Journal of Financial Services Research* 8: 123–150.

Kawai, Masahiro. 1992. Internationalization of the yen [En no Kokusai-ka]. In *Current Status of International Finance* [*Kokusai Kin-yu no Genjo*], ed. T. Ito. Yuhikaku.

Kindleberger, Charles P. 1995. *Manias, Panics, and Crashes: A History of Financial Crises.* Wiley.

Kishimoto, Koichi. 1982. *Politics in Modern Japan.* Japan Echo.

Kohno, Masaru, and Yoshitaka Nizhizawa. 1990. A study of the electoral business cycle in Japan: Elections and government spending on public construction. *Comparative Politics* 22, January: 151–166.

Konya, Fumiko. 1994. The rise and fall of the bubble economy: An analysis of the performance and structure of the Japanese stock market. In *The Structure of the Japanese Economy.*, ed. M. Okabe. Macmillan.

Konya, Fumiko, and T. Wakasugi. 1987. Tobin's q and stock prices [in Japanese]. *Research on Securities* 80: 149–162.

Kreps, David, and Robert Wilson. 1982. Reputation and imperfect competition. *Journal of Economic Theory* 27, August: 253–279.

Kyland, Finn, and Edward C. Prescott. 1977. Rules rather than discretion: The inconsistency of optimal plans. *Journal of Political Economy* 85, June: 473–492.

Lachler, Ulrich. 1982. On political business cycles with endogenous election dates. *Journal of Public Economics* 17: 111–117.

Marston, Richard C. 1987. Real exchange rates and productivity growth in the United States and Japan. In *Real-Financial Linkages among Open Economies,* ed. S. Arndt and J. Richardson. MIT Press.

McCallum, Bennett T. 1978. The political business cycle: An empirical test. *Southern Economic Journal* 44: 504–515.

McCallum, Bennett T. 1990. Inflation: Theory and evidence. *Handbook of Monetary Economics* 2: 963–1012.

Meltzer, Allan H. 1985. Variability of prices, output and money under fixed and flexible exchange rates: An empirical study of monetary regimes in Japan and the United States. *Monetary and Economic Studies* (Bank of Japan Institute for Monetary and Economic Studies) 3, December: 1–46.

Mieno, Yasushi. 1995. Issues facing the Japanese economy and the roles of central banks. *Bank of Japan Quarterly Bulletin* 3, February: 5–14.

Michelacci, Claudio. 1993. Central Bank Involvement in the Supervision of the Banking System and of Financial Markets: A Comparative Analysis. Centre for Monetary and Financial Economics, Bocconi University.

Nakajima, Zenta, and Hiroo Taguchi. 1995. Toward a more stable financial framework. In *Financial Stability in a Changing Environment,* ed. K. Sawamoto et al. St. Martin's.

Nakao, Masakki, and Akinari Horii. 1991. The Process of Decision-Making and Implementation of Monetary Policy in Japan. Special Paper 198, Bank of Japan.

Nishimura, Kiyohiko G. 1990. The mechanism of land price determination in Japan [Nihon no chika kettei mechanism]. In *Japanese Stock and Land Prices* [*Nihon no kabuka chika*], ed. K. Nishimura and Y. Miwa. University of Tokyo Press.

Noguchi, Yukio. 1989. *Economics of Land* [*Tochi no keizaigaku*]. Nihonkeizai Shinbunsya.

Nordhaus, William D. 1975. The political business cycle. *Review of Economic Studies* 42: 169–190.

Nordhaus, William D. 1989. Alternative approaches to the political business cycle. *Brookings Papers on Economic Activity* 2: 1–68.

Organization for Economic Cooperation and Development. 1969. *Economic Survey of Japan.*

Ostrom, Douglas. 1992. A savings and loan-style crisis for Japan? *Japan Economic Institute Report*, October 2.

Ostrom, Douglas. 1994a. G-7 confab fails to resolve policy differences. *Japan Economic Institute Report*, March 4.

Ostrom, Douglas. 1994b. Intervention brakes yen's ascent against dollar but questions remain. *Japan Economic Institute Report*, May 13.

Packer, Frank. 1994. The disposal of bad loans in Japan: A review of recent policy initiatives. Presented at Current Developments in Japanese Financial Markets, University of Southern California.

Patrick, Hugh, and Henry Rosovsky, eds. 1976. *Asia's New Giant: How the Japanese Economy Works.* Brookings Institution.

Pempel, T. J. 1987. The unbundling of 'Japan, Inc.': The changing dynamics of Japanese policy formation. *Journal of Japanese Studies* 13, Summer: 271–306.

Pigott, Charles. 1980. Wringing out inflation: Japan's experience. *Economic Review* (Federal Reserve Bank of San Francisco), summer: 21–46.

Posen, Adam S. 1995. Declarations are not enough: Financial sector sources of central bank independence. *National Bureau of Economic Research Macroeconomic Annual 1995:* 253–276.

Quirk, Peter. 1977. Exchange rate policy in Japan: Leaning against the wind. *International Monetary Fund Staff Papers* 4: 642–664.

Rogoff, Kenneth. 1984. On the effects of sterilized intervention: An analysis of weekly data. *Journal of Monetary Economics* 14: 133–150.

Rogoff, Kenneth. 1985. The optimal degree of commitment to an intermediate monetary target. *Quarterly Journal of Economics* 100(4): 1169–1190.

Romer, Christina. 1986. Is the stabilization of the postwar economy a figment of the data? *American Economic Review* 76: 314–334.

Sakakibara, Eisuke. 1991. The Japanese politico-economic system and the public sector. In *Parallel Politics*, ed. S. Kernell. Brookings Institution.

Salomon Bothers, Tokyo. 1992. *Japanese Economic/Market Analysis.* November 2.

Sawamoto, Kuniho, Zenta Nakajima, and Hiroo Taguchi, eds. 1995. *Financial Stability in a Changing Environment.* St. Martin's.

Schaede, U. 1989. Forwards and futures in Tokugawa-period Japan. *Journal of Banking and Finance* 13: 487–513.

Schiffer, Hubert F. 1962. *The Modern Japanese Banking System*. University Publishers.

Schumpter, Joseph. 1939. *Business Cycles: A Theoretical, Historical, and Statistical Analysis of the Capitalist Process*. McGraw-Hill.

Shimamoto, Reiichi. 1982. Monetary control in Japan. In *Central Bank Views on Monetary Targeting*, ed. P. Meek. Federal Reserve Bank of New York.

Shionoya, Tsukumo. 1962. *Problems Surrounding the Revision of the Bank of Japan Law*. Beckhard Foundation.

Short, Genie D., and Jeffery W. Gunther. 1989. The Texas Thrift Situation: Implications for the Texas Financial Services Industry. Federal Reserve Bank of Dallas.

Suzuki, Yoshio. 1980. *Money and Banking in Contemporary Japan*. Yale University Press.

Suzuki, Yoshio. 1985. Japan's monetary policy over the past 10 years. *Monetary and Economic Studies* (Bank of Japan Institute for Monetary and Economic Studies) 3, September: 1–18.

Suzuki, Yoshio. 1986. *Money, Finance, and Macroeconomic Performance in Japan*. Yale University Press.

Suzuki, Yoshio, ed. 1987. *The Japanese Financial System*. Clarendon.

Tabellini, Guido. 1985. Centralized Wage Setting and Monetary Policy in a Reputational Equilibrium. Manuscript, University of California, Los Angeles.

Tachibanaki, Toshiaki. 1991. Economics of regulation and deregulation on financial industry in Japan. Presented at Recent Changes in the Financial Structure, Tokyo.

Taguchi, Hiroo. 1994. On the iInternationalization of the Japanese yen. In *Macroeconomic Linkage*, ed. T. Ito and A. Krueger. University of Chicago Press.

Takagi, Shinji. 1991. Foreign exchange market intervention and domestic monetary control in Japan, 1973–89. *Japan and the World Economy* 3: 147–180.

Takeda, Masahiko, and Phillip Turner. 1992. The Liberalization of Japan's Financial Markets: Some Major Themes. Economic Paper 34, Bank for International Settlements.

Tamaki, Norio. 1995. *Japanese Banking: A History, 1859–1959*. Cambridge University Press.

Tavlas, George S., and Yuzuru Ozeki. 1992. *The Internationalization of Currencies: An Appraisal of the Japanese Yen*. International Monetary Fund.

Teranishi, Juro. 1990. Financial System and the Industrialization of Japan: 1900–1970. Presented at Money Markets and Monetary Policy in the Pacific Basin, San Francisco.

Taguchi, Hiroo. 1992. On the internationalization of the Japanese yen. In *Macroeconomic Linkage: Savings, Exchange Rates, and Capital Flows*, ed. T. Ito and A. Krueger. University of Chicago Press.

Tsutsui, William M. 1988. *Banking Policy in Japan: American Efforts at Reform during the Occupation*. Routledge.

Tufte, Edward R. 1978. *Political Control of the Economy*. Princeton University Press.

Ueda, Kazuo. 1990. Are Japanese stock prices too high? *Journal of the Japanese and International Economies* 14, December: 351–370.

Walsh, Carl E. 1994. Short-Run Output-Inflation Tradeoffs and Central Bank Independence: Evidence from the Industrial Countries. Manuscript, University of California, Santa Cruz.

Walsh, Carl E. 1995a. Recent central-bank reforms and the role of price stability as the sole objective of monetary policy. *National Bureau of Economic Research Macroeconomic Annual 1995:* 237–252.

Walsh, Carl E. 1995b. Is New Zealand's Reserve Bank Contract of 1989 an optimal central bank contract? *Journal of Money, Credit and Banking* 27, November: 1179–1191.

Walsh, Carl E. 1995c. Optimal contracts for central bankers. *American Economic Review* 85, March: 150–167.

Walsh, Carl E. 1996. Inflation and Central Bank Independence: Is Japan Really an Outlier? Manuscript, University of California, Santa Cruz.

Watanabe, Tsutomu. 1994. The signalling effect of foreign exchange intervention: The case of Japan. In *Exchange Rate Policy and Interdependence: Perspectives from the Pacific Basin,* ed. R. Glick and M. Hutchison. Cambridge University Press.

Watson, Mark W. 1994. Business cycle durations and postwar stabilization of the U.S. economy. *American Economic Review* 84, March: 24–46.

White, Lawrence J. 1991. *The S&L Debacle.* Oxford University Press.

Willett, Thomas, ed. 1988. *Political Business Cycles.* Duke University Press.

Yoshida, Tomoo. 1990. On the stability of the Japanese money demand function: Estimation results using the error correction model. *Monetary and Economic Studies* (Bank of Japan Institute for Monetary and Economic Studies) 8, January: 1–48.

Yoshida, Tomoo, and Robert Rasche. 1990. The M2 demand in Japan: Shifted and unstable? *Monetary and Economic Studies* (Bank of Japan Institute for Monetary and Economic Studies) 8, September: 9–30.

Yoshino, Naoyuki. 1996. Effects of financial liberalization on banks, corporations, and monetary policy: Asset price inflation and money flow from Japan. In *U.S.-Japan Macroeconomic Relations: Interactions and Interdependence in the 1980s.* University of Washington Press.

Index